ESSAYS RELATING TO IRELAND

BIOGRAPHICAL

HISTORICAL AND TOPOGRAPHICAL

KENNIKAT PRESS SCHOLARLY REPRINTS

Ralph Adams Brown, Senior Editor

Series In

IRISH HISTORY AND CULTURE

Under the General Editorial Supervision of

Gilbert A. Cahill

Professor of History, State University of New York

ESSAYS
RELATING TO IRELAND

BIOGRAPHICAL

HISTORICAL AND TOPOGRAPHICAL

BY

C. LITTON FALKINER

WITH A MEMOIR OF THE AUTHOR

BY

EDWARD DOWDEN, LL.D.

KENNIKAT PRESS
Port Washington, N. Y./London

ESSAYS RELATING TO IRELAND

First published in 1909
Reissued in 1970 by Kennikat Press
Library of Congress Catalog Card No: 74-102600
SBN 8046-0777-X

Manufactured by Taylor Publishing Company Dallas, Texas

KENNIKAT SERIES IN IRISH HISTORY AND CULTURE

MEMOIR

The accident near Argentière, in the Chamonix Valley, of August 5, 1908, which caused the death of Cæsar Litton Falkiner, not only carried sorrow into a happy home and brought a deep sense of deprivation to friends who regarded him with honour and affection, but was felt as a public calamity by lovers of literature, and especially by those who are interested in the history and the literature of Ireland. He died when all his powers were at the full, before he had completed his forty-fifth year, and when he was actively engaged in several literary undertakings of importance. I shall set down in the briefest way some facts of a happy, laborious, and well-spent life.

He was born in Dublin, September 26, 1863, the second son of the late Sir Frederick Richard Falkiner, Recorder of Dublin and Privy Councillor, Ireland. His mother was a daughter of Mr. Sadlier, of Ballinderry Park, Co. Tipperary. The 'Litton' of Falkiner's Christian name had been the maiden name of his grandmother; the 'Cæsar' came from a friend, and, I believe, a kinsman of the family, the Rev. Cæsar Otway, an antiquary and a writer of popular books on Irish topography, who had projected a History of Ireland and an edition of the works of Sir James Ware. For a time Falkiner was a pupil in the Royal School, Armagh. In Trinity College, Dublin, where he graduated B.A. in 1886, M.A. in 1890, his career was not undistinguished. He took a prominent part in the discussions of the Philosophical Society, whose composition prize was awarded to him for an essay on Macaulay. At a later time he referred to the 'juvenility' of this essay, though he retained a certain respect for his early achievement; in truth it is mature in judgment beyond the writer's years, and already shows something of the judicial character of his mind. The esteem in which he was held by his fellow-students is evidenced by the fact that they elected him President of the Society—a coveted honour—for the session 1885–86. His opening address, delivered before a large and distinguished audience, entitled in its printed form 'The New Voyage to Utopia,' is a kind of appeal from the New Whigs to the Old. The spirit engendered by the recent Reform Act, and that expressed in a still more recent political manifesto of Mr. Gladstone, supplied the text for Falkiner's discourse. Utopian visions, rash designs of innovation, the temper of change for the sake of change, and the consequent sense of insecurity and the violations of justice to minorities were the subjects of his criticism.

In 1887 Falkiner was called to the Bar. I knew him in those days and earlier days, and I imagined that in order to be a great advocate it would be needful for him to strive against his own judicial temper. Yet letters addressed by several Irish judges to his father testify to their high opinion of Falkiner's conduct of cases in their Courts. And he could vigorously take a side in controversy, for, when deliberation had resulted in convictions, those convictions were steadfast and became the basis of action. In the year after that in which he was called to the Bar he began to take an active part in political work in connexion with the Unionist Registration Associations for the City of Dublin and the South County Dublin. Of the former association he was for many years an honorary officer, secretary or treasurer, and threw himself into the work with the energy and practical ability which were characteristic of him. At the same time he was engaged in politics as a regular contributor of leading articles to a Dublin newspaper—the *Daily Express*. Such dealings with contemporary politics doubtless had their influence upon him afterwards, when he became a historical student of the past. He felt more vividly the living spirit in and behind external events; history could not appear to him as a mere accumulation of inanimate facts piled up by scientific coral-insects.

He acquired much knowledge of the inner working of party government, and a sense of those forces with which the legislative has to reckon. He developed a feeling for the values of personal influences in politics. And while untiring in historical research, and aware of the importance of those minute contributions to knowledge which delight the specialist, he saw the necessity of co-ordinating such facts under ideas and wider views, which can be appreciated, at least in a measure, by all intelligent readers.

At the General Election of 1892 Falkiner as a Unionist candidate contested South Armagh, making the best poll that has ever been recorded for a candidate of his political persuasion. Again in 1895 he was invited to contest the same constituency, and also that of East Donegal, but he was unable to accept either of these invitations in consequence of the task of organising the extensive campaign of the Irish Unionist Alliance at the General Election of that year—a task for which his zeal, his energy, his caution, and his sound judgment eminently qualified him, and which he conducted to the most successful results.

Before this date a great happiness had come to Falkiner. On August 4, 1892, took place his marriage to Henrietta Mary, only daughter of Sir Thomas Newenham Deane, the eminent architect, to whom Ireland owes its Art Museum and National Library, and Oxford its University Physiological Laboratory and Anthropological Museum. Even if it were possible, this is not the place to tell of the incalculable gains added to his life by his marriage and by the birth of two daughters.

In 1896 he became a member of the Royal Irish Academy. Having served for some years on the Council, he was elected secretary to that body in 1907, a position which he held until the close of his life. His successor in that office, Dr. L. C. Purser, in noticing the losses of the Academy during the session 1908–09, spoke of Falkiner's work thus: 'His work (in the secretaryship of the Council) was indefatigable and thorough-going, and was always inspired by the consciousness of the dignity and high position which the Academy holds in the world of learning. He contributed various papers to the Academy relating to the history of Ireland ; and the object at which he aimed in his works was twofold, to help in determining the degree in which the progress of the constitutional and administrative history of the country and the evolution of its social condition have been influenced by the accidents of its local development and of its physical characteristics, and to show that Irish history is adorned with episodes in which all sections of Irishmen can take an honourable pride. . . . A wide and general knowledge of the sources for the elucidation of Irish history, which was second to that of no other scholar, an impartial sympathy with all forms of excellence, a practical acquaintance with administration, remarkable judgment in the selection of materials, and a singularly graceful and lucid style—all combined to render his historical writings models of accuracy, research, and exposition.' The first part of Falkiner's 'Illustrations of Irish History and Topography' (1904) is formed in the main from papers read before the Royal Irish Academy, and to the President and members of that body the volume is dedicated. It fell to his lot as secretary to survey the work of two distinguished Presidents of the Academy, who died during the session 1907–08—J. Kells Ingram and Robert Atkinson. A more detailed memoir of Ingram was read by Falkiner before the Statistical and Social Inquiry Society of Ireland (November 1, 1907). This, which was printed and published as a pamphlet, forms—together with the bibliography by Mr. T. W. Lyster—the least inadequate existing record of the work of that remarkable thinker, poet, and scholar.

Falkiner's literary interests were by no means confined to history, topography, and political biography. Of the many contributions which he made to the 'Dictionary of National Biography' not a few are concerned with Irish writers whose work lay in other provinces than these. In the third volume of the last edition of 'Chambers's Cyclopædia of English Literature' his articles deal chiefly with the poets of Ireland. He edited in 1903 the poems of Charles Wolfe, and in the same year appeared in 'The Golden Treasury Series' his selection from the poems of Thomas Moore. I will not deny myself the pleasure of mentioning that Falkiner associated my name with his own through the dedication of this little volume. Shortly before his death he had begun to make preparations for a complete edition of Moore's Poetical Works to be published by the Clarendon Press. He knew the disrepute into which much of Moore's once popular poetry has fallen, and he recognised that in the revenge of Time there was a certain justice; but he held that the 'Irish Melodies' still live and deserve to live, and he assigned a high place to Moore as a satirist who wielded deftly a scourge of small cords. In the poetry of what is styled the Irish Literary Revival of recent years Falkiner took an interest, but he regarded some of the verse which is supposed outside Ireland to possess a characteristic Irish 'glamour' as in truth eminently foreign to the Irish character and genius. I remember two delightful visits to my study, in one of which Falkiner sketched in outline the scheme for a series of volumes on Irish Men of Letters, in the other the scheme for a series of public lectures dealing with the same themes. I can recall that he assigned to me Henry Brooke, the author of 'The Fool of Quality.' Difficulties arose and neither design was accomplished. Such visits were a pleasure of a rare kind, for Falkiner spoke on a subject in which he was a master, and he gave more play in conversation than he often gave in his writings to the gift of humour which he possessed—humour not boisterous, but alert, intelligent, and shrewd.

He was appointed in 1898 an Assistant Legal Land Commissioner. The appointment at first was temporary, but in 1905 he was placed on the permanent staff. The ability, discretion, and impartiality with which he performed his duties were recognised in the highest quarters and by his colleagues in the Land Commission. For the first half of his period of service his work lay in the western counties, for the latter half in the southern counties. During the earlier years he acquired a special knowledge of the Congested Districts, which he turned to good account in some of his published articles. His official position, of course, brought to a sudden close his work in connexion with political organisations; it did not withdraw him from literature, but he laboured under all the disadvantages of public duties, which were often exacting, much railway travelling, frequent absences from his own collection of books and from public libraries. Under such conditions it is really surprising to see how large a body of work, often involving detailed research and always of high excellence, was achieved. Within the last ten years of his life he contributed twenty articles to the *Edinburgh Review,* three to the *Monthly Review*, three to the *English Historical Review,* a series of articles to the *Saturday Review,* and seven important papers to the *Proceedings of the Royal Irish Academy.* Nor does this list nearly exhaust the sum of his labours. In 1899 Falkiner was appointed in the room of Sir John Gilbert an inspector under the Historical Manuscripts Commission, with the duty of editing the 'Ormonde Papers.' He went to work with his usual diligence and sense of responsibility. The five volumes of the 'Ormonde Papers,' which appeared from 1902 to 1908, contain not far from 3000 pages—a great contribution to the materials of history; the Introductions show the editor's mastery of his subject, and that mastery is also evident in the Essay 'An Illustrious Cavalier,' included in the present volume. Materials for a sixth volume of the 'Ormonde Papers' (now in the press) had been selected by Falkiner before his last midsummer holiday. With such a heavy pack upon his shoulders of the literary work in which he rejoiced, he never seemed to suffer from hurry and flurry; he was always, it seemed to me, well poised for work; and certainly he was always ready to answer a query or solve a doubt, even at the cost of some distraction or loss of time, if thereby a deserving fellow-labourer in the field of his own studies could be guided or assisted. He recognised, moreover, the claims made upon him by institutions connected with education and culture in Ireland, even at the loss of a portion of his cherished hours of study. He was a visitor of the Science and Art Museum, Dublin, a member of the Erasmus Smith Board, of the Board of the King's Hospital, and a Governor of the Incorporated

Society for Promoting Protestant Schools in Ireland. With reference to his work in the last of these positions the Rev. H. Kingsmill Moore writes: 'He did not rest until he had mastered the whole system; alike in visiting the different schools, and in studying the various problems which they presented, his exertions were untiring. It followed naturally that the Governors were learning to attach the highest value to the advice of one in whom they found both the wisest of helpers and the truest of friends.'

He had indeed a gift for friendship. Where he gave affection, he gave it with all the strength, sincerity, and steadfastness of his nature. As his closest friend I cannot be wrong in naming the editor of the present volume, Mr. F. Elrington Ball, a colleague of Falkiner in much of his political work, and a specialist, like Falkiner, in the field of Irish topographical research. Among the many and various labours which occupied Falkiner during the last year of his life was an edition of the collected letters of Jonathan Swift. It is a happiness to think that this important undertaking will not be allowed to drop, and that the completion of Falkiner's work has been entrusted to skilled and competent hands—those of his most intimate and faithful friend.

The end came in a moment. On a glorious morning, August 5, 1908, he started alone from his hotel at Tréléchant, near Argentière, for a walk to the Flégère, intending to return in the early afternoon. He must have strayed, probably when returning, from the path to a point where the cliff edge wears a deceptive appearance of safety. Death was instantaneous. In what followed kind help was given by many. His body was laid to rest in the English cemetery at Chamonix. His friends, in response to a movement initiated by Colonel Edward Macartney-Filgate, and with the approval and sympathy of the Very Reverend Dean Bernard, have made arrangements to place a memorial tablet to Falkiner in St. Patrick's Cathedral, Dublin.

Not very long before his death he was actively engaged as secretary to the Committee of the Lecky Memorial, which placed near the Library of Trinity College, Dublin, the statue of that eminent historian. Had Falkiner lived it is probable that he would have ranked, among the students of Irish history of the younger generation, as Lecky's immediate successor. His chief work, apart from the 'Ormonde Papers,' which are the possession of specialists rather than of the general reader, and apart from those articles which dealt with contemporary social and political questions, is comprised in the three volumes of collected essays—'Studies in Irish History and Biography,' 1902, 'Illustrations of Irish History and Topography,' 1904, and the present volume. Falkiner's view as to how history should be written is expressed in an article contributed to the *Monthly Review* for May 1904. He stood between the elder school of historians and those of recent years who claim that history should be not literature but a branch of science. Accuracy in the ascertainment of facts he recognised as a chief duty of the historian. Every historical student, he held, should train himself to a certain intellectual detachment—'the faculty of discarding native prepossessions, of trying innate prejudices by the touchstone of principle, and of submitting every historical problem to the same test.' But he did not believe that any mere accumulation of minute facts deserves the name of history. He feared that the so-called 'scientific' school in its research after fact might ignore the great fact of life in things otherwise dead, the great fact of the spirit which animates what is material. He admitted the duty of historical impartiality, but impartiality, he thought, does not mean indifference or suppression of opinion—it means that the historian should be a judge, who delivers his charge, and not an advocate for this party or for that. Even in the selection of facts, essential for the intelligent presentation of truth, a certain personal element cannot but enter into historical work. Finally, Falkiner dared to think that if history is to be read it should be readable, and that, however 'scientific,' it yet should not fail to be literature. His suggestions as to special provinces of study and research in Irish history, which had peculiar claims upon students of the present day, may be found in the Preface to the 'Illustrations'; they were set forth more fully in an unpublished lecture delivered before the National Literary Society not long before his death.

Animated by such views as these, Falkiner studied and revived the past. His first collected volume, 'Studies in Irish History and Biography,' is a substantial addition, and one of enduring value, to our knowledge of the history of Ireland from the days of Grattan to those of O'Connell. Each study presents in a form attractive to a reader who is not necessarily a specialist the results of careful and often full investigation; documents previously unpublished are exhibited in appendices. While dealing with passages of history and figures of historical importance around which controversy had been violent and harsh, the writer, whose own convictions are decided and unfaltering, gives an example, rare at least until recent years, of an exponent of Irish history who does not fail in justice, temperance, and charity. He corrects incomplete or erroneous views not so much by direct polemical methods as by replacing these with fuller knowledge and a more exact setting forth of the truth. 'Our homage to moral grandeur, intellectual power or great achievement,' he writes in the Preface, 'need not be limited by our predilections or prejudices. To insist on the importance of Plunket's share in the struggle for Catholic Emancipation is not to rob O'Connell of the aureole of his genius, nor is the majestic figure of Grattan dwarfed by dwelling on the great qualities of the Earl of Clare.' The essay on Frederick Hervey, Earl of Bristol and Bishop of Derry, is noteworthy not only as a contribution to history but as a psychological study of character in the case of one whose great wit was near allied to madness.

The 'Illustrations' consist in part of original papers, historical and topographical, in which an attempt is made to exhibit 'the manner and degree in which the local and general history of the country are intertwined'; in part of a carefully selected series of descriptions of Ireland in the seventeenth century from published and manuscript writings by seventeenth century authors. 'The book originated,' Falkiner writes, 'in the desire to realise for myself the social condition of Ireland at a period singularly pregnant of lasting effects upon her history. . . . The difficulty I have experienced in finding the materials for my purpose has led me to believe that a collection of the less accessible descriptions of Ireland for the period under consideration may not be unwelcome to fellow students in the same field.' The value of the work was recognised by a highly qualified critic, Mr. Robert Dunlop, in the *English Historical Review.*

During the years while he was thus exploring the past, Falkiner, through articles contributed to the *Edinburgh Review,* and less frequently to another leading Review became an adviser to the British public—an adviser exceptionally well-informed and judicious—on matters relating to the political and social welfare of contemporary Ireland. His wide acquaintance with facts, the historical tendency of his mind, and his generous recognition of what is excellent even in opponents, saved him from merely partisan views; his temperament and his experience would not permit him to err through over-sanguine expectations; he was a meliorist, not an optimist. Assured that the best interests alike of Great Britain and Ireland are bound up with the maintenance of the legislative Union, he was unfaltering in his opposition to every scheme which might tend to disintegrate the political nucleus of the Empire; but the policy on which rested his hopes was not one of mere resistance or negation. Prepared for difficulties and occasional disappointments, he yet was confident that the gradual operation of measures, at once generous and prudent, would in the end yield satisfactory results. When in 1895 Lord Salisbury returned to power with a commanding majority, Falkiner's chief desire was that a great opportunity should be seized by the Unionist party, not so much for the advancement of their cause as for the good of the country. He pleaded for the creation of a Department of Agriculture and Industry in Ireland; an extension of the powers and resources of the Congested Districts Board; the provision of an effective system of industrial education; the encouragement of extensive forestry operations in the waste lands of the West; the further development of light railways, and the reorganisation through State intervention of the Irish railway system ; and such an arrangement of the respective duties of the Viceroyalty and the Chief Secretaryship as would make it possible that the functions of the Viceroy should be undertaken by a member of the Royal Family. I recite his proposals as they are summarised by himself in a published article of 1896. He interpreted the principle of equality of treatment as between the Three Kingdoms with a comment on the word 'equality' called for, as he believed, by the circumstances and conditions of his own country : 'Equality of treatment is not justice to Ireland if it only means the same treatment ; for that is not true equality which is applied with procrustean indifference to objects essentially dissimilar. To succeed at all, equality of treatment must be accompanied by an endeavour to produce as close an approximation of conditions as the inexorable disparities prescribed by Nature will allow. In the dealings of a rich country with a poor one, generosity is involved in the idea of justice.' It was not because he desired to range the youth of Ireland into separate camps, each regarding the other with mutual distrust, that Falkiner advocated the establishment of a Roman Catholic College or University : it was because, as he believed, nothing better would meet the conditions of the case ; and he would have preferred that a denominational institution, if created, should wear no disguise, but be frankly and courageously described as that which in fact it is. He hoped much from the gradual creation of a peasant proprietorship, but he demanded justice to existing rights as a condition ; he did not expect good results from raw haste, 'the sister of delay' ; and he saw the futility of enlarging uneconomic holdings into holdings a little less large but still uneconomic. Parliamentary compulsion having been already resorted to in the creation of dual ownership, he did not regard with horror the compulsory destruction of such ownership, subject to the conditions imposed by justice and prudence. He did not raise an outcry against emigration in so far as it was a natural result of the economic conditions of the world. He sympathised with some of the professed objects of the Gaelic League, but not with that hostility to England and English institutions which drew the literary and artistic movement towards a connexion with politics. He did not disapprove efforts to preserve the ancient language of Ireland as the spoken tongue in districts where it still survives; but he regarded 'the task of re-creating the Irish language, in a country from which it has almost died out, as the living language of a people which the last seven centuries have left perhaps the most mixed in Europe,' as best designated in words which he quotes from Lord Russell of Killowen: 'absolutely futile and impracticable.' It need hardly be added that Falkiner was no admirer of a lax administration; whatever remedial measures might be desirable, he regarded the vigorous maintenance of social order as a prime condition of success. Such in a brief summary were some of the opinions which he expressed on the contemporary affairs of Ireland. It will be perceived that he lived sufficiently long to see the fulfilment of some of his hopes.

This notice, slight as it is, could not have been written without help received from Mr. F. Elrington Ball, for which I desire to thank him.

EDWARD DOWDEN.

NOTE

In the selection and arrangement of the Essays included in the present volume the aim has been to obtain the unity and historical sequence which mark the author's former works. The greater number of the Essays appeared originally in the *Edinburgh Review*. Their reproduction has been generously permitted by Messrs. Longmans, Green, & Co. The Essay on Dublin is inserted with the consent of Professor Cole, acting on behalf of the Publication Committee of the British Association for 1908, and the Essays on the other Irish towns are included with the approval of the Editor of the *Saturday Review*, while leave has been granted by the Council of the Royal Irish Academy for the use of the notes and appendices to the Essay on Irish Parliamentary Antiquities, which appeared in connexion with papers published in the Academy's Proceedings.

F. E. B.

Dublin,
September 21, 1909.

CONTENTS

APPENDICES

Errata

Page 14, line 10, *for* Rowland Eustace *read* James Eustace.
„ 38, „ 24, „ this great *read* the great.

I

STUDIES IN IRISH BIOGRAPHY

SPENSER IN IRELAND

The large part which, in recent times at least, has been played by Irishmen on the imperial stage of Great Britain is among the most familiar of commonplaces whenever the relation of Ireland to the Empire is mooted. We are constantly reminded how, not merely in the field of war and action, but in the realm of letters and the world of affairs, some of the greatest places have been filled by men of Irish birth and Irish genius. Not to take any account of contemporary figures, the history of the last hundred and fifty years supplies abundant examples in every sphere of action and of effort of this honourable eminence of distinguished Irishmen in the roll of British fame. In the senate, Burke and Sheridan; in the camp, Wellington; in letters, Swift, Goldsmith, and Moore are examples that at once occur to the mind of great reputations achieved by Irishmen in purely British surroundings. It is not so often recalled that, in earlier times, a reciprocal opportunity was afforded by Ireland to English men of letters and of politics. Especially was this the case with many of the later Elizabethans. In an age when pen and sword were wielded with equal facility by the accomplished courtiers of a sovereign whose favour might be won as readily by a sonnet as at a siege, Ireland had its full share in the activities of those versatile servants of the Crown who were equally ready to serve in Court or in camp. The names of Barnaby Googe, the poet, and Barnaby Rich, the pamphleteer; of Sir Geoffrey Fenton, the translator of Bandello and Guicciardini, and of Bryskett, one of the lyrists of 'Astrophel,' by no means exhaust the list of those literary stars of lesser magnitude which shone in the Viceregal Courts of Sussex, of Sidney, or of Grey.

Of the part which Ireland played in the fortunes of much more illustrious men, Mr. Sidney Lee's 'Great Englishmen of the Sixteenth Century'[1] reminds us very forcibly. Of the six representative Elizabethans discussed in that volume, two were identified in the closest and most direct manner with the wars and politics of Ireland, while to a third, as the son of a statesman who thrice held the reins of Irish Government, the sister kingdom must have been a familiar theme. But of the three great careers of Spenser, Raleigh, and Sidney, it is that of the poet of the 'Faery Queene' which was most closely connected with Irish affairs, and which was most largely influenced by the connexion. Sidney, though he visited his father in Ireland in 1577, soon passed to the wider arena in which he was to find his untimely fate. To Raleigh, though his earliest successes were achieved there, and though he acquired in the Munster confiscations a princely territory whose development might well have filled the interests and absorbed the energies of a less mercurial temperament, Ireland was never an abiding home. But to Spenser, from his twenty-eighth year, Ireland was the place of his actual residence and the sole scene of his struggles for worldly advancement.

It would, perhaps, be an exaggeration, though hardly a grave one, to assert that no poet of equal fame is less read than the author of the 'Faery Queene.' The poet's poet, as Charles Lamb truly called him, Spenser has indeed received the fullest meed of fame in the unstinted admiration he has won from so many of the most illustrious of his descendants in the great line of English poets. But, though he has unquestionably found fit audience, it cannot be pretended that the students of his poetry have ever been numerous. And, having regard to the place which he admittedly occupies of right in the history of English literature, it is quite remarkable how little attention has been bestowed either upon the circumstances under which his work was produced, or upon a study of the influence exerted by those circumstances, not merely upon the form and direction which Spenser's art assumed, but upon the actual texture of his poetry.

[1] Lond. 1904.

That this is so is, doubtless, due in part to the extreme length of the work on which Spenser's fame mainly depends. Not all of those who open their Spenser at the first canto of the 'Legend of Holiness' are in, as Macaulay put it, at the death of the Blatant Beast. And Macaulay's reference to that incident proves, as has been pointed out, that the brilliant essayist had not himself reached, or if he reached it, had not accurately remembered, the unconcluded conclusion of this most elaborate and longest drawn of allegories. For the Blatant Beast, though subdued, is not slain. But in part, also, the comparative superficiality of the study given to Spenser's poetry, even by those who have felt the poet's spell most strongly, may be attributed to the scantiness of our knowledge of the facts of the poet's life. For above two centuries from his death not much more was known of the circumstances of Spenser's career than of Shakespeare's. Indeed, in certain material respects the record of the elder poet was the more scanty of the two; the facts as to Spenser's origin and early life resting as they did on a few vague autobiographical allusions scattered through his own works, and on the unsubstantiated traditions recorded by such antiquaries as Aubrey and Oldys. That the poet was a Londoner; that his birth took place somewhere about 1552; that he was somehow connected with the ancient house of Spencer; that he was educated at Pembroke Hall, Cambridge; and that shortly after he had graduated at the University he retired into the North of England for some years—this was as much as was certainly known on these points. Who his father was and whence his origin; where the poet's school-days had been passed, and in what locality his earlier manhood had been spent; who was the fair 'Rosalind' of the 'Shepherd's Calendar,' so long, so passionately, and so vainly wooed; and what was the scenery which formed the setting of Colin Clout's pastoral lamentations: who, again, was Rosalind's late found but more complaisant successor, the last of his trinity of Elizabeths:

> The third, my love, my life's last ornament,
> By whom my spirit out of dust was raised—

these were all of them questions which long remained not only unanswered but almost unasked, so thick was the obscurity which veiled all the more intimate associations of the poet's career. That some time after leaving the University he made the acquaintance of the gifted Philip Sidney, the Astrophel of his famous elegy; that either through the influence of this powerful friend, whose father was one of the most eminent of Elizabethan Viceroys of Ireland, or through that of Sidney's uncle, Leicester, he was appointed to an official position in the sister kingdom, and subsequently accompanied Lord Grey de Wilton to that country; that he received successive grants of land there, and was subsequently visited at his castle of Kilcolman by Sir Walter Raleigh, by whom, as the poet himself relates in 'Colin Clout's Come Home Again,' he was brought to Court and graciously received by Elizabeth; that he married towards the close of his career the fair unknown to whom the 'Amoretti' are addressed, and whom he adorned with such wealth of worship in that 'song made in lieu of many ornaments,' the 'Epithalamion,' with its splendid ritual of impassioned adoration; and that finally, with fortunes overwhelmed by the lava of the Irish volcano, he died in London at the age of forty-six—these are substantially all the facts which the wreck of time had left us knowledge of prior to the patient discoveries of nineteenth century research.

In years still recent, however, the diligence of a few Spenserian enthusiasts has added very considerably to the number of authenticated facts concerning the poet's career. From the date of Archdeacon Todd's edition of the poet's works, first published a century ago,[1] to that of Dr. Grosart's monumental and elaborately annotated 'Life and Works,' issued some twenty-five years since,[2] a continuous stream of discovery has poured fresh light on many long hidden incidents in Spenser's career. The last-mentioned editor, in particular, devoted many years of assiduous industry to the patient exploration of fresh sources of knowledge, and the careful co-ordination of evidence already available. Dr.

[1] *The Works of Edmund Spenser*, edited by Henry J. Todd.
[2] *The Complete Works of Edmund Spenser*, edited by Alexander B. Grosart.

Grosart's tireless zeal was rewarded by the discovery or independent corroboration of a number of facts which not only add materially to our knowledge of the actual course of Spenser's life, both before and after his coming to Ireland, but shed an informing light on the development of Spenser's poetical genius. By a careful analysis and comparison of the facts previously ascertained; by a diligent search through State papers, legal records, parish registers, and so forth; and especially by a minute etymological study of the archaic vocabulary of the 'Shepherd's Calendar,' Dr. Grosart succeeded in establishing a number of interesting and valuable certainties which greatly add to the clearness of our conception alike of the poet and his writings. It is true that, like all his predecessors, Dr. Grosart has failed to conclusively identify the poet's father, or to do more than confirm the evidence already available of Spenser's connexion with the Spensers of Hurstwood, near Clitheroe, in North-East Lancashire, a family of respectable and long-established position, though its precise relationship to the 'house of ancient fame' with which the poet claimed to be allied has not been established. But he has shown beyond question that the country district in 'the north parts' to which Spenser retired after leaving Cambridge was Pendle Forest, near Clitheroe, on the borders of Lancashire and the West Riding of Yorkshire; and he has established the identity of much of the idiom of the 'Shepherd's Calendar' with the north country provincialisms of that neighbourhood. If the editor's efforts to identify 'Rosalind' with a supposed Rose Dineley—conjectured to have been the daughter of a yeoman of that name known to have resided in the district in Spenser's time—can hardly be accepted as successful, Dr. Grosart has undoubtedly recovered for us the name and lineage of the poet's wife. That lady he has proved to have been Elizabeth Boyle, of Youghal, and a near kinswoman of that remarkable personage who, succeeding Spenser in his office of Clerk of the Council of the Presidency of Munster, was busy during the poet's last years in Ireland in laying the foundations of the splendid fortunes of the Great Earl of Cork.[1]

[1] The evidence of the identity of Spenser's wife is furnished by the Earl of

But while Dr. Grosart's labours have placed lovers of Spenser under a heavy obligation, the value of his services has not been fully commensurate with the labour he bestowed on his researches. Privately printed in two elaborate editions, which together numbered no more than two hundred and fifty copies, his volumes are necessarily known only to students; and even in this form the series of volumes which he proposed to devote to the edition remains incomplete. A large mass of laboriously acquired information intended to form the tenth volume has never reached even the limited public for whom it was designed. Again, the minute attention bestowed by Dr. Grosart upon the earlier poems, and the microscopic comparison of the descriptions and language in the 'Shepherd's Calendar' with the scenery and dialect of Pendle Forest and its neighbourhood, have not been paralleled in the case of the poet's later and more important work. Though a visit to Youghal and its neighbourhood probably contributed to his identification of the poet's wife, Dr. Grosart's knowledge of Ireland was certainly not as great as his familiarity with North-East Lancashire. He was unable to criticise the descriptions in the 'Faery Queene' from the same topographical standpoint which served him so well in dealing with the earlier work of the poet. And although Dr. Grosart's zeal led him to explore with all the enthusiasm of an editor the most minute scraps of Spenser's extant reports as an Irish official which can be traced in the Record Office or elsewhere, he has given comparatively little attention to the evidences which the poems contain of the influence exerted upon Spenser's genius by his Irish surroundings.

Dr. Grosart is not alone in his disregard of the effects of Spenser's Irish environment upon the character of his work. Indeed, it is not an aspect which has been much noticed by any recognised editor or critic of the poet. In an admirable article, which deserves to be better known, contributed

Cork's diary, edited by Dr. Grosart, and by an entry in the Council Book of the Corporation of Youghal. The facts are summarised in his introductions to both series of the *Lismore Papers*, in which Lord Cork's diary is printed. It may be noted that the *Lismore Papers* are not cited among the authorities for Spenser's life in the notice of the poet in the *Dictionary of National Biography*.

thirty years ago to *Frazer's Magazine*,[1] Dr. P. W. Joyce has examined elaborately and with a wealth of local knowledge Spenser's account of the Irish rivers in the eleventh canto of the fourth book of the 'Faery Queene,' as well as the references to the streams in the neighbourhood of Kilcolman which are so prominent in 'Colin Clout 's Come Home Again.' The late Mr. Keightley, too, in some valuable contributions published many years ago in *Notes and Queries*, has dwelt upon the same topic, and asserted the title of Spenser to be viewed as in a special sense the poet of Ireland.[2] But with these exceptions little or nothing has been written on the subject of Spenser's indebtedness to the country in which his later lot was cast for much of the scenery, many of the allusions, and even some of the topics handled in the 'Faery Queene' and others of his poems. Dean Church, indeed, in the admirable monograph [3] which he contributed to the 'Men of Letters Series' has some excellent remarks on the similarity between the actual Ireland of the sixteenth century and the imagined world of Spenser's romantic invention. But he has not attempted to work out the parallel either in regard to the political significance or the descriptive realism of Spenser's poetry. And even so profound and capable a student as Mr. Sidney Lee, in his admirable essay cited above, alludes to Spenser's Irish experiences in connexion with his prose work, rather than with his poetry. In such circumstances an attempt to trace in some detail the connexion of the poet of the 'Faery Queene' with the Ireland of Elizabeth may not appear wholly superfluous.

That Spenser was himself conscious of the influence exerted upon his poetry by the conditions of his Irish career, and that he felt his work to be impressed in a marked degree with the stamp of his surroundings, is apparent from his own language. Whether he was right in representing the 'Faery Queene' as having lost something of grace and perfection of form through his Irish exile, or whether his deprecatory

[1] N.S. vol. xvii. pp. 315–33.
[2] *Notes and Queries*, Ser.'4, vol. vii. p. 317.
[3] *Spenser*, by R. W. Church, Dean of St. Paul's.

expressions are to be taken as the merely conventional language of affected modesty, it is certain that many such sentiments are to be found in his later writings. In the dedicatory sonnets prefixed to the 'Faery Queene' this language of self-deprecia-tion is frequently employed, and always in relation to the misfortune of his situation, remote from the culture and charm of the Court of Elizabeth. Thus, in the sonnet addressed to his principal patron in Ireland, the ex-Viceroy Lord Grey de Wilton, he apologises for his poetry as no better than

> Rude rhymes, the which a rustic Muse did weave
> In salvage soil, far from Parnasso Mount
> And roughly wrought in an unlearned loom.

Again, in addressing the Earl of Ormond, one of the most eminent of contemporary Irishmen, and a kinsman through the Boleyns of Elizabeth herself, the poet holds almost identical language :

> Receive, most noble Lord, a simple taste
> Of the wilde fruit which salvage soil hath bred,
> Which being through long wars left almost waste
> With brutish barbarism is overspread.

Nor indeed was this kind of language peculiar to the poet of the 'Faery Queene.' It was the common form of every writer connected with Ireland in Spenser's day. To the subjects of Elizabeth the sister kingdom seemed a place as far apart from England as though it were situate in another hemisphere. Its trackless forests and unexplored fastnesses were a fit theatre for the malign enchantments of fairy land. There, as Dean Church puts it, 'men might in good truth travel long through wildernesses and great woods given over to the outlaw. There might be found, in most certain and prosaic reality, the ambushes, the disguises, the treacheries, the deceits and temptations, even the supposed witchcrafts and enchantments against which the fairy champions of the virtues have to be on their guard.' In the estimation of the courtiers of Elizabeth, and indeed in that of every subject of the Queen of gentle birth, Ireland was no better than unreclaimed backwoods, wholly given over to savagery and 'incivility,' little fit for the habitation of people of character and refinement, but to which in the last resort a spendthrift or a scapegrace might perhaps venture to repair, to restore his shattered fortunes in the vast area of its confiscated lands, or to win reputation in its incessant wars. It is of such a one that Bishop Hall speaks, in his 'Virgidemiarum,' in the lines

> So slips he to the wolvish western isle
> Among the savage kerne in sad exile.

And it is of a piece with this conception of Ireland that in the fourth book of the 'Faery Queene' Sir Arthegall, the knight who is afterwards charged with the task of succouring Irena, the fair princess in whom Ireland is personified in the allegory, is introduced under the designation of 'the Salvage Knight,' all whose armour

> was like the salvage weed
> With woody moss bedight, and all his steed
> With oaken leaves attrapped, that seemed fit
> For salvage wight.

To realise adequately the extent to which the poetry of the 'Faery Queene' was influenced by Spenser's surroundings in Ireland, it is necessary to examine a little carefully the course of his career as a servant of the Crown in that country, and to compare his successive migrations with the stages of the composition of his great poem. The poet's connexion with Ireland certainly began as early as 1577, when, as already noted, he was appointed to the position of secretary to Sir Henry Sidney. Neither then, nor later under Lord Grey de Wilton's Viceroyalty, does Spenser's name appear in the lists of viceregal officers; the Secretary of State under both Sidney and Grey being John Chaloner, who in 1581 was succeeded by the well-known Sir Geoffrey Fenton. Evidently Spenser's position was only that of private secretary. Sidney left Ireland in August 1578, and Spenser did not remain behind him; so that the poet's first connexion with Ireland must have been of the briefest. Some of his biographers have even doubted whether he came over. But though no document of any sort survives to attest the fact, it is impossible to doubt the poet's own statement in his 'View of the State of Ireland,' that he was present at Limerick 'at the execution of a notable traitor Murrough O'Brien,' an event which is known to have taken place in July 1577.

This first brief visit to Ireland can have given Spenser but few opportunities of learning his way about the country. He was certainly absent from Ireland between 1578 and 1580, that is, from the retirement of Sidney to the appointment of Grey. He may, indeed, have acquired just such an impression of the country as an untutored wilderness, filled with wild and semi-civilised people, as would suggest his making its solitudes of wood and waste and mountain the background or scenery of the action of the great allegory he was already meditating. But it was impossible that he could learn enough in so short a stay to enable him to give those intimate descriptions of familiar scenes which are abundant in the later books of the 'Faery Queene' and elsewhere in his later poetry. In the summer of 1580, however, Spenser entered definitely upon that Irish career which was to last until his death. Except for occasional visits, sometimes lengthened, but still never more than visits, to England, Ireland was henceforth his continuous, though no doubt uncongenial, residence, and in the fullest sense his home. We know from a letter to Gabriel Harvey, written in April 1580—four months, that is, before his coming to Ireland for the second time—that before that date he had already begun work on the 'Faery Queene.' Some portions of the poem had been drafted, though probably not precisely in the form in which they ultimately appeared. But evidently no great progress had been made; for he writes to his literary confidant and critic, 'I will in hand forthwith with my "Faery Queene," which I pray you heartily send me with all expedition.' In the years immediately following his appointment, and in fact throughout his chief's tenure of the Viceroyalty, Spenser can have had little leisure to cultivate the Muse. The Deputy was constantly moving about, and for the first six months his secretary had abundant opportunities of seeing rural Ireland. He was present with Grey at Smerwick, and as is evident from the 'View of the State of Ireland,' was perpetually at his chief's elbow until his duties were terminated by the Viceroy's recall, precisely two years after his coming over. Meantime, he had been appointed, in March 1580–81, to the office of Registrar or Clerk of the Faculties in the Court of Chancery, a position of considerable importance, and probably proportionate emolument, in Dublin. He was succeeded in this office in 1588 by Arland Ussher, father of the great Primate, and it may have been in this connexion that the latter formed the acquaintance to which he testified heartily many years afterwards, as Aubrey relates, by his indignation at Sir William Davenant's slighting remarks on his 'old friend Edmund Spenser.'[1] For six years from this date, until he took over from his brother poet, Ludovic Bryskett, the office of Clerk to the Council of the Munster Presidency, Spenser's head quarters must have been in Dublin. In the same year in which he acquired his Chancery post he received his first grant of Irish property, procuring a lease of 'the house of Friars

[1] None of Spenser's biographers, not even the industrious Dr. Grosart, have been at much pains to investigate the nature of the office in the Irish Court of Chancery to which Spenser was appointed, shortly after his arrival in Ireland. There is certainly nothing in the title of that office or the enumeration of its duties which suggests that it can have had much attraction for the poet. It was, however, a position of considerable importance and substantial emolument; and so far as regards this office, and his later post in Munster, Mr. Lee's remark that 'the record of Spenser's worldly struggles is sordid and insignificant' is hardly warranted. The office of 'Registrar or Clerk in Chancery for the Faculties' was constituted by the Act of Faculties, 28th Henry VIII. Chapter 19. This statute was levelled against the 'intollerable exaction of great sums of money by the Bishop of Rome' for dispensations, licences, and faculties. After repudiating the Pope's authority it declared the authority of the King and Parliament to dispense upon due occasion with the laws, and provided that such dispensations should be given under faculties to be obtained under the Great Seal, or the seal of the Archbishop of Dublin. For the due performance of its prescribed functions, the Act further provided for the appointment of 'one sufficient Clerk, being learned in the course of Chancery, which shall always be attendant on the Lord Chancellor or the Lord Keeper of the Great Seal, and shall make, write and enroll the confirmations of all such licences, dispensations, instruments and other writings as shall be brought under the Archbishop's seal, there to be confirmed or enrolled, taking for his pains such reasonable sums of money as hereafter, by this Act, shall be limited for the same.' What the precise remuneration amounted to does not appear, as it was paid out of the fees charged on the faculties. With this office was united the cognate office of Registrar of Ecclesiastical Appeals, constituted as a separate post under the Act, but which in practice was amalgamated with the Registrarship of Faculties.

of Enniscortie, the Manor of Enniscortie, and a ruinous castle and weir there.' Of this he was only three days the master, parting with it to one Richard Synot, who some years later transferred the lands to Sir Henry Wallop, ancestor of the Earls of Portsmouth, by whose descendants they are still held. But he was not long in acquiring a similar interest in property more conveniently situated, being granted in August 1581 a lease of 'the site of the House of Friars called the New Abbey, co. Kildare,' which had lapsed to the Crown through the attainder of Rowland Eustace, Lord Baltinglass, the head of a family whose distinction it has been to supply at a distance of two centuries two eminent occupants of the Irish Woolsack. He likewise acquired the custodiam of the lands of Newlands in the same neighbourhood, and a lease for six years of the same nobleman's Dublin residence. New Abbey was a house of the Franciscans which had been founded by the ancestors of Lord Baltinglass in 1460, and had been regranted to that peer on the dissolution of the monasteries. Seven years later this property had passed out of Spenser's hands, being leased to one Thomas Lambyn, from whom it passed within a few years to Sir Henry Harington. The poet had by that time settled in Munster, and had no further need of it. But there is evidence that it remained for some years in his hands, and must often have been visited by him, even if he did not actually reside there. In 1583 and 1584 Spenser is named in successive commissions to the principal gentry of Kildare as one of the commissioners of musters for that county.[1] New Abbey lay within riding distance of the metropolis, the river Liffey flowing through its grounds, and adjacent to the north-eastern border of the great Bog of Allen. At least two passages in the 'Faery Queene' are reminiscent of its surroundings. The well-known line in the descriptive of the Irish rivers in the fourth book—

> There was the Liffey rolling down the lea,

is strictly applicable to the aspect of the river at this part of its course, where, having left its mountain sources, it assumes the proportions and the vigour of an ample stream. And

[1] See *Calendars of Fiants* and *State Papers, Ireland.*

a passage in the ninth canto of the second book, which may be presumed to have been written about the period of his residence in this district, and prior to his residence at Kilcolman, bears still stronger testimony to the poet's familiarity with the neighbourhood :—

> As when a swarme of gnats at eventide
> Out of the fennes of Allan do arise,
> Their murmuring small trompets sounden wide,
> Whiles in the air their clustring army flies,
> That as a cloud doth seeme to dim the skies ;
> Ne man nor beast may rest nor take repast
> For their sharpe wounds, and noyous injuries,
> Till the fierce northerne wind with blustring blast
> Doth blow them quite away and in the ocean cast.

Spenser's earlier biographers seem to have considered that his connexion with Ireland ceased for some years with his patron's withdrawal from the country. But this suggestion is unwarranted by what we now know of the facts. The documents just referred to in connexion with New Abbey show him to have been resident in Ireland in the summer of 1584, and the fact that he retained his appointment as Registrar of the Court of Chancery till 1588, only resigning it within a week of his being gazetted Clerk of the Munster Council, affords a strong presumption that he remained continuously resident in or near Dublin. The date of the well-known meeting of Spenser and other friends, many of them persons of distinction, at Bryskett's cottage near Dublin, at which time the poet is known to have been busily at work upon his poem, cannot have been earlier than July 1584, and may have been a year later. Spenser must manifestly have been resident in Ireland when, in June 1586 in the articles for the Munster Undertakers, he was set down for the lands of Kilcolman, for in this year he addressed a sonnet from Dublin to his old friend Harvey. From the date of the poet's acceptance of the Munster Secretaryship, and actual settlement at Kilcolman, our knowledge of Spenser's career is sufficient to enable us to say that he was almost continuously in the South of Ireland. From 1588, when he succeeded Ludovic Bryskett, until about

1593, when he appears to have surrendered his office to a deputy, he must have passed his time between Limerick, the official seat of the Presidency, and his own home at Kilcolman, his only absences being occasioned by his visits to London with Raleigh in 1589 or 1590, when he arranged for the publication of the first three books of the 'Faery Queene,' and again in 1595, in connexion with the publication of the last books of the same work.

It is plain from the foregoing analysis of the known facts of Spenser's official career in Ireland that his residence there falls into two clearly marked periods. In the first, which extended from his arrival in August 1580 to his acceptance of the office in Munster in 1588, he was in general resident in Dublin, though his duties took him frequently into the country. During a part and perhaps the greater part of this period he had an alternative residence in a country seat not far from Dublin, in which he could at times enjoy the sylvan scenery in which he delighted. But it is evident that while he would thus have acquired an excellent general knowledge of Ireland, he was not in a position to acquire an intimate familiarity with any particular locality. In the second period, on the other hand, he was in uninterrupted occupation of a permanent home, and enjoying a comparative leisure which would enable him to explore the whole of the neighbouring country. For although his official position must have rendered it a matter of obligation that his head quarters should be in Munster, it did not of necessity involve residence in Limerick, where the routine duties of the Secretaryship were discharged by a deputy.

These differing characteristics of the two main periods of Spenser's Irish life will be found to be closely reflected in his poetry. In the first three books of the 'Faery Queene,' the *genius loci* is indeed apparent, not only in the general setting of the imagery, but in many specific allusions; but there is no detailed description of familiar haunts. In the second portion of the poem, on the other hand, the scenery and the associations of Kilcolman and the South of Ireland colour the whole texture of his work, and the concluding books abound in passages wherein not all the poet's idealism nor the veil of his elaborate allegory can conceal the influence of his actual surroundings, both upon the trend of his fancy and the form in which that fancy found expression. And what is true of the 'Faery Queene' is true of Spenser's minor poetry. In the poems written between 1580 and 1590 the local allusions, though not entirely wanting, are few and far between, and they are the allusions of a stranger in a strange land; in his later pieces they are frequent and even elaborate. Thus in 'Astrophel' the forest of Arlo, which he afterwards celebrated so affectionately, is mentioned only to be contrasted with the more peaceful woodlands of England.

So wide a forest and so waste as this
Nor famous Arden, nor fowl Arlo is.

But in the fragment on 'Mutability' this synonym for the terrible is transformed by 'the magic of ownership' into a paradise, and represented as having been anciently

the best and fairest hill
That was in all their holy island's heights,

though transformed by wars and the hand of man into a wilderness.

In illustration of these remarks it is worth while to examine the 'Faery Queene' with some attention from the point of view of its topographical allusiveness. In the first three books, as already remarked, there are to be found by the careful reader reminiscences of Irish scenery and of Irish social conditions which are tolerably distinct. Thus in the 'Legend of Temperance,' it is sufficiently obvious that in the description of the attack on Sir Guyon and his comrades we have a picture of the lawless banditti who commonly formed the bodyguard of an Irish chief, much as they are represented by Derricke in his 'Image of Irelande,'[1] or by Spenser himself in his prose works, and as they are depicted in the almost contemporary drawings which accompany Derricke's work:

Thus as he spoke, lo, with outrageous cry
A thousand villeins round about them swarmed
Out of the rocks and caves adjoining nigh;

[1] *The Image of Irelande*, edited by John Small. Edin. 1883.

Vile caitiff wretches, ragged, rude, deformed,
All threat'ning death, all in strange manner armed ;
Some with unwieldy clubs, some with long spears,
Some rusty knives, some staves in fire warmed ;
Stern was their look, like wild amazed stears,
Staring with hollow eyes and stiff upstanding hairs.[1]

Again, in the two following quotations it is plain that the poet is drawing not from imagination but from memory :

As when a foggy mist hath overcast
The face of heaven, and the clear air engrost,
The world in darkness dwells ; till that at last
The watery south-wind, from the seaboard coast
Upblowing, doth disperse the vapour loos'd,
And pours itself forth in a stormy shower :
So the fair Britomart, &c.[2]

In the lines just quoted we may have a reminiscence of Kilcolman, which lies not very far from the sea, and it is little to be doubted that in the following we have a picture of the vale of Arlo :

Into that forest far they thence him led,
Where was their dwelling ; in a pleasant glade
With mountains round about environed,
And mighty woods which did the valley shade,
And like a stately theatre it made,
Spreading itself into a spacious plain ;
And in the midst a little river played
Amongst the pumy stones, which seemed to plaine
With gentle murmur that his course they did restrain.[3]

The witch's cottage in the same book is plainly reminiscent of an Irish cabin of Spenser's day :

There in a gloomy hollow glen she found
A little cottage, built of sticks and reeds
In homely wise, and walled with sods around ;
In which a witch did dwell in loathly weeds
And wilful want, all careless of her needs.[4]

[1] Book II. Canto ix. Stanza 13.
[2] Book III. Canto iv. Stanza 13.
[3] Book III. Canto v. Stanza 39.
[4] Book III. Canto vii. Stanza 6.

While the lordlier apartment, described in the 'Legend of Holiness,' may well have been drawn from the hall of one of the greater Irish castles, even if the scene depicted be not the Earl of Ormond's 'brave mansion' at Kilkenny:

> And forth he comes into the common hall;
> Where early waits him many a gazing eye,
> To weet what end to stranger knights may fall.
> There many minstrels maken melody;
> To drive away the dull melancholy;
> And many bards that to the trembling chord
> Can tune their timely voices cunningly;
> And many chroniclers that can record
> Old loves, and wars for ladies done by many a Lord.[1]

Many similar illustrations might readily be adduced from the earlier books of the 'Faery Queene,' to show the degree in which Spenser's imagination was haunted by the wild charm of the 'salvage soil' in which he found himself, even where the context shows that he had no express concern with Ireland in the evolution of his allegory. But these must suffice. It is to be noticed, however, concerning these and all similar passages, that however obvious the reflections of the sights and scenes of Irish life which they exhibit, it is only in the earliest cited example, the description of the gnats of the fens of Allen, that any express use is made of Irish scenery or that an Irish name is used. With that exception it is only in the later books that the scenery of Ireland is avowedly introduced. In those books, however, and in those of his minor poems which can confidently be ascribed to the last decade of the poet's life, the references to the rivers, hills, and woods of Ireland are many and widely scattered, though it is curious that the account of Sir Arthegall's 'adventure hard' in the 'Legend of Justice,' in which Lord Grey de Wilton's Irish experiences are almost undisguisedly commemorated, contains no mention of the country in which it is represented as occurring more express than the anagram Irene for Ierne, in which the parable is subtly indicated. With the exception already specified, the first clear

[1] Book I. Canto v. Stanza 3.

note of Spenser's acquaintance with Ireland which is heard in the 'Faery Queene' occurs in book four, and refers appropriately to the Irish Channel. It is to be found in canto one stanza forty-two, where the shock of the onset of the two knights in the encounter between Blandamour and Scudamour is likened to

two billows in the Irish sounds
Forcibly driven with contráry tides.

The next, in canto three stanza twenty-seven, of the same book, is also an aquatic simile for a knightly duel. It will be found in the story of Campbell's fight with Triamond, and is borrowed from the tidal conflict of sea and river in the estuary of the Shannon, which Spenser must often have noted during his official visits to Limerick:

Like as the tide, that comes fro' the ocean main,
Flows up the Shannon with contrary force,
And, over-ruling him in his own reign,
Drives back the current of his kindly course,
And makes it seem to have some other source;
But, when the flood is spent, then back again
His borrowed waters forced to redisburse,
He sends the sea his own with doubled gain
And tribute eke withal, as to his Soveraine.

But by far the most famous of the Irish passages in the 'Faery Queene' is of course the well-known catalogue of the Irish rivers, who are represented as attending the spousals of the Thames and the Medway, which, often as it has been quoted, must be quoted here once more:

Ne thence the Irish rivers absent were,
Sith no less famous than the rest they be.

. . . . . .

There was the Liffey rolling down the lea;
The sandy Slane; the stony Aubrian;[1]
The spacious Shenan spreading like a sea;
The pleasant Boyne; the fishy, fruitful Ban;

[1] 'The Stony Aubrian' has puzzled Dr. Joyce and all the topographical critics. May it not be the Owenbrin which flows into Lough Mask, a river certainly known to the Elizabethan captains who soldiered in Connaught and to whom Spenser was certainly indebted for some of his local knowledge? The epithet 'stony' is particularly applicable to this river.

Swift Awniduff, which of the English man
Is cal'de Blackewater, and the Liffar deepe ;
Sad Trowis, that once his people overran ;
Strong Allo, tumbling from Slewlogher steep ;
And Mulla mine, whose waves I whilom taught to weep.

And there the three renowned brethren were :
. . . . .

The first and gentle Shure that making way
By sweet Clonmell adorns rich Waterford ;
The next the stubborn Newre, whose waters gray
By faire Kilkenny and Rossponte boord,
The third the goodly Barow, which doth hoord
Great heapes of salmons in their deepe bosome :
All which, long sundered, do at last accord
To joyne in one, ere to the sea they come ;
So flowing all from one, all one at last become.

There also was the wide embayed Mayre ;
The pleasant Bandon, crowned with many a wood ;
The spreading Lee, that, like an island fair,
Encloseth Cork with his divided flood ;
The baleful Oure, late stained with English blood,
With many more whose names no tongue can tell.[1]

Dr. Joyce, in the article in *Fraser's Magazine* already mentioned, has dealt, with great fulness and intimate knowledge of the local geography of Ireland, with this enumeration of the Irish rivers, as also with the detailed references to the neighbourhood of the poet's home, which are so numerous in the largely autobiographical poem of 'Colin Clout 's Come Home Again,' and in the fragmentary cantos of 'Mutability.' We have no intention of entering here into a detailed examination of the use made by the poet of the scenery of Kilcolman. The pictures of his home in the former poem and in the 'Epithalamion' are photographic in their accuracy to anyone who has viewed the scene for himself, though its aspect to-day is of course less homely, since, of the once substantial building only the gaunt peel tower of the castle remains, and almost all

[1] Book IV. Canto xi. Stanzas 40–44.

traces of its precincts are lost. For the wild solitudes of Kilcolman, with its lonely lake and barren marsh, peopled only by wild-fowl, and the desolate levels of moor and bog which stretch between the mountains and the mere are not less but more a solitude to-day than in the poet's time. Those familiar with its present appearance will hardly agree with Mr. Lee that 'the surrounding scenery has gained in fulness and in richness of aspect' in the interval. This reminiscence of the poet ruminating in his farm is more attractive than the present-day reality, though it testifies to his unaffected enjoyment of his home:

> One day (quoth he), I sat (as was my trade)
> Under the foot of Mole, that mountain hore,
> Keeping my sheep amongst the cooly shade
> Of the greene alders by the Mulla's shore.[1]

Similarly the panegyric on the stream at Kilcolman as an angler's joy, though it may perhaps exaggerate the piscatory qualities of the Awbeg as we now know it, expresses all the pride of an owner in the attractions of his home, and recalls with accurate suggestiveness the surroundings of Kilcolman:

> Ye nymphs of Mulla, that with careful heed
> The scaly river trouts do tend full well,
> And greedy pikes which use therein to feed;
> (Those trouts and pikes all others do excel)
> And ye likewise which keep the rushy lake
> Where none do fishes take,
> Bind up the locks, the which hang scattered light.
> . . . .
> And eke ye lightfoot maids which keep the dore
> That on the hoary mountain use to toure:
> And the wild wolves which seek them to devour
> With your steele darts do chace from coming near.[2]

But neither the express references to the poet's home, nor the specific descriptions of the natural features and scenery of Ireland already quoted, exhaust the illustrations which Spenser's poetry affords of the influence exerted upon his

[1] *Colin Clout's Come Home Again.* [2] *Epithalamion.*

literary development by the circumstances which cast his lot in Ireland. There are also clear indications of the effects produced by his official experience upon his opinions on the political problems presented by the Ireland of his day. Of Spenser's official connexion with Ireland, by far the most important memorial is his prose 'View of the State of Ireland.' But scarcely less remarkable, and even more minute in its references to the actual scenes in which the poet participated, is the narrative already referred to of the 'Adventure of Irene,' in the fifth book of the 'Faery Queene.' It has been observed, and not unjustly, that the pure allegory of the poem is much more perfect in the earlier than in the later books, and that the vividness of Spenser's purely poetical imagination is injured in some parts of the poem by the substitution of the historical for the strictly romantic allegory. That is no more than to say that even the astonishing wealth and fecundity of Spenser's imagination were not absolutely inexhaustible, and could not be entirely independent of the pabulum supplied by the actualities of life in the material world in which he lived and moved. But the poetry as poetry is none the worse for this. It is doubtless true that if we insist on dissecting the poetry, and on laying bare the political moral which may be found to underlie it, our appreciation of the poetry is likely to be effected by our sympathy with or dislike for the political or religious ideals of the poet. But there is no reason why the reader who comes to the 'Faery Queene' for its poetry should trouble himself about its politics, real or supposed. It is only from the point of view from which we are now writing that the hidden or obscure allusions to contemporary persons and events are of any serious interest. It is, however, precisely those portions of the poem which are most obviously historical that are the most likely to yield sidelights on the poet's personal history. And there is no portion of the 'Faery Queene' or of any of Spenser's works more charged with autobiographical significance than the 'Legend of Justice.'

As everyone knows, the 'Legend of Justice' portrays in the person of its hero, Sir Arthegall, Spenser's political chief in Ireland, Lord Grey de Wilton. Already in the 'Legend of

Britomartis' he had hinted not obscurely at Elizabeth's dissatisfaction with Grey in the early part of that statesman's career, when, for some now unknown offence, the Queen imprisoned him in the Fleet, and he had eloquently vindicated his patron through the mouth of the Redcross Knight :—

> Faire martial maid,
> Certes ye misadvised been to upbraid
> A gentle knight with so unknightly blame ;
> For weet ye well of all that ever played
> At tilt or tourney, or like warlike game,
> The noble Arthegall hath ever borne the name.[1]

Spenser had also drawn in the same canto a splendid portrait of his hero. But although in the fourth canto Sir Arthegall is again introduced and his restoration to the Queen's favour is intimated in the knight's relations with Britomartis, the poet does no more at that stage of his story than foreshadow his intention of dealing with the episodes of his patron's Irish career, by representing the knight as leaving his lady in quest of the 'hard adventure' he had long propounded, and the 'Legend of Friendship' is concluded without any development of Arthegall's adventures in Irene's behalf. In all probability what determined Spenser's choice of the topic of the fifth book was the death of Lord Grey. This event, which occurred in October 1593, must have been nearly coincident with the date at which the 'Legend of Justice' was commenced. The book must certainly have been written about this period, and it is easy to imagine that the death of his friend and former patron, to whom, amongst others, he had dedicated the earlier portions of his poem, and for whom he lost no opportunity of evincing a warm and grateful regard, would have given a fresh impulse to the poet's Muse, and led him to commemorate Grey's career. It is certain that in the 'Legend of Justice' and especially in the portrait of Sir Arthegall there is a personal note which is wanting elsewhere, and which intimates how closely the poet's sympathies were aroused in this part of his narrative. It is at once an elegy on

[1] Book III. Canto ii. Stanza 9.

his much admired patron and an assertion of the principles upon which, in Spenser's judgment, the government of Ireland could alone be successfully conducted, principles by which Grey had certainly been animated, but of which little trace was to be found in the administration of his successors.

The twelfth canto of the fifth book recounts accordingly, under a thinly veiled disguise, the stirring incidents of Lord Grey's vigorous government, the hostilities with the Spanish force, whose landing at Smerwick had been almost coincident with Lord Grey's arrival in Ireland, their annihilation by the Viceroy's army, the reduction of the country by a stern enforcement of the law, and the vacillation of Elizabeth and her ministers in England, by which his policy was thwarted and which soon led to his recall and disgrace. Of these latter aspects of his patron's career in Ireland the poet's views are expressed in these nervous stanzas :

> During which time that he did there remain,
> His study was true justice how to deal,
> And day and night employed his busy pain
> How to reform that ragged commonweal :
> And that same Iron Man, which could reveal
> All hidden crimes, through all that realm he sent,
> To search out those that used to rob and steal
> Or did rebel 'gainst lawful government,
> On whom he did inflict most grievous punishment.
>
> But ere he could reforme it thoroughly,
> He through occasion called was away
> To Faerie Court, that of necessity
> His course of justice he was forced to stay,
> And Talus to revoke from the right way
> In which he was that Realm for to redresse.
> But Envye's cloud still dimmeth virtue's ray !
> So having freed Irene from distress
> He took his leave of her, there left in heaviness.[1]

Spenser has been reproached in relation to Irish politics with an arrogant contempt for Ireland, and Mr. Lee censures

[1] Book V. Canto xii. Stanzas 26, 27.

his 'View of the State of Ireland' as 'a mere echo of the hopeless and helpless prejudices which infected the English governing class.' But whatever may be said of the narrowness of Elizabethan views of the Irish question, this picture of the difficulties of an Irish Viceroy is intensely modern. So little difference have three centuries wrought in Ireland, so perennial are the problems that at recurring periods compel the attention of English statesmen, that they might with equal applicability have been written by some uncompromising Unionist of the present day in reference to Mr. Arthur Balfour's Chief Secretaryship and his administration of the Crimes Act.

The political motive of the 'Legend of Justice,' and especially of Sir Arthegall's adventure with Irene, has of course been often noticed, and indeed is almost too obvious to be missed by any reader at all acquainted with the history of the time. But the like intention has not been so generally recognised in the two cantos of 'Mutability.' Yet their applicability to Ireland and to the changes in the attitude of English policy after Lord Grey's recall is too striking to be merely accidental. It would seem as though the 'Legend of Constancy' of which these fragments were meant to be a part was designed to furnish that supplement to the 'Legend of Justice' which is promised in the last stanza of the fifth book. It is at any rate manifest that the evils which the poet bewails in these cantos are precisely those which the ex-official deplored in his 'View of the State of Ireland,' and which the Munster Undertaker reprobated in the last known writing of Spenser, that letter addressed to the Queen which he either brought with him on his last journey to London, or composed as he lay sick in King Street on what proved to be his death-bed.

The parallel between the two works is indeed astonishingly close. The chief burden of the 'View' in its constructive suggestions, is the need for consistency in the policy to be pursued by the Crown in Ireland. Spenser's ideal administration was the stern and inflexible but never purposeless severity of the administration of Lord Grey. He could conceive no greater injustice to Ireland, nothing more injurious to the well-being of his adopted country, than the making her the sport of English politicians, or the arena for the rivalries of the English courtiers who contended for the favour of Elizabeth. Inconsistency or inconstancy in action, lack of purpose and vacillation on the part of the representatives of the Crown, he considered injurious alike to both the English and the Irish elements of the population. Spenser's acute sense of the mischief wrought by this unfortunate feature in a system of government whose working he thoroughly understood, and whose actions he had had the best means of noting during fifteen years' residence in Ireland, is stated with great clearness and emphasis in the remarkable passage in his prose treatise in which he reviews the motives and conduct of successive Deputies :

> The sequel of things doth in a manner prove, and plainly speak so much, that the governors usually are envious one of another's greater glory, which if they would seek to excel by better governing it should be a most laudable emulation. But they do quite otherwise. For this (as you may mark) is the common order of them, that who cometh next in place will not follow that course of government, however good, which his predecessors held, either for disdain of himself, or doubt to have his doings drowned in another man's praise, but will straight take a way quite contrary to the former : as if the former thought (by keeping under the Irish) to reform them ; the next, by discountenancing the English, will curry favour with the Irish, and so make his government seem plausible, as having all the Irish at his command : but he that comes after, will perhaps follow neither the one nor the other, but will dandle the one and the other in such sort as he will suck sweet out of them both, and leave bitterness to the poor country, which if he that comes after shall seek to redress, he shall perhaps find such crosses as he shall hardly be able to bear, or do any good that might work the disgrace of his predecessors.

Such is the burden of the song which was continually on Spenser's lips as often as he referred to Irish problems, and such is the significance of the stanzas of ' Mutability,' which sound like its musical accompaniment. The date at which these posthumously published cantos were written is not known, but they almost certainly belong to that period of trouble and disorder in which the poet's closing years were spent, and were inspired by the apprehension of that calamitous rising in which the Munster plantation was overwhelmed and his own fortunes ruined. So read, and it is impossible for anyone who knows the historical facts to read them otherwise, they are full of a melancholy personal significance from the commencement to the close. The metrical argument prefixed to each canto indicates not obscurely the motive of the allegory and its application to the ills of Ireland, while the fact that the scenery of both cantos is laid in Munster, and that the machinery moves in the solitudes of the Galtee mountains, is even more clearly indicative of the poet's meaning and purpose.

> Proud change (not pleased in mortall things
>   Beneath the moon to reign)
> Pretends as well of gods as men
>   To be the sovereign.
>
> 'Pealing from Jove to Nature's bar
>   Bold alteration pleads
> Large evidence ; but Nature soon
>   Her righteous doom areads.'

The first stanza of canto six, with the two stanzas which have alone reached us of the 'unperfite' eighth canto, plainly bespeak the pessimism of the poet in his latter days. Convinced of the ultimate triumph of the principle of constancy in the moral and spiritual world, he yet despairs of witnessing the effective assertion in the actual world in which he moved of the principle of unswerving consistency of purpose and action. These cantos are the dirge of the system of selfish, unprincipled and purposeless methods of government which had lasted through the poet's Irish career, and which were to be replaced, as a result of the anarchy which they inevitably produced, by the very different scheme of administration and of settlement which Spenser did not live to see.

What man that sees the ever-whirling wheel
Of Change, the which all mortal things doth sway,
But that thereby shall find, and plainly feel
How Mutability in them doth play
Her cruel sports to many men's decay.[1]

. . . .

When I bethink me of that speech whileare
Of Mutability, and well it way!
Me seems that though she all unworthy were
Of the heavens' rule; yet very sooth to say,
In all things else she bears the greatest sway;
Which makes me loath this state of life so tickle,
And love of things so vain to cast away;
Whose flowring pride, so fading and so fickle,
Short Time shall soon cut down with his consuming sickle.

Then 'gin I think on that which Nature said,
Of that same time when no more change shall be.
But steadfast rest of all things, firmly stayed
Upon the pillars of Eternity,
That is contrayr to Mutability:
For all that moveth doth in change delight:
But thenceforth all shall rest eternally
With Him that is the God of Sabaoth hight,
O! thou great Sabaoth God, grant me that Sabaoth's sight.[2]

As the larger moral of this concluding portion of Spenser's great poem is plainly to assert the faultiness of the methods of government employed by English statesmen in their dealings with Ireland, so the machinery of the allegory is utilised to indicate its effects in producing or helping to produce the desolation which the resulting anarchy in the Irish provinces had wrought in Munster and in the near neighbourhood of his own home. Of the affection he had grown to feel for Kilcolman and his surroundings abundant references throughout the poem are eloquent. But nowhere is this trait more

[1] Canto vi. Stanza 1. [2] Canto viii. Stanzas 1, 2.

apparent, though his language in the latter reference is charged with melancholy and foreboding, than in the first of these cantos of 'Mutability,' the scene of which is laid amid the hill and vale of Arlo. After adverting to the old days—

When Ireland flourished in fame
Of wealth and goodness far above the rest
Of all that bear the British islands' name,[1]

the poet narrates how Cynthia, as 'sovereign queen professed of woods and forests,' had chosen Arlo for her home:

But mongst them all as fittest for her game
(Either for chase of beasts with hound or bow
Or for to shroud in shade from Phoebus flame
Or bathe in fountains that do freshly flow
Or from high hills, or from the dales below)
She chose this Arlo.[2]

Then after explaining by what offence against her modesty Diana was driven from her loved resort, he gives the picture of its modern desolation:

Natheless Diana full of indignation,
Thenceforth abandoned her delicious brook,
In whose sweet stream, before that bad occasion,
So much delight to bathe her limbs she took;
Ne only her, but also quite forsook
All those fair forests about Arlo hid;
And all that mountain which doth overlook
The richest champain that may else be rid,
And the fair Shure in which are thousand salmons bred.

Them all, and all that she so dear did way,
Thenceforth she left; and, parting from the place,
Thereon a heavy, hapless curse did lay;
To weet, that wolves, where she was wont to space
Should harboured be, and all those woods deface,
And thieves should rob and spoil that coast around,

[1] Canto vi. Stanza 38.
[2] Stanza 39.

Since which, those woods, and all that goodly chase
Doth to this day with wolves and thieves abound :
Which too-too true that lands indwellers since have found.[1]

Such and so melancholy are the last references to Ireland to be found in Spenser's verse. It is significant that they are also the last lines of all his poetry that have reached us.

[1] Stanzas 54–55.

SIR JOHN DAVIS

In the previous article occasion was taken to observe on the remarkable degree in which the careers of many among the most famous Elizabethans were involved in the affairs of Ireland. Men of action and men of letters alike found on Irish soil a field for adventures and an opportunity for advancing their fortunes, and flocked to it in numbers. The careers of many of the most famous figures in the Courts of Elizabeth and James the First were moulded, often to a large degree, and sometimes finally, by their Irish experiences. Sidney and Sussex, Mountjoy and the ill-fated Essex among statesmen, are all of them examples of men whose fortunes were made or marred in Ireland. Among men of action and affairs there is the striking instance of Richard Boyle, 'the great Earl of Cork,' a man whose acquisitive and constructive genius must have won him enduring fame as an empire builder, had he carried it to any country but Ireland. And in the sphere of letters there are the yet more splendid names of Spenser and of Raleigh, and the less eminent but still remarkable figure of the subject of this article.

But there is this distinction between the case of Sir John Davis and the others we have mentioned, that whereas in the case of the latter their Irish experiences formed no more than an episode, however important, in the career of each, in that of Davis his Irish service made up the main interest and importance of a life in which all other incidents were secondary. It is true, indeed, that before he had entered on his sixteen years' service as an Irish official Davis was already famous enough to be greeted by James the First at that monarch's accession to the English Crown as a poet of acknowledged celebrity, and that at its conclusion he devoted himself to a legal career in England, which had just led him to the great place of Lord Chief Justice when death put its abrupt close on his ambitions. But neither his literary eminence, though it was considerable, nor his legal attainments, though these were of a high order, would have sufficed to give Davis the lasting fame he acquired had his career not included the period of his life in which he was the animating spirit of the Irish Government at an epoch of singular importance in Irish history. For not merely was Davis the trusted and most efficient instrument of the Irish policy of King James and his Ministers from the morrow of that suppression of Tyrone's rebellion which was the last act in the long agony of Elizabeth's Irish wars, but he was in a large degree the guiding spirit of the Irish administration by which that policy was directed.

Davis's connexion with Ireland was marked by three great and far-reaching developments in its administrative, its social, and its parliamentary history. And in each of these great and pregnant transactions he himself bore a principal part. It was during his tenure of the Irish attorney-generalship that the machinery of local government was first effectively organised through the definitive demarcation of the four Irish provinces and the final settlement of the boundaries of the counties embraced in each. It was during his term of office, and largely under his direction and supervision, if not under his immediate inspiration, that the tremendous operation of the Plantation of Ulster was conceived and executed. And finally it was under his advice and guidance that the parliamentary system of Ireland was modelled and developed from the very primitive organisation which had sufficed even as late as Tudor times into the actual scheme of representation which prevailed for almost two centuries from his time.

To the proper understanding of the tangled story of Ireland under Charles the First and Cromwell, an accurate knowledge of the Ireland of the first quarter of the seventeenth century is essential. This is a period which has too often been passed over by the historians, and no adequate account of it has yet been written. But Dr. Mahaffy in his book on Trinity College, Dublin,[1] has handled with much felicity and gift of historical insight some, at least, of the problems which belong to the Ireland of Davis. And Mrs. Townshend in her 'Life of the Great Earl of Cork'[2] recalls both the peculiar social conditions of the time and the characters of the leading personages.

Sir John Davis[3] was the son of Edward Davis, a small country gentleman of Welsh extraction and owning a patrimony in Wiltshire, whither his ancestor had accompanied the Earl of Pembroke early in the sixteenth century. John Davis was the third son, and was born about the year 1570. He was educated at Winchester and Queen's College, Oxford, where he graduated in 1590. Early designed for the law, Davis was admitted a student at the Middle Temple in 1587, and was called to the Bar in 1595. His progress, both academic and legal, was marked by many irregularities. He had a taste for practical joking and rough horseplay, which at Oxford caused his expulsion from Commons; and in early life at least he displayed a warmth of temper and a disregard for social conventions which, within three years of his admission to the Bar, had nearly wrecked his career. He was intemperate enough to publicly chastise a quondam friend, one Richard Martin, in the hall of the Middle Temple in presence of the assembled benchers. For this offence he was very properly disbarred and expelled the society, and but for the intervention of a powerful friend his legal prospects must have been for ever ruined. But after three years of disgrace Lord Chancellor Ellesmere procured his restoration, and on making public profession of repentance Davis was readmitted to practice.

But the three years of seclusion had not been wasted. As early as 1593 Davis had written his first poem 'Orchestra, or a Poem of Dancing': a work which was dedicated to the same Martin with whom he subsequently quarrelled so

[1] *An Epoch in Irish History*, by John Pentland Mahaffy.

[2] *The Life and Letters of the Great Earl of Cork*, by Dorothea Townshend.

[3] Davies is the more correct form of the name, and is the spelling adopted in the notice in the *Dictionary of National Biography;* but the form long consecrated by familiar usage has been retained throughout this article.

disastrously, and which Mr. Bullen, in his Introduction to Professor Arber's collection of longer English poems,[1] justly praises as 'a graceful monument of ingenious fancy.' On being prohibited from practice, Davis resumed his devotion to the Muses, and, retiring to Oxford, produced his well-known 'Nosce Teipsum,' a poem 'Of the Soul of Man, and of the Immortality thereof,' which he was encouraged by his friend and patron, Lord Mountjoy, to dedicate to Elizabeth. Of this poem Hallam, in his 'History of Literature,' says that 'perhaps no language can produce a poem extending to so great a length of more condensation of thought, or in which fewer languid verses will be found,' and that 'very few have been able to preserve a perspicuous brevity without stiffness or pedantry so successfully as Sir John Davis.' What was of more importance to the poet than the posthumous praise of even the most eminent of literary Solomons, the poem procured him the favour of the Queen, to whom it was introduced by Mountjoy, and the opportunity of chanting his gratitude in no fewer than twenty-six 'Hymns to Astræa': acrostic verses of sixteen lines each, in which the initial letters of each line formed the words *Elizabetha Regina*. Better still, the same poem which won the favour of Elizabeth's setting sun procured the author equal praise from the rising orb of her successor. King James was delighted with the poem. Anthony à Wood, the Oxford antiquary, has preserved the anecdote of the first introduction of Davis to King James. He tells how the poet, proceeding in Lord Hunsdon's train to Scotland to notify the monarch of his accession, was presented by Hunsdon to the King, 'who straightway asked was he "Nosce Teipsum" Davis, which, being answered in the affirmative, James graciously embraced him and conceived a considerable liking for him.'

Meantime the poet had succeeded in entering the House of Commons. Under the auspices, doubtless, of Mountjoy, he had been returned to the last and short parliament of Elizabeth as member for Corfe Castle. James had been but a short time on the throne when the recommendation of

[1] *Some Longer Elizabethan Poems*, with an Introduction by A. H. Bullen.

the same statesman, joined to the favour of his sovereign, procured the nomination of Davis as Solicitor-General for Ireland. He received his patent of appointment on November 25, 1603, and, immediately proceeding to Ireland, received the honour of knighthood at the hands of his patron the Viceroy. He at once entered on a career as an Irish law officer of almost unexampled duration and of quite unrivalled importance. But before entering on his achievements in that capacity it will be convenient to recount briefly the main passages in his subsequent career.

Davis's Irish preferment did not involve complete severance from the English Bar. In 1606, the year which saw his advancement to the office of Attorney-General for Ireland, he was called to the degree of serjeant-at-law in England. At that time it was the custom for newly made serjeants to present rings, and Davis chose for his the motto, 'Lex publica lux est.' In 1612 he became First Serjeant. Davis remained constantly in Ireland until 1616, when, returning to England, he resumed regular practice at the English Bar. But he retained his official post in Ireland until 1619. He was counsel for the Crown in the trial of the Countess of Somerset for the murder of Lord Overbury, and as First or Prime Serjeant was frequently sent to preside at assizes. Some of his charges on circuit survive in manuscript in the British Museum. In 1620 he was again returned to the House of Commons, this time for Newcastle-under-Lyme. His name occurs in the printed debates of this Parliament chiefly in connexion with Irish affairs, in which he never lost interest. He opposed the Bill of that year restraining the importation of Irish cattle to England, and was an advocate of the continuance of a separate Irish currency. In one of his speeches he touches on the perennial controversy between the two kingdoms, maintaining on the one hand the dependence of Ireland on the crown of England, but, on the other, asserting 'that this kingdom cannot make laws to bind that kingdom, for they have there a Parliament of their own,' a sentiment which was certainly becoming in one who had been Speaker of the Irish House of Commons.

The crowning triumph of Davis's career was lost in the tragical anti-climax of his sudden death. As the brief 'Notes' of his life, which survive in the Bodleian Library, put it, 'He was made Chief-Justice of England, and had not death seized on him, he had sat that day he died on the Bench.' In November 1626, by one of the earliest of Charles the First's unfortunate exertions of arbitrary power, Chief Justice Sir Randolph Crew was discharged from his office for refusing to recognise the legality of forced loans. Davis, who had written in defence of the exaction, was nominated to the vacancy. His robes of office were actually ordered. On the night of December 7 he supped with the Lord Keeper apparently in vigorous health, and received congratulations on his advancement to this great dignity. Next morning he was found dead in his bed. He had succumbed to apoplexy: no unexpected fate, except for the dramatic manner of its overtaking him, for physically he was a very Falstaff. A contemporary has left a very unflattering picture of his awkward gait, describing him as 'waddling in a most ungainly fashion, and walking as if he carried a cloakbag behind him.'[1]

No account of Sir John Davis may entirely omit mention of his wife, Lady Eleanor Audley, daughter of George, Earl of Castlehaven, grandfather of the well-known Irish statesman and writer of that name. She belonged to a family of great social consideration in that day. But however largely the alliance may have contributed to the consolidation of Davis's position in Court circles, it did little to procure him domestic happiness. In Lady Eleanor's generation there was an evident touch of madness in her family, from which she was not exempt. Her brother figures notoriously in the 'State Trials' as the subject of an unsavoury prosecution, and she herself, eccentric at all times, ultimately developed complete insanity. She had a turn for prophecy based on scriptural anagrams. Most of her vaticinations were unhappily melancholy. Among other predictions she claimed to have foretold her husband's death. 'His doom I gave him in letters of his own name

[1] *Manningham's Diary*, published by Camden Society, p. 168.

(John Daves—Jove's Hand) within three years to expect the mortal blow, so put on my mourning garments from that time; when about three days before his sudden death, before his servants and friends at the table, gave him part to take his long sleep, by him thus put off: "I pray, weep not while I am alive, and I will give you leave to laugh when I am dead."' But with all her disadvantages this unhappy Cassandra was attractive enough to get a second husband, who, however, deserted her.

Heylin, in his 'Life of Laud,' tells a good story of Lady Eleanor. She was brought, it appears, into the Court of High Commission, on charges arising out of her claims to prophetic powers, which she grounded on an anagram of her name, Eleanor Davis—Reveal, O Daniel.

> 'And though,' says Heylin, 'it had too much by an L, and too little by an S, yet she found Daniel and Reveal in it, which served her turn. Much pains was taken by the Court to dispossess her of this spirit; but all would not do, till Lamb, then Dean of Arches, shot her through and through with an arrow borrowed from her own quiver. For whilst the Bishops and Divines were reasoning the point with her out of holy Scriptures, he took a pen in his hand and at last hit on this excellent anagram, viz. *Dame Eleanor Davys —Never so mad a lady!* [1]

It is, of course, by this great historical treatise, first published in 1612, towards the close of the author's active work in Ireland, that Davis's connexion with that country is best remembered and most clearly emphasised. As the climax of that work is the plantation of Ulster, and its primary object the glorification of the measures of King James for the

[1] In Bishop Goodman's *Court and Times of Charles I* some curious particulars are given of the later eccentricities of this unfortunate lady. The Cathedral of Lichfield was the scene of one of her most whimsical misdemeanours. In 1636 the Cathedral had lately been beautifully adorned with arras hangings and other decorations. The demented lady appeared one morning, 'with a kettle in one hand and a brush in the other,' to sprinkle the hangings and the bishop's seat with what she called holy water, but which proved to be 'a composition of tar, pitch, sink puddle, and water and such kind of nasty ingredients.' 'This,' says the narrator, 'being the act of a madwoman, the lords to prevent further mischief have given out two warrants, the one to bring the lady to Bethlehem, the other to the keeper of Bethlehem to receive her.'

pacification of Ireland, it is easily forgotten that a large part of its author's administrative work had been achieved before the plantation of Ulster had been rendered possible by the flight of the Earls, and that a further very important phase of it was subsequent to that event. In truth, his most important work lay not in the plantation of Ulster, but in the setting, to use his own words, of the clock of civil government in Ireland, and the harmonising of the strings of that Irish harp which it was the business of the civil magistrate to finger.[1] The story of the Plantation of Ulster has been often written, and though much still remains to be said in elucidation of some of its incidents, it is not our purpose to re-tell the story now. But it is worth while to endeavour to realise more clearly than has yet been done the civil and social state of Ireland at the date of the accession of the first Stuart and the arrival of Sir John Davis in Ireland. It is, therefore, to the first and third of thc three great achievements with which Davis was connected that attention will be directed here.

Not the least remarkable feature in the state of Ireland at the opening of the seventeenth century was the primitive, not to say amorphous, condition of the administrative organisation provided by its rulers. Not merely was the machinery of government inefficient, but even the framework of an administrative system was non-existent in a great part of Ireland. It is indeed astonishing to reflect how little progress had been made by the representatives of the Crown in applying English law to Irish lawlessness between the days of King John and those of Elizabeth. The early Plantagenets, indeed, had made some progress. They had divided the country into provinces, and even, in theory at least, into counties. As early as Henry the Third's reign the sheriff, that pioneer of the laws of England, exercised his functions

[1] It is curious to note Davis's fondness for this image. He had used it many years earlier, and before he had set foot in Ireland, in his poem of *The King's Welcome*, addressed to James on his accession :

> On, for thee birds will help to fill thie songe,
> wherto all english harte stringes doe agree ;
> And the Irish harpe stringes, that did iarre soe long
> to make the musicke full, nowe tunèd be.

in every one of the districts into which the island had been parcelled, either as the direct functionary of the Crown itself, or as the agent and nominee of the great earls palatine, who in feudal times did so much of the work of government as well in England as in Ireland. But the feebleness of Henry's grandson, Edward the Second, allowed the process to be arrested. It is scarcely an exaggeration to assert that the independence of Scotland, vindicated on the field of Bannockburn, was really consolidated in Ireland, where the invasion of Edward Bruce struck a signal blow at the prestige of the English crown. That invasion undermined English authority not merely with the Irish chieftains, but with the great Norman lords on whom the English sovereigns had till then depended for the administration of a large part of the country. Of this truth no more striking illustration can be given than the fact that from the date of the wars of the Bruce in Ireland to the middle of the reign of Henry the Eighth, for a period that is of two full centuries, not a single addition was made to the list of Irish counties. On the contrary, the effective authority of the Crown vanished from all but four of the twelve counties created by King John, until, in the quaint language of the historian Stanyhurst, the boundaries of the English Pale were 'cramperned and crouched into an odd corner of the country named Fingal, with a parcel of the king's land of Meath and tho counties of Kildare and Louth.' In every quarter of Ireland the functions of government were wrested from their nominal owners. In Connaught the Burkes enjoyed complete independence. In Ulster the Anglo-Norman colonies of Lecale and Antrim practically ceased to exist; and the show of homage rendered to the Crown under the later Plantagenets by the great Earls of Ormond, Desmond, and Kildare but thinly concealed the complete indifference of the country at large to a sovereignty that was at best an unenforced and scarcely enforceable suzerainty. So far had the sense of the English ownership of Ireland vanished from the minds of the nominal lords of the island, that as late as 1537 the Irish Council addressed to Henry the Eighth's English advisers a 'Memorial for the winning,' not of Ulster, Munster, or

Connaught, but of Leinster itself. They actually began this document with a definition of the extent of the metropolitan province, with the extraordinary averment that 'the country called Leinster and the situation thereof is unknown to the King and his Council.' Even after the Act of 1541, constituting Henry the Eighth king of Ireland, had shown the resolution of that masterful sovereign to convert his nominal overlordship of Ireland into an effective supremacy, little progress had been made in the formal subdivision of the country into administrative units. To the end of Henry's reign the proverb quoted by Sir John Davis in his 'Discovery' continued to hold good, that 'Whoso lives by west of the Barrow lives west of the law;' and three-fourths of Ireland, if not exactly unconquered, was at all events ungoverned. The short reign of Edward the Sixth witnessed little or no progress in the business of reintroducing English legal and administrative procedure; and though that of Mary saw the first step in the process of forming a proper administrative system through the island by the erection of the districts of Leix and Offaly into the King's and Queen's Counties, it was not until Elizabeth had succeeded to the throne that any substantial advance was made in the shiring of Ireland, a work which, as a succession of deputies had long seen, lay at the root of all real administrative reform. And in fact although two Acts of Parliament, one of Mary and the other of Elizabeth, had been passed to empower the deputies 'to convert and turn divers and sundry waste grounds into shire ground,' it is probable that the objects of this legislation would have long remained unaccomplished had not Sir Henry Sidney, perhaps the ablest in the great succession of Elizabeth's Irish Viceroys, devised a new and potent administrative instrument, which in his hands and in those of his successor, Sir John Perrot, was destined to produce vast effects in winning back Ireland to what was called in that day 'civility.'

Sidney, whose vigour and energy made him a marvel of activity both military and administrative, united with his Irish government the Presidency of Wales. In the political system of the Principality he found a model for a scheme of administrative devolution which he aimed at applying to the whole of Ireland, and which he successfully established in two of its provinces. No single act of Elizabethan policy had more important or more satisfactory results than the institution of the Presidencies of Munster and Connaught, not only because the gradual demarcation of the counties of both these provinces as they now exist was largely effected by their means, but because it was by their example that Davis was guided when, a generation later, he effected the final shiring of Ulster. It may be worth while to devote a brief paragraph to an account of an institution devised, in Davis's own language, 'to inure and acquaint the people again with English government.'

The first idea of these instruments of government may be traced to the reign of Mary, if not to the time of Edward the Sixth, when a scheme was devised for the appointment of separate Presidents for each of the three provinces of Munster, Connaught, and Ulster. Sidney was then in Ireland in a subordinate position, as the friend and adviser of his brother-in-law Sussex, then Lord Fitzwalter. But although Sussex had a clearly defined scheme for the institution of the system, nothing was done during his government to give effect to it. It was not until Sidney's first administration in 1565 that a practical shape was given to his plan. In that year, the constitution of what for the next century were known as the Presidencies of Connaught and Munster was formally drafted. The presidency included not only a president answerable directly to the Lord Deputy for the military security of the province entrusted to him, but a provincial council composed of the prelates and nobles whose dioceses and estates lay within the district. It had also a separate legal machinery composed of the provincial chief justice, two puisne judges, and an attorney-general; and it was provided with a treasurer, clerk of the council, and other administrative officers. The powers and functions exercised by these Councils appear very fully from the detailed instructions issued by Mountjoy and the Irish Privy Council to Sir George Carew which are printed in 'Pacata Hibernia.'

It is a matter of great regret, and a serious loss to the

historian of the Ireland of Elizabeth and the early Stuarts, that the records of these provincial presidencies have long since perished. They seem to have been lost in the anarchic years succeeding the rebellion of 1641; and, indeed, the presidency system did not long survive that cataclysm. Though they were revived at the Restoration as part of the *status quo ante* existing at the time of the rebellion which the Ministers of Charles the Second desired, as far as possible, to re-establish, the presidencies were not regarded by the Restoration viceroy, the Duke of Ormond, as necessary instruments of government. Their efficacy, in fact, ceased with the final establishment of a strong central executive; and in 1672, during the viceroyalty of Lord Essex, the system was abolished.

But though the era of their utility was comparatively brief, the presidencies were invaluable aids to that policy of restoring the power of the Crown through the remoter districts of the south and west, which was the chief object of solicitude to the Irish Government in the latter half of the sixteenth century. It was under Sidney and his successors that the provinces of Munster and Connaught, and by consequence of Leinster, assumed their present shape. To Sidney himself belonged the credit of the shiring of Connaught and the division of that province, which throughout the Middle Ages was treated as but one shire, into its five modern counties of Galway, Mayo, Sligo, Leitrim, and Roscommon. The same administrator had also the honour of devising, though not of completing, those additions to the area of Leinster by which the final shape of the eastern province was determined. The business of shiring Munster was in the main accomplished by Sir John Perrot, and was the principal achievement of a distinguished term of office as president of the province, though it was not until Perrot had succeeded to the higher office of deputy that his work in this respect was completed.

But, successful as were the Elizabethan deputies in the settlement of the southern and western provinces through the agency of the presidential administrations, they could make no similar progress in Ulster. The conditions, indeed, of the northern province forbade the application of that method of government to the solution of its problems. Thanks to the success with which the O'Neills and O'Donnells, and other chieftains of the north continuously asserted their independence of the Crown, the great northern territories remained down to the very end of the seventeenth century practically *terra incognita* to the Viceroys, and preserved all the primitive characteristics of the scarcely more than nomadic civilization of Ulster. At the close of the sixteenth century the greatest woods and fastnesses which remained in Ireland were to be found in Ulster. And the thoroughly Celtic character of its civilization was emphasised by the fact that the whole province did not contain a single town of the smallest importance, with the exception of Armagh, which, being a centre of English influence, was continually harried by the O'Neills. It was significant of this state of things that when Sidney appointed the presidents of Munster and Connaught he made no attempt to create a similar office for Ulster, but contented himself with constituting the military office of marshal. The O'Neills succeeded in keeping this and all other Anglicising institutions at bay for close on half a century longer, and, indeed, one of the circumstances which is held to have most directly influenced Tyrone to his flight in 1607 was the threat or rumour that such an administration was to be at length established.

In 1575 Sir Henry Sidney made a journey into Ulster for the purpose of dividing the province into shires, but failed to effect his object, and Perrot's endeavour in the same direction some ten years later was no more than a settlement on paper of the boundaries of the new counties he desired to create. It is best described in Sir John Davis's own language: 'Sir John Perrot reduced the unreformed parts of Ulster into seven shires, namely, Armagh, Monaghan, Tyrone, Coleraine, Donegal, Fermanagh, and Cavan, though in his time the law was never executed in these new counties by any sheriffs or justices of assize; but the people left to be ruled still by their own barbarous laws and lords.' Perrot's work was thus effective only in the sense that his division became the basis of the allocation of territory carried out by Davis fully twenty years later, and that his nomenclature of the Ulster counties is that which, with the substitution of Londonderry for Coleraine, still distinguishes the shires of the north.

Nor was this independence of authority confined to those districts of the northern province which were dominated by the O'Neills. South-western Ulster was equally remote from the influence of the central government. East Breny, the modern Cavan, was described by the Marshal, Sir Nicholas Bagnal, as 'a territory where never writ was current,' which it was 'almost sacrilege to look into'; and a Commission appointed about the same time, by virtue of the same enactments under which the Presidents of Munster and Connaught had been constituted, for reducing Ulster to shire ground, had been entirely unable to proceed. Thus it came about that until the eve of the accession of James the First, Ireland as a whole was in all essentials less amenable to the authority of the British Crown than it had been in the days before the wars of the Bruces: a state of things which suggests at once the important influence exerted on the consolidation of English power in Ireland by the union of the English and Scottish Crowns.

There can be little question, indeed, that the success of the northern province in prolonging its independence long after the rest of Ireland had submitted in more or less sullen acquiescence to the assertion of English power, was due in no small measure to its geographical position, and to its neighbourhood to the independent kingdom of Scotland. In the early days of English rule, indeed, no inconsiderable progress had been made in colonising the north, and especially the north-east of Ireland. The settlements of Lecale and the Ards in Down, and of Carrickfergus in Antrim, were flourishing colonies in the reigns of the early Plantagenets; and the existence of Down and Antrim as separate administrative entities, if not as counties in the full sense of the word, can be clearly traced to a period prior to that of Edward the Second. But from the date of the assertion of Scottish independence, and of the overrunning of Ulster by Edward Bruce and his army, down to Tudor times, these settlements, though never perhaps altogether uprooted, had ceased to expand. Communication between Dublin and the colonies in Antrim and Down was carried on by sea only. There can be little doubt that a main cause of the failure to revive English influence north of the Boyne lay in the sense of the propinquity of Ulster to the northern kingdom, and in the ease with which, in times of trouble between England and Scotland, the northern chieftains could secure support from their neighbours and kindred across the Irish Sea. It is certainly something more than a coincidence that the anglicising of Ulster, arrested in the fourteenth century by the Scottish invasion, was never effectually resumed until the hostile exertion of Scottish power had ceased to be a possibility through the accession of James the First to the English Crown.

The failure of all attempts to establish a semblance of English administration in Ulster even in late Tudor times only serves to emphasise the merit of the performance which the energy and determination of Davis successfully carried through. And it is to be noted that his shiring of Ulster, unlike his other great achievements, was accomplished before and not after the flight of the Earls. It is true that the actual series of 'inquisitions' by which every 'bordering territory whereof doubt was made in what county the same should lie was added or reduced to a county certain,' was not completed till 1610; and that, as noticed already, the delimitation of one or two of the counties was directly affected in some important respects by the Plantation. But the direct personal investigation by Davis himself, by which the process had been preceded, had been begun at a time when, to all appearance, Tyrone's continuance in Ireland in a position of comparative prosperity was assured. It may perchance have been a perception on the part of that clear-sighted adversary of British power of the effects of the direct introduction of English laws and institutions into the Irish territories that precipitated the fatal step that ended in final exile. The flight of the Earls has indeed never been adequately accounted for. As Disraeli said of Newman's secession from the Anglican communion, 'it has been apologised for, but it has never been explained.' It was no doubt the result of the sum of many causes operating in the same direction. But the strongest motive in the heart of this strenuous adversary of English rule may well have been the feeling that the efforts of a lifetime to stem the tide of alien innovation were at last on the verge of exhaustion and failure. Cultivated though he was, this great representative of a vanishing ideal must have looked on the onward march of English institutions with feelings not very different from those with which the aborigines of the American continent beheld the advance of the stranger from the East. It was doubtless a desperate determination to appeal to the Spanish King to assist him in arresting what he regarded as a fatal process that led Tyrone to take this step. And no doubt but for the accidents of European politics the step might have been successful. For months, if not for years, after the flight of the Earls from Ulster the direct intervention of the Spanish King was everywhere expected. Had hostilities been suspended on the Continent within a year or two of the flight, an invasion of Ireland would almost certainly have followed. '"Peace in the Netherlands means war in Ireland" has become a proverbial saying here.' So wrote the ambassador De la Broderie from London in the spring of 1608. As it was, the war in the Netherlands dragged on until Philip's energies and resources were too far exhausted for further adventures. And so the flight of the Earls to win foreign succour for their native land, instead of bringing the desired help, only fastened the chains upon those they left behind, and facilitated the process which Davis was a foremost agent in carrying out. No wonder that their exodus, precipitate, rash, and inconsiderate as it was, prompted that eloquent and impressive lamentation of the Four Masters which is the last dirge of Irish independence: 'Woe to the heart that meditated, woe to the mind that conceived, woe to the council that decided on the project of their setting out on this voyage, without knowing whether they should ever return to their native principalities or patrimonies to the end of the world.'

The last, and in some respects the most important, of the

three great acts of policy with which Sir John Davis was intimately associated was the reform of the Irish Parliament. It is indeed not a little curious that it is to the man who was the central figure in a great popular commotion, who stood, in fact, for all that was most objectionable to the Irish leaders of the day, that the parliamentary system of Ireland in a later century owed much of its organisation. No episode in the seventeenth-century history of Ireland is better known than the story of the election to the Speakership in the Parliament called in Ireland by Sir Arthur Chichester in 1613. On that occasion, after an unseemly struggle, not unmarked by the appearance, if not the reality, of physical violence, on the floor of the House of Commons, Davis, who had been recommended from the Throne for the office, was elected Speaker by a majority composed of 127 Protestant votes, as against 97 'recusant' or Roman Catholic votes. His competitor was Sir John Everard, an ex-judge who had left the bench rather than subscribe to the oath of supremacy. But though in this controversy Davis was the official candidate of the English Government, and as such in direct opposition to the popular party, it had been his business, prior to the election, to devise the Parliamentary system under which, with little alteration, the Grattan Parliament subsequently sat, and which lasted down to the Union. Moreover, it was his part to pronounce, in his address to the Viceroy, following on his election as Speaker, the most eloquent vindication of the history of the Irish Legislature which has ever been put on record.

It was natural enough that, upon the morrow of the great operation of the plantation of Ulster, when the issue which most moved men in Ireland was the momentous issue of religion, objection should have been taken to the selection as Speaker of a great Crown lawyer and the chief adviser of the English interest. But it is impossible to deny either the pre-eminence of Davis's qualifications for the post or the conspicuous ability with which he discharged its duties. When the first and only Irish Parliament of James the First met, the very name of Parliament was little more than a memory in the country. For nearly a generation none had been called.

The three Parliaments held in the reign of Elizabeth, those of 1560, 1569, and 1585, had been summoned for specific purposes—the attainder of Shane O'Neill and the Earl of Desmond in the first and third cases, and the raising of revenue in the second—and had sat for a very short time. There were few, if any, alive in 1613 who had sat in an Irish House of Commons, and still fewer who had any knowledge of parliamentary procedure in England. The records of former Parliaments were scanty and inadequate, and in order to ascertain the precedents a diligent search through such journals as survived had been essential. Such an inquiry could hardly be profitably conducted save by an investigator with a lawyer's training, and in fact it had been undertaken by Davis himself. The actual record of his inquiry is still extant among the Huntingdon papers preserved in the Bodleian Library. Its more matured fruits remain in the speech addressed by Davis to Chichester on presenting himself at the head of the Commons of Ireland for the ratification of his election as their Speaker. It may not be out of place to preface an account of his singularly complete analysis of Irish Parliamentary history by some reference to the actual character of the formal proceedings at the opening of an Irish Parliament in the seventeenth century.

Parliament was summoned by writs addressed to the lords spiritual and temporal, and to the sheriffs of counties, mayors and sovereigns of cities and boroughs, to elect knights of the shire and burgesses of the cities and boroughs to attend the King's deputy in Parliament, on Tuesday, May 18, 1613. The place of meeting was the Castle of Dublin, a choice to which exception was taken by the popular party, on the ground, which was scarcely tenable, that it was contrary to custom to meet there, and that troops had been brought into the city by the deputy to overawe the assembly. A further objection was based on the alleged fear of the explosion of the powder and ammunition stored in the Castle, which, in the view of the objectors, was like to occasion such alarm as had been felt at Westminster on a still recent Fifth of November. This last objection was set aside by Chichester, who with some adroitness turned the tables by reminding those who put it forward 'of what religion they were that had hatched such cockatrices' eggs.' As for the presence of the soldiers, their utility was quickly evidenced by the disorders which ensued. The scene when Parliament met has been graphically painted in a contemporary letter: [1]

'Upon the 18th of May, being Tuesday, the lord deputy with all the peers of the realm, and the noblemen, the clergy, both bishops and archbishops, attired in scarlet robes very sumptuously, with sound of trumpets; the lord David Barry, Viscount Buttevant, bearing the sword of estate; the earl of Thomond, bearing the cap of maintenance; and after all these the lord deputy followed, riding a most stately horse, very richly trapped, himself attired in a very rich and stately robe of purple velvet which the King's Majesty had sent him, having his train borne up by eight gentlemen of worth: and thus in a most stately and sumptuous manner they rode from the Castle of Dublin to the Cathedral Church of St. Patrick, to hear divine service, and a sermon preached by the reverend father in God, Christopher Hampton, D.D., archbishop of Armagh, and primate of all Ireland.'

The chronicler of the proceedings further informs us, with picturesque detail, how the Lord Deputy, having returned with his train to the Castle, 'ascended up into the high house of parliament, where he sat down in his chair of estate; likewise the Lord Chancellor sat down according to his estate, also the nobility of the kingdom, the lords spiritual and temporal, everyone sat down accordingly.' After which, 'when the whole high court of Parliament was assembled,' the Lord Chancellor delivered what was in effect a 'King's speech,' 'setting forth many great and worthy causes of estate, there to be debated upon for the good of the kingdom and for the commonwealth thereof.'

Of the struggle with which the actual proceedings of the Parliament opened more than one account has been left by actual eye-witnesses and participants in the scene. The Roman Catholic party, aware that, owing to the re-distribution of seats due to the creation of new counties and the erection

[1] *State Papers, Ireland*, James I, 1613, May 29; Ryves to Dunn.

of fresh boroughs, they would find themselves in a minority, and dreading that legislation inimical to their creed would be proposed and carried by the Government, resolved to bring the proceedings to naught. Since they would be powerless in any division, the tactics resolved on were to obstruct the introduction of legislation by creating a preliminary discussion. Accordingly, when the House of Commons, after hearing the Lord Chancellor's speech, was dismissed to elect a Speaker, a scene of the utmost and apparently the most calculated disorder ensued. Sir John Davis having been proposed by the Court party, on the recommendation of the Crown, Sir John Everard was proposed by the Opposition. After an attempt had been made to procure a postponement of the election pending an investigation into the returns for several of the seats, the validity of which was challenged by the popular party, a division was called. Some uncertainty existing as to the mode of division, Sir Oliver St. John, a member of the English House of Commons and a supporter of Davis, who three years later became Lord Deputy, gave the House the benefit of his experience at Westminster. 'The use of Parliament,' he said, 'is to decide controversies by questions, and questions by the numbering of voices; and for trial thereof I know by experience that they who are of the affirmative part are to go out of the House to be numbered, and to leave those that are of the negative part to be numbered within the House.' St. John's suggestion was acted upon, and the supporters of Davis withdrew to be numbered. But the Opposition, refusing to appoint tellers, and taking advantage of the accident which left them in possession of the House, proceeded to elect Everard by acclamation, and placed him in the Speaker's chair. The sequel to this disorderly violation of all the conditions of parliamentary procedure and decorum is best told in the quaint language of the eye-witness already quoted, Dr. Thomas Ryves:

'Which when we saw,' i.e. the placing of Everard in the chair, 'we entered the House again and propounded for Sir John Davis, and finding ourselves to be the major part by twenty-eight voices or thereabouts, having named him, two knights took him and put him also in the Speaker's chair and set him down in the other's lap; and because he would not remove they took him fairly out of the chair and kept Sir John there. I cannot express what a cry was raised thereupon, but the recusants, seeing they could not prevail, left the House, and being sent unto by us refused to return, but went every man to his lodging; and shortly after we caused the mace to be borne up before our Speaker and carried him to his home. This is the true sum of that which passed that day; no man doubteth but that had the Parliament been kept in the town, the whole town had been drawn in upon us, and we had all fallen to cutting of throats. But in the Castle they durst not stir so far.'

It was before an assembly thus constituted that three days later, having emerged successfully from the stormy scenes which attended his election to the Speaker's chair, Sir John Davis addressed to the Lord Deputy the remarkable oration in which he reviewed with admirable succinctness, yet with essential fulness, the parliamentary history of Ireland. In the course of this address, to the essential completeness of which modern research has added few facts of importance, Davis pointed out the circumstances which made the House of Commons of which he was the spokesman representative for the first time of the whole of Ireland. For the space of one hundred and forty years after Henry the Second had become possessed of the lordship of Ireland, and of forty from the establishment of an effective representative system by Edward the First, there had been no separate Irish Parliament, the laws passed in England being transmitted into Ireland under the Great Seal to be enrolled as laws of the realm. Oddly enough it was not until the decline of English power, in the reign of Edward the Second, that the first formal Parliaments of Ireland were called by Sir John Wogan, a name of much importance in the history of the Irish legislature. The Parliaments of the later Plantagenets were, of course, mainly occupied with legislation which, like the famous Statute of Kilkenny, was designed to enforce the views of the Norman or English minority upon the Irish majority, and to keep up the distinction between the King's English servants and his Irish enemies. In point of fact the Parliaments of the Plantagenets were Parliaments in which the lords of the ever-shrinking English Pale sought to legislate for the exclusive benefit of the English colony. At one period, indeed, the four shires of the Pale were the only districts of the country which returned any members. The Parliament, both Lords and Commons, was returned exclusively by the Pale. To the Parliament called by Lord Gormanston in 1493, under Henry the Seventh, the other shires were not even summoned to return members, an illegality so flagrant that Poynings' Parliament caused its Acts to be repealed. These Parliaments were, of course, as Davis showed, entirely unrepresentative, and though he did not say so, it was due to his exertions more than to those of any single individual that it had become possible to elect a representative Parliament in the sense of a Parliament, the constituencies of which embraced all the geographical and administrative divisions of the island. And not only was the Parliament of James in very truth the first in which every district of the country was directly represented, but it was the first in which representatives of Irish blood and Irish opinion had any real place. Down to the 33rd of Henry VIII none but those of English blood or English title were admitted to the House of Commons. For, as Davis put it, 'The mere Irish of those days were never admitted, as well because their countries, lying out of the limit of counties, could have no knights, and, having neither cities nor boroughs in them, could send no burgesses to the Parliament. Besides, the State did not as then hold them fit to be trusted with the Council of the kingdom.' As regards the shires represented, it had been impossible, prior to the effective settlement of the Irish counties, to secure any proper system of county representation. Down to the year 1541, as we have already seen, there were no more than twelve shires in being. In Mary's reign there were fourteen, and in the first Parliament called by Elizabeth there were seventeen. But even when Elizabeth, through the instrumentality of Sidney and Perrot, had raised the number considerably, the representation was still deficient; for the Ulster shires, having no sheriffs, returned no members. The state of the borough representation was even more unsatisfactory. Only thirty boroughs returned any members, and the entire body of the House of Commons was less than a hundred in number. Davis raised the total membership to two hundred and thirty-two, of whom eighty sat for the new boroughs created to counterbalance the additions made to the county representation, which was predominantly patriotic in feeling. He thus provided and fixed the shape of the House of Commons as it remained with little or no alteration for close on two centuries.

It is true that by this great measure of parliamentary reform Davis provoked one of the fiercest parliamentary storms that has ever agitated Ireland. The Parliament of 1613 was the first in which the King's servants were confronted by an anti-English opposition, and this opposition was strong enough to make itself felt. The addition to the borough members was accordingly denounced by the Roman Catholic party as devised merely for the purpose of overwhelming the opinion of the country gentlemen by the votes of the place men and nominees of great officials returned for the new boroughs. And the controversy was in the end referred to the determination of the sovereign in person. The career of Sir John Davis in Ireland, indeed, abounds in matters which touch closely the root of the perennial controversies of Irishmen, and his policy, in most if not all of its aspects, was one necessarily offensive to the national aspirations which in his time were beginning to find organised constitutional expression for the first time. For the final overthrow of the last Irish chieftain who was strong enough to wrestle with England in the field was followed almost immediately by the first effective coalition between the Anglo-Irish of the Pale and the native inhabitants of the rest of the country. Down to the close of the sixteenth century the old English throughout the island had continued to feel for the ancient race the contempt with which for four centuries their fathers had looked down upon 'a barbarous people, void of civility and religion.' Had Tyrone maintained his independence, the Pale would doubtless have remained fixed in its traditional attitude, and continued to support English authority against Irish revolt. But the practical annihilation of purely Irish ideas in their last stronghold, the advent in Ulster of a new race of English and Scottish colonists equally hostile to the aboriginal and the acclimatised Irishmen, and the opposition in the vital element of religion between the old inhabitants and the newcomers, produced within but a few years that unity which many generations had hitherto failed to effect. Davis left Ireland at the moment when these new conditions had for the first time made themselves apparent, and it is not to be denied that for the new and unhappy shape which the Irish difficulty assumed in his time he must bear his share of the responsibility. That he fully concurred in the views of his colleagues and superiors in the Irish Government and the English Council as to the propriety of the measures with which he was associated there can be little doubt, and he would have been the last to disavow his share in the framing of the policy which it was his business to carry out. But it is not with these matters that we are mainly concerned here. It is upon the part played by Davis as an administrator rather than as a statesman that we have sought to dwell. What gives to Davis his great importance in the history of Ireland is not so much the share he took in devising policies as the immense administrative capacity with which he carried out these policies, and made them real and operative. Let history decide as it may on the wisdom or unwisdom of the whole scheme of British policy in the Ireland of James the First, it can never weaken the claims of Davis to our admiration in this regard. Whether it was well or ill to have consolidated the social organisation of Ireland on a frankly English model; whether it was wise or foolish to destroy rather than seek to conciliate the last governing leaders of the Irish race; whether it was a bold expedient or only a base one to contrive a Parliament technically representative of the whole Irish nation without distinction of race, but actually subservient to the will of the English Council—these propositions may be controverted. What can never be questioned is that the man who rightly or wrongly achieved all this has as just a title to admiration as a great executive officer as any public functionary who in any century has served the English Crown.

AN ILLUSTRIOUS CAVALIER

Among the voluminous labours of the Historical Manuscripts Commission by no means the least considerable place must be assigned to the already numerous volumes devoted to the Marquess of Ormonde's very extensive collection of historical documents. These volumes consist almost entirely of transcripts from the papers of that well-known statesman James Butler, twelfth Earl and first Duke of Ormond, of whom it has been justly observed that 'the history of Ireland for nigh half a century may be read in the life, actions, and adventures of this able, virtuous, and illustrious man.' Ormond was one of those who consider that 'papers are the jewels of a family,' and few statesmen have ever taken more pains to preserve their correspondence. Yet the papers now at Kilkenny, numerous as they are, do not, as is well known, by any means exhaust the documentary remains which the sedulous solicitude of the Duke of Ormond, during an active participation in public affairs which extended over half a century, has preserved for the information of posterity. At least as many more are to be found in the Bodleian Library among the papers of the Duke's biographer, Thomas Carte. Taken together, the documents preserved at Kilkenny and at Oxford form something like a continuous series of papers relating to public affairs in Ireland from the outbreak of the Irish rebellion of 1641 to the arrival of Cromwell in Ireland, and from the Restoration to the close of the reign of Charles the Second. They are full of information alike in regard to the history of the great events of this period and to the more minute details of administration. It may, indeed, be said without exaggeration that the annals of English Government in Ireland during the middle period of the seventeenth century are illustrated by a greater mass and variety of extant documentary evidence than can be matched in the case of any other period. And it is, at any rate, certain that the manuscript collections of the Duke of Ormond relating to the affairs of his own times exceed both in value and in volume those of any of his contemporaries, with the exception of his friend and colleague, the indefatigable Clarendon, whose tireless industry as a correspondent has, perhaps, never been paralleled among statesmen.

The value of these extensive remains has, however, been considerably marred by their separation into two widely sundered portions. Our gratitude to Carte for his 'Life of Ormond,' a work which, in spite of some obvious literary imperfections which have not escaped the inexorable judgment of Dr. Johnson, is too thoroughly done to be ever superseded, must not blind us to the injury done through the splitting up of a great homogeneous collection into two confused and disordered parts. The history of the transference of the larger and in some respects the more valuable portion of the Duke's papers from Kilkenny to Oxford may rank among the curiosities of literature; and, as it has been the subject of some misconception, must be briefly noticed here.

A biography of Ormond on a large scale had been long contemplated by members of his family and friends, but thirty years had passed from the date of the Duke's death before the task of writing it was entered on by Thomas Carte, a Jacobite author, whose first contribution to literature had been a vindication of Charles the First from the charge of having instigated the Irish Rebellion of 1641, and who saw in the career of Ormond the opportunity for a defence of the House of Stuart at a time when the failure of the Old Pretender to recover the throne his father had forfeited had covered the fallen dynasty with every form of obloquy. When Carte embarked on his task Ormond's grandson and successor in the title was an exile at Avignon, having paid the penalty of a too reckless participation in the schemes of Harley and St. John, and the family was represented by Charles, Earl of

Arran, the younger brother of the attainted Duke. To Arran Carte addressed himself, and by him was not only entrusted with a large quantity of his grandfather's, the first Duke of Ormond's, letters and papers, which had already been brought to England in connexion with earlier biographical projects, but was authorised to visit Kilkenny and select from the collection there such documents as he might find suited to his purpose. The liberal interpretation which Carte placed on this permission must be given in his own words :—

'The success was answerable to my wishes; I found in the Evidence Room at Kilkenny, about fourteen wicker bins (each large enough to hold a hogshead of wine in bottles) covered with unwieldy books of steward's accounts, but which, upon examination, appeared to be full of papers and to contain a series of papers of state, orders, resolutions, and letters of the Privy Council of Ireland, the despatches of the king and secretaries of state in England, his Grace's own letters and those of other great men who corresponded with him, from before the Restoration of King Charles II to the year 1686. There being no bookbinder at Kilkenny, I was forced to transport these in three Irish cars to Dublin, where I was continually employed for several months in digesting them, in order to have them bound up like the others. Such papers as upon perusal did not appear useful to my subject I sent back to Kilkenny, and bound up the rest in volumes.' [1]

The volumes so bound up, to the number of not less than a hundred, were brought to England, and were never returned. They were retained by Carte with the rest of an enormous collection of manuscripts accumulated by him for the purposes of his other historical undertakings until very shortly before his death in 1754; and it was long supposed that, as stated by Nichols in his 'Literary Anecdotes,' they had passed to Carte's widow under the terms of his will and had by her been left to the University of Oxford. That lady did in fact make a will by which she bequeathed, subject to a life estate in her second husband, Nicholas Jernegan, 'all the manuscripts of my late husband, Mr. Thomas Carte, or which did belong to him, to and for the use of the University of Oxford,' and the papers so demised were deposited in the Bodleian in 1778.

[1] *Life of Ormond*, by Thomas Carte, Oxford, 1851, vol. i. p. iv.

It was long imagined that these papers included the Ormond manuscripts, in which Carte had no sort of ownership, and that the biographer had been guilty of one of those misappropriations of manuscript materials from which the history of literature shows that many otherwise honourable men have not been exempt. The researches of the historian of the Bodleian have, however, wholly exonerated Carte from the imputation of literary kleptomania. Mr. Macray has shown that the Ormond collection was in fact handed over to the keeping of the University of Oxford by Carte himself in the year 1753; and, further, that Carte in 1754, very shortly before his death, placed in the Bodleian numerous other manuscripts relating to Irish affairs in the seventeenth century. No record has been preserved of the circumstances under which the gift was made or of the concurrence of the representatives of the Ormond family in this disposition of the great Duke's papers. But there is strong warrant for the presumption that this arrangement had the sanction of the nobleman from whom Carte had received his original authority. Lord Arran was still alive in 1753, and was moreover, like his grandfather and brother before him, Chancellor of the University of Oxford. In that year the University had become the recipient of a cognate gift of great importance in the bequest by the descendant of the great Earl of Clarendon of a large portion of the manuscripts of that statesman; and, although these papers did not actually reach Oxford till six years later, nothing appears more probable than that the gift to the University of the papers of the historian of the Great Rebellion should have suggested to Carte a like destination for the very similar manuscripts of Clarendon's great friend and colleague. That Lord Arran, as custodian of the manuscripts, should have assented to an arrangement in which as Chancellor of the University he must have willingly acquiesced is an entirely natural supposition; and it is difficult to believe that the transaction could have been completed without his cognisance in either or both capacities.

From the very extensive nature of Carte's selections it follows that the papers of the great Duke remaining at Kilkenny are comparatively deficient in historical interest, and it is the highest tribute to the completeness of Carte's labours that the most careful investigation of the sources he consulted, though it enables us not seldom to supplement his statements with interesting particulars, in no way supersedes his work. Accurate in his statements of fact, even where he is most prejudiced in his opinions, the reader may quarrel with Carte's conclusions, but is obliged to accept his premises. Nevertheless there have been found at Kilkenny, over and above the many documents which were probably known to Carte, some which he appears to have overlooked, and which throw no inconsiderable light on his hero's career, while there are others which, having come into the Ormond collection since Carte's day, could never have been known to the biographer. In what we have here to say of the career of the Duke of Ormond it is proposed to draw more particularly upon those portions of these fresh sources of information which throw light upon the personal character of Ormond, the limits of an article scarcely admitting of an adequate survey of the political aspects of a career which is part of the texture of more than half a century of English history. Chief among these sources may be mentioned some particulars of the Duke's early life, apparently compiled shortly after his death with a view to his biography, a number of letters from the Duchess to his half-brother, and the Duke's letters in the last two years of his life to his close friend and henchman Sir Robert Southwell.

Of all the statesmen of the seventeenth century the great Duke of Ormond, as he is commonly called, had the longest career. The Courts of Charles the First and Charles the Second contained no more conspicuous or imposing figure than his whom Macaulay has described as 'the most illustrious of the cavaliers of the Great Civil War.' Ormond was continuously occupied in public affairs for more than half a century, and his public life spans the history of his country from Strafford to Tyrconnell. More than forty years elapsed between his first appointment to the Government of Ireland by Charles the First and the termination of his third tenure of the same great office just before the accession of James the Second. In the words of his friend and correspondent Sir Robert Southwell 'he was fifty-five years in councils and business, which comprehends all the last age.' Thus the record of his participation in public affairs forms, in the words of the same admirer, 'a little map of a great country.' And this lengthened career was marked throughout by an unswerving consistency, inspired by an indomitable loyalty. Hence it is that Ormond has impressed even those who have little sympathy with the cause he supported with a sense of his absolute honesty. Even his hero-worship of Cromwell could not blind Carlyle to the 'distinguished integrity, patience, activity, and talent' of the chief supporter of the royal cause in Ireland; and Lord Morley, in his 'Life of Cromwell,' has characterised Ormond in terms which it would be difficult to improve on as 'one of the most admirably steadfast, patient, clear-sighted, and honourable men in the list of British statesmen.'

James Butler, twelfth Earl and first Duke of Ormond, was born, according to his own belief—for the date of his birth is not otherwise attested—on October 19, 1610, at Clerkenwell, then a fashionable quarter of London, in which the town residence of his maternal grandfather, Sir John Poyntz, of Acton, in Gloucestershire, was situated. Though the scion of a stock among the most ancient in Europe there was nothing in the circumstances in which he was born to suggest that the infant would become the possessor of the vast patrimony of the Earls of Ormond, or live to excite the envy of the most powerful of English nobles as the wealthiest subject of the British crown. At the moment of young James Butler's birth the hereditary honours of the house of Butler were held by the well-known tenth Earl, the veteran warrior of the perpetual conflicts which had torn his country under Elizabeth. 'Tom Duff' or 'Black Tom,' as this earl was commonly called, was without male heirs, and his presumptive successor was his eldest nephew, Theobald, Viscount Tulleophelim, who had married the Earl's only daughter. Young James Butler, who was but the son of a younger nephew, was thus only a contingent successor to the family honours when he was brought to Ireland as a child of three.

On this occasion the boy was taken by his parents to visit the old Earl in the stately mansion of Carrick-on-Suir, in which the veteran passed his latter years, and where, as the interlaced monogram of his sovereign's initials and his own on a still remaining ceiling certifies, he had once prepared to receive a visit from Elizabeth. Young as he then was, the future Duke in after years could often recall the patriarchal aspect of old Earl Thomas, as he sat sightless in his chair with flowing beard and his jewelled George about his neck. There is a pretty story which, though it rests only upon the tradition preserved by some ancient retainer of the family, and contains some obvious inaccuracies, has yet an air of verisimilitude in its essentials sufficient to justify its acceptance. On the last Christmas before his death, so the story runs, Earl Thomas kept Christmas at Carrick, in the midst of a large family gathering:

> 'The table being full, and no room for the younger James Butler to sit at it, he, being then a sprightly boy, entertained himself by whipping his gig (top) in the dining-room, just behind the Earl of Ormond's chair.'

The old man, inquiring and being told the cause of the noise, bade the servant put the boy upon his knees, when, stroking the child's hair, he is reported to have predicted the family misfortunes which, in fact, followed his own demise, and the ultimate advancement of his name to more than its former splendour in the person of the child upon his knee.

> 'Upon which prophetical expression by the Earl,' says the family chronicler, 'the Lord Viscount Tullogh, who then sat near him, and was his nephew and son-in-law, and was to be his successor in the earldom, being a very proud, conceited man, he in great indignation put back his chair and rose up and flung from the table.'

The Earl again inquiring and ascertaining the cause of the second noise, and being told that his nephew had left the room in dudgeon, predicted his early demise, and the consequent succession of the boy James to the heirship of the family honours.[1]

Whatever degree of credence may be attached to this story

[1] *Manuscripts of the Marquis of Ormonde*, N.S. vol. ii. p. 346.

it is certain that the Earl's death was followed by twenty years of melancholy family vicissitudes. The Lady Elizabeth, the widowed daughter and heiress to the entailed estates of Earl Thomas, becoming by her father's death a ward of the crown, was given in marriage by James the First to a Scotch favourite, the playfellow of his childhood, James Preston, Lord Dingwall. Created Earl of Desmond by his sovereign, the Scotch peer immediately instituted claims on behalf of his wife to the greater part of the Ormond estates, in defiance of the rights of the owner of the Ormond title. A long and expensive lawsuit followed, which King James, who actively assisted his favourite, ultimately undertook to terminate by an award. But the terms of the settlement were so onerous that Walter, Earl of Ormond, refused to abide by it. He was accordingly thrown into the Fleet, where he lay for eight years. The King, not satisfied with this injustice, arbitrarily resumed the ancient grant of the county palatine of Tipperary, which had been enjoyed for above four centuries by the Earl's family, and the splendid fortunes of the house of Butler were for a time completely eclipsed.

Meantime young James Butler was being brought up in London. Earl Walter, the new head of the family, joined to his other offences against King James's predilections a warm devotion to the Roman Catholic religion, to which faith the lad's parents and almost all his immediate relatives also belonged. Accordingly, on the death of his father, which occurred when he was ten years old, the lad, who had thus become by courtesy Viscount Thurles, was removed to England by the King's direction and placed under the care of the Archbishop of Canterbury at Lambeth, to be brought up in the Protestant faith. No provision, beyond the scanty allowance of forty pounds a year, appears to have been made for his maintenance; but though Primate Abbot troubled himself as little as possible about his charge this expedient answered the King's purpose. Though always thoroughly tolerant of every form of religious opinion Ormond appears to have become imbued at this period with a sincere attachment to the Church of England, to whose principles he ever afterwards constantly and conscientiously adhered. In his government of Ireland after the

Restoration, his tolerance of Roman Catholics was more than once a source of embarrassment to Ormond, and in the ferment excited by Oates's Plot his kindness to his numerous relatives of that creed even threatened to lead to an impeachment. In a letter addressed at this period to his confidential correspondent, Sir Robert Southwell, Ormond vindicates himself from the aspersions and suspicions which were then rife, with a firmness and manliness entirely honourable to him :

'I know well that I am born with some disadvantages in relation to this present conjuncture, besides my natural weakness and infirmities, and such as I can no more free myself from than I can from them. . . . My father and mother lived and died Papists, and bred all their children so, and only I, by God's merciful providence, was educated in the true Protestant religion, from which I never swerved towards either extreme, not when it was most dangerous to profess it and most advantageous to quit it. . . . My brothers and sisters, though they were not very many, were very fruitful and obstinate (they will call it constant) in their way. Their fruitfulness hath spread into a large alliance, and their obstinacy has made it altogether Popish. . . . But I am taught by nature, and also by instruction, that difference in opinion concerning matters of religion dissolves not the obligations of nature ; and in conformity to this principle I own not only that I have done but that I will do my relations of that or any other persuasion all the good I can.'[1]

Great as was the hostility between the Earls of Ormond and Desmond, consequent on the acute family quarrel which had arisen between them, the costs of a protracted lawsuit disposed both parties, after some years, to seek the means of an accommodation. As the Countess of Desmond had but one child, the Lady Elizabeth Preston, who was the sole heiress to whatever rights the daughter of Earl Thomas might ultimately be found to possess, an obvious mode was presented of reconciling the family differences by uniting the rival claims in the persons of the respective heirs of the disputants. As early as 1621, while both parties to the suggested contract were still children, respectively aged eleven and seven, articles of agreement were concluded between Walter, Earl of Ormond,

[1] *Manuscripts of the Marquis of Ormonde*, vol. ii. p. 280.

and the Earl and Countess of Desmond for the union of Viscount Thurles and his cousin as soon as they should attain marriageable age. Doubts and differences, however, prevented this arrangement from taking effect; the proposal was broken off, and was not renewed until after the death of both the parents of the young lady. Meantime, the cousins having made each other's acquaintance, mutual inclination had combined with mutual interest to forward an alliance so obviously desirable. There is a pretty story of the young Viscount's courtship of his cousin which represents him as 'going in disguise (as a romantic lover) through Kensington, with a pedlar's pack on his back,' with the object of gaining an interview. The Lady Elizabeth condescending to inspect the wares of the supposed pedlar,

> 'he presented to her a pair of gloves, into one of which he had before conveyed a letter, which she in drawing on the glove perceiving, pretended to have no money in her pocket to pay for the gloves, and notwithstanding the young ladies offered to lend her money yet she retired to her chamber to fetch money, and, being there, perused the letter, and soon after returned with the gloves again (into which she had as cunningly conveyed an answer) which she returned to the amorous pedlar, pretending they had an ill smell.' 'What were the contents of these letters,' the narrator of the tale continues, 'can be no otherwise guessed at (because they were so secretly contrived as all amorous intrigues are) than by the success.' [1]

The young couple were shortly afterwards married, and removing into Ireland in 1630 resided there until the death of Earl Walter in 1634 left his youthful grandson the unchallenged master of the long disputed heritage of Earl Thomas.

At this point a word may be fitly said of the lady who for fifty-four years was Ormond's helpmeet. Her character fitted her alike in prosperity and in adversity for such a partnership. Her letters, of which a good many remain, show her to have been, in Carte's words, 'a person of excellent capacity and good sense, who could write on matters of business with great clearness and strength of expression.' That she possessed both intrepidity and energy was shown by her activity in rescuing the Protestant refugees in the neighbourhood during

[1] *Manuscripts of the Marquis of Ormonde,* N.S. vol. ii. p. 350.

the rebellion, and by the capacity with which, during her husband's long absence abroad with his exiled sovereign, she continued to assert her own rights as an heiress and to induce Cromwell to respect them. Her possession of a proper feminine spirit was shown by the firmness with which, as a great lady at Court, she declined to recognise the pretensions of the mistresses of Charles the Second. She refused to wait on the imperious Barbara Villiers, and when the beautiful Louise de Kéroualle sent word she was coming to dinner the Duchess of Ormond, though she received her with hospitality, put her grandchildren out of the house, that they might not meet the frail favourite of the sovereign. She was, however, exceedingly magnificent in her notions of hospitality, and her extravagance caused her husband a good deal of embarrassment. To entertain Charles the Second at supper she is said to have spent two thousand pounds, an expenditure which, measured by the different standard of value, was as colossal as that of any modern millionaire on a like occasion. Her *protégé*, Lady Fanshawe, relates in her 'Memoirs' that the Duchess of Ormond, on her leaving for Ireland in 1662 on the Duke's reappointment as Viceroy, gave her a turquoise and diamond bracelet, and to her husband a diamond ring, and that she never parted from the Duchess on a journey without receiving some present from her. Her love of magnificence occasionally drove the Duchess to odd expedients. Thus on one occasion she was driven to pawn 'a pair of diamond pendants and a diamond fasset ring' to raise £500; and when her son, the gallant Ossory, was honoured with the Garter for his naval success, she presented him with a diamond George worth £200, which she had subsequently some difficulty in paying for.

Ormond's first appearance in public life was made shortly after Strafford's entry on his Irish career. The familiar story of that defiance of the masterful Lord Deputy which was the foundation of a cordial friendship illustrated both the strength and the adroitness in circumstances of difficulty which were Ormond's characteristics throughout his long career. On the occasion of the calling of his first Parliament Strafford, fearing that the hot temper and embittered feeling prevailing among parties in Dublin might easily lead to a breach of the peace, had issued an order forbidding members of either House of Parliament to wear their swords. The order was generally respected, the peers as they entered their chamber handing their weapons to Black Rod. But the young Earl of Ormond, on being called on to do the like, coolly told this official 'that if he had his sword it should be through his guts, and so marched to his seat, and was the only peer who sat with a sword that day in the House.' Strafford was not the man to permit such a defiance of his will, and sent for the offender to appear before the Privy Council. Ormond promptly attended and serenely gave this explanation: He 'acknowledged that he knew of the order and had seen the proclamation, but added that if he disobeyed both it was out of deference to a more particular command and to an higher authority, to which all his obedience and duty were due, and then produced the King's writ which summoned him to come to Parliament *cum gladio cinctus*.' However unwelcome such a display of independence may have been to Strafford, the Deputy bore no resentment; on the contrary, the incident was the commencement of a close friendship. Strafford formed a high opinion of Ormond's capacity, giving him important command in the army raised in Ireland, and in his commendation of the young Earl to the King may be found the origin of that reliance which Charles subsequently placed on Ormond's devotion to his service. The friendship between the two men was thoroughly reciprocal, and endured to the end of the great Viceroy's career. In the dark days, before his trial, Strafford had no more staunch friend than Ormond, who exerted himself strenuously to delay the proceedings for his impeachment in the Irish Parliament, and successfully retarded their progress for several days by devices which prove him to have possessed considerable adroitness in using the forms of Parliamentary procedure for the purpose of what is now known as obstruction. That Strafford warmly appreciated the loyal friendship extended to him in his adversity is proved by his having made it one of his last bequests to his royal master that his own Garter should be bestowed upon Ormond; and Ormond, in later years, never lost an opportunity of expressing his regard for the memory of his early friend.

Although Ormond had been sworn of the Privy Council as early as 1634, and had accepted from Strafford various military commissions, it was not until after the fall of that statesman that he seriously entered upon active public service. When the Lord-Lieutenant quitted Ireland in 1640 he had left Ormond in command of all the forces of the Crown in that country. It thus befell that on the outbreak of the Rebellion, in October 1641, it was upon Ormond that the actual conduct of the measures devised for its suppression immediately devolved. He was thus at once placed in a position of the utmost prominence and responsibility. The rapid development of the military situation, and the resort of both parties to the civil quarrel in England to the arbitrament of the sword, led directly to the rapid advancement of Ormond to a position of authority in the Royalist counsels. Though possessing, through his position and connexions, a vast influence with all classes of Irish society, Ormond had as yet been scarcely tried in the serious business of State. Henceforward he remained, despite all the vicissitudes of the royal fortunes, for more than forty years to follow, the central figure in the affairs of Ireland, and earned a resplendent reputation as perhaps the most illustrious servant of the Crown that has ever held the sword of state in that country. Into the details of that long and varied career, in the course of which he was thrice the ruler of Ireland, and twice a fugitive and exile; which witnessed the complete disruption of social order in his own country, and its resettlement upon a basis which was to outlast him by exactly two centuries; and which embraced alike long periods in which he was a principal counsellor of his exiled sovereign and others in which that sovereign, forgetful in prosperity of the services faithfully rendered in adversity, ostentatiously ignored his most devoted subject; it is impossible to enter within the compass of an article in this review. But something may be said of its leading features, and of those aspects of it which are most in evidence in the additional materials for his biography which are contained in the Ormonde Papers.

Although Ormond's participation in public affairs extended, as has been already noted, over something like half a century, his direct concern with the politics of his own country was interrupted by the long break of eleven years which were spent in exile. The period of his actual responsibility for Irish affairs is thus sharply divided into two unequal parts. In the first of these, which, speaking broadly, lasted from the fall of Strafford to the death of Charles the First, he was engaged in a patient, sustained, but always hopeless struggle to hold Ireland for the Crown; in the second, which, again speaking broadly, lasted, with but one considerable break, from the Restoration to the accession of James the Second, he was occupied with the scarcely less difficult task of evolving social order from the chaos to which long years of the bitterest internecine faction had reduced the country, and of reorganising the whole administrative edifice in Ireland on a new foundation. It can hardly be said that either period has hitherto been adequately handled by the historians.[1] Dr. Gardiner has, indeed, explored the State Papers of the earlier time with marvellous patience and minuteness. The Irish chapters of his great works together constitute the most lucid and impartial examination of a singularly tangled story which has yet been attempted, and indeed have been so written that they might easily be detached from their context and published as a separate book, to the great advantage of the general reader. But with Dr. Gardiner the history of the Rebellion and of the war of the Confederation in Ireland was necessarily only an episode, though a profoundly important one, in the larger history of the Civil War, and it is full time that its incidents should be examined afresh and in detail in an independent work. For such a work the Ormonde Papers, in spite of their necessarily fragmentary character, provide considerable additional materials. Chief among these are the letters of the Irish Lords Justices and Privy Council to the English Government from the commencement of the Irish Rebellion, in October 1641, to the appointment of Ormond to be Lord-Lieutenant at the end of 1643, letters which

[1] Since this passage was written Mr. Richard Bagwell's *Ireland under the Stuarts* has been published.

have not hitherto been available in anything like complete sequence.

No episode in Irish history, as has been remarked in the Introduction to these letters, has been more heavily canvassed than the Rebellion of 1641.

> 'The extent to which the rising was organised and premeditated, the degree in which the accounts of the massacre are entitled to credence, and the question to what extent the spread and violence of the insurrection may have been aggravated by the policy of the Lords Justices'[1]

are all of them matters which remain to a great extent unsettled by the historians, but upon which these letters of the Irish Privy Council shed a considerable light. Being only concerned at present with Ormond's share of the business, we have no intention of discussing here a topic which, in the words of Lecky, 'is still the favourite field of writers who desire to excite sectarian or religious animosity'; nor do the letters themselves do much to resolve the long vexed question of the real extent of the murders by which the Rebellion was accompanied. The gravity and magnitude of these outrages have of late been as absurdly minimised as they were at one time scandalously exaggerated. There can be no question that, taken at the lowest, they were quite numerous enough to excite the liveliest alarm in an age to which the notion of a religious massacre was a conception by no means far-fetched or novel. But as a contribution to the biography of Ormond the letters go to show what a serious misfortune it was alike for the future peace of Ireland and for the cause of his master in the wider conflict between King and Commons that Ormond's authority was subordinate to that of the self-seeking and unscrupulous and withal essentially weak hands to which the reins of government had been confined on Strafford's departure from Ireland. Although in command of the military forces engaged in suppressing the Rebellion Ormond was subject at every step to the civil authority, and that authority was exerted unfortunately in more than one instance in the attempt to control the conduct of military affairs, which ought properly

[1] *Manuscripts of the Marquis of Ormonde,* N.S. vol. ii. p. viii.

to have been left to the discretion of the commander. Even more disastrous was the exercise of the authority of the Lords Justices in their legitimate sphere of action. It has been often imputed to Parsons and Borlase that they deliberately discouraged the speedy and effective suppression of the insurrection, with the sinister motive of driving the Lords of the Pale into rebellion; and it is far from clear that they can be absolved from the guilt of so detestable a policy. But even if the most favourable view be taken, and their mistakes excused as due to no greater fault than the violence of incompetence, it must still be deplored that the conduct of affairs should have been left at a moment so critical to men who were wholly incapable of appreciating or utilising the materials which lay ready to their hands for effecting a pacification. Had the government of Ireland, as well as the command of the army, been in the hands of one not less devoted to the authority of the Crown than sympathetic with the great territorial interests represented by the Lords of the Pale, interests which were traditionally attached to the English connexion and hostile to the ideals of the Ulster leaders, it is far from unlikely that the rising would have been suppressed long before the outbreak of hostilities between the Parliament and the King. Could the moderating influence of Ormond, which even under the adverse conditions which afterwards prevailed was so often able to produce combinations impossible to others, have exerted its full effects in the early stages of the Irish troubles, the history of the next few years and the issue of the great civil conflict might well have been altogether different. When, after two years of vacillation, during which the flames of a local disorder had been fanned, whether by accident or design, to a conflagration involving the whole island, the government of Ireland was placed in Ormond's exclusive charge, it was too late to effect a pacification. By that time the Irish leaders had found in the political situation across the Channel such encouragement to the pursuit of separatist ideals as Irish leaders have at no time been able to resist. Then, as so often before and since, England's difficulty appeared to them to be Ireland's opportunity.

The light thrown by the Ormonde Papers on the second of

the two periods to which we have referred is less steady and concentrated than that which is shed upon the first, though the mass of extant correspondence is considerably larger. There is no such sequence of letters for the period of Ormond's second Irish administration as the letters of the Lords Justices. In any case the circumstances connected with the passing of the Irish Act of Settlement and the subsequent difficulties arising from the impossibility of satisfying the just demands of all who had at one time or another enjoyed or acquired a legal right to Irish land have been much more clearly narrated by historians than the complex politics of the earlier time. The fresh materials now available simply go to emphasise the difficulties of a problem which was really insoluble. It needed, indeed, but a simple sum in arithmetic to demonstrate the impossibility of meeting the engagements which Charles the First on the one hand, had entered into with the Roman Catholics, and which the Parliament, on the other, had contracted with the adventurers; yet which Charles the Second at the Restoration was equally pledged to satisfy. The utter hopelessness of satisfying demands which were not only mutually inconsistent with each other, but of which the hard statistical facts of the case decisively forbade the settlement, were plain from the first to Ormond. It is, indeed, impossible to state the insuperable nature of the difficulty more incisively than did the Lord-Lieutenant when he applied himself to the drafting of the Act of Explanation.

'I confess,' he wrote to the Lord Chancellor, 'I am not able to see to the end of a settlement. For if the adventurer and soldier must be satisfied to the extent of what they suppose intended them by the Declaration, and if all that accepted and constantly adhered to the Declaration of 1648 must be restored, as the same Declaration seems also to intend, there must be new discoveries made of a new Ireland, for the old will not serve to satisfy their engagements. It remains then to determine which party must suffer in the default of means to satisfy all, or whether both must be proportionably losers.'[1]

The latter alternative was that which Ormond preferred, and could he have had his way he would have enforced a *pro rata*

[1] Carte, *op. cit.* vol. iv. p. 81.

abatement of the rival claims. But circumstances were too strong for him. The Cromwellian interest was too powerful and too determined to be withstood. The King had no intention of going on his travels again. The sacrifice of the old proprietors was the line of least resistance, and it was the line that was followed. This determination had a disastrous effect on the influence of Ormond in Ireland, and was the true cause of his being superseded in the government in 1669. By advocating fair play to the old owners he offended the Cromwellians ; by failing to secure that fair play he won the hostility of the Roman Catholics ; and, as the poverty of Ireland, after long years of exhausting wars, forbade the raising of any considerable revenue, he was unable to maintain himself in the good graces of the King. The papers of this period contain many illustrations of the urgency and importance of the financial difficulties of the Irish Government in the years following the Restoration ; difficulties which were not lessened by the facility with which royal warrants for large sums charged on the Irish Revenue were procured from the sovereign, any more than they were solved by the subsequent manipulation of the revenue in the hands of the greedy speculators to whose hands the control of the finances of Ireland was confided by the King after the recall of Ormond.

Among the most interesting of the letters in the latter portion of the Ormonde Papers are those of the once famous Earl of Ossory, whose somewhat remarkable course has hardly been sufficiently appreciated by modern writers. It is, at any rate, impossible in any summary of Ormond's career to omit a reference to his eldest son, that *preux chevalier* who enjoyed in the seventeenth century a prestige for personal prowess something akin to that won, through similar gifts, in the eighteenth by the perhaps better-known Marquis of Granby. Thomas Butler, Earl of Ossory, is indeed entitled to a higher meed of praise than that which is due to mere dare-devil gallantry, such as he displayed in many a hand-to-hand encounter aboard ship, and on the field of Mons at the head of the English contingent. For his is a figure of considerable interest in the history of the English navy. Having acquired some knowledge of naval tactics during a five years' residence in Holland before the Restoration, Ossory was given a subordinate command under the Duke of York at the outbreak of the first Dutch war of Charles the Second, and in the five days' action off the Suffolk coast he so distinguished himself as 'to become the darling of the kingdom and especially of his seamen, who called him the preserver of the navy.' Later, in 1672, he held important command as rear-admiral of the Blue Squadron. In the fight at Sole Bay and other naval actions of this war he played a most conspicuous and distinguished part, displaying a dash and gallantry worthy of the best traditions of the navy. His valour and conduct in this war, to use the language of Anthony Wood, were 'beyond the fiction of a romance.' They evoked a signal mark of royal favour, the King and his Consort visiting Ossory on board his ship, and subsequently conferring the Garter upon him in recognition of his services. This is the first of the only two instances in which the Garter has been given for a naval victory, the other being the blue riband bestowed by George the Third on Lord Howe, more than a century later, for the triumph of the Glorious First of June. The Duke of Ormond had long ago received the same Order, and, as Ossory had, some years earlier, been called to the House of Lords as Baron Butler of Moor Park, both father and son now sat together as Peers of Parliament, and both Gartered; a circumstance probably without a parallel.

That Ossory possessed a daring worthy of the old Elizabethan sea dogs, combined with that impatience of any insult to the national honour which was the mark of Drake and Nelson, is shown by his plan for a descent on Helvoetsluys while that port was guarded by a fleet of twenty-two Dutch ships, in order to recapture or destroy the *Royal Charles* and other trophies of the first Dutch war, which lay in the harbour. There is the true Nelson touch about Ossory's declaration to Sir John Narbrough, his captain and his colleague in the design, that 'he would fire the Dutch ships with a halfpenny candle, or should place his head upon Westminster Hall by Cromwell's, for the greatest traitor that ever breathed.' That this 'man of great honour, generosity, and courage,' as Burnet calls him, carried the like virtues into other spheres of action appears from his once celebrated encounter with Shaftesbury in the House of Lords. That subtle statesman, in the height of the ferment produced by the Oates plot, was posing as the champion of the Protestant interest, and in that capacity had made some reflections from his place in the Lords on the inadequacy of Ormond's measures for suppressing Roman Catholic sedition in Ireland. Ossory was present, and at once rose to defend his father. Having recalled the Duke's services, and demonstrated the improbability of his being lacking in fidelity to the Established Church, he carried the war into the enemy's country, winning the delighted applause of Shaftesbury's numerous ill-wishers by these spirited sentences :—

'Having spoke of what he (Ormond) has done, I presume to tell your Lordships what he has not done. He never advised the breaking of the Triple League ; he never advised the shutting up of the Exchequer ; he never advised the declaration for a toleration ; he never advised the falling out with the Dutch and the joining with France ; he was not the author of that most excellent position of *delenda est Carthago*, that Holland, a Protestant country, should, contrary to the true interest of England, be totally destroyed.'[1]

It was Ossory's curious fortune to be on terms of the closest intimacy with the two princes who, a few years after his own death, were to contend for the crown of the Three Kingdoms. And, despite the extraordinary contrast between the characters of James the Second and William the Third, he appears to have entertained an equal affection for both, and equally to have won their regard. To the former, under whom, as Duke of York, he had served in the Dutch wars, Ossory was united by ties of professional brotherhood. The personal courage of James the Second has often been impugned ; but it is difficult to impute cowardice to one whose demeanour in action won the unstinted admiration of a sailor brave to the point of recklessness. James's intimacy with Ossory seems to have been cordial and unreserved, and in some of his extant letters he writes in the most familiar and unconventional terms both about naval matters and about his own matrimonial projects.

[1] Carte, *op. cit.* vol. v. p. 136.

With William Ossory's relations were even closer. Ossory had spent much of his youth in Flanders. He had married, in 1659, the daughter of the governor of Sluys, a nobleman allied in blood to the Princes of Orange, and he had early become acquainted with the young Stadtholder. In 1674 he was chosen by Charles to be the negotiator of the match between the Prince of Orange and the Princess Mary when that alliance was first suggested. When William came to England three years later, to resume the negotiations for his marriage, Ossory was among the Prince's principal attendants. Though it had hung fire for three years the affair was quickly settled when once the Prince had made up his mind, and, as Sir Henry Coventry wrote to Ormond, it was 'quicker than ordinary that a Prince should come and woo, marry, bed, and carry away the Princess Mary in less than a month's time.' Just before this visit to England Ossory had fought with William at the siege of Charleroi, and the next year found him at Mons fighting by his side as general of the British auxiliaries raised by the States-General. It was evidently with entire sincerity that, when leaving England with his bride, William, in acknowledging Ossory's services, wrote that among all his friends the latter could have none more devoted than his 'très affectionné serviteur, Prince d'Orange.' With such associations and memories it was perhaps fortunate for Ossory that he did not live to witness the Revolution, and so was spared the necessity of determining into which scale he should throw the weight of his influence, or to which of the contending Princes he should lend the not less weighty encouragement of his sword.

His exploits at Mons, where, besides advising the attack and directing the tactics, he displayed remarkable personal gallantry, formed Ossory's last experience of active service on sea or shore, an appointment to a command against the Algerian pirates who, in those days, were the scourge not merely of the Mediterranean but of the Channel, not being taken up. In the last months of his life, having been already specially attached to the service of Queen Catherine of Braganza as her Chamberlain, he was appointed governor of Tangier, but before he could proceed thither he was seized with fever and died. No public misfortune has ever been more sincerely or more widely deplored in England than this premature close of a career whose brilliance had caught the popular imagination. The letters are still extant in which King Charles and his Consort condoled with the bereaved parents, and Ossory was made the subject of innumerable elegies. Of these the most elaborate was the Pindaric Ode of Thomas Flatman. But, though Ormond's munificence rewarded the author with fifty guineas and a diamond ring, posterity would contentedly exchange it for one of that poet-painter's miniatures. A more enduring metrical monument was raised in the splendid condolence addressed by Dryden to Ormond in one of the finest passages in 'Absalom and Achitophel.' In these lines the poet deplores Ossory as

> Snatched in manhood's prime
> By unequal fates and Providence's crime:
> Yet not before the goal of honour won,
> All parts fulfilled of subject and of son;
> Swift was his race, but short the time to run.
> Oh, narrow circle, but of power divine,
> Scanted in space, but perfect in thy line.
> By sea, by land thy matchless worth was known,
> Arms thy delight, and war was all thy own.

To Dryden's stately if formal verses must be added the more feeling tribute of John Evelyn, who had known Ossory from his boyhood, and who, having lived with him on terms of the warmest affection, and attended his death-bed, was able to affirm that

> 'his Majesty never lost a worthier subject, nor father a better or more dutiful son.' 'Unhappy England,' Evelyn went on to say,[1] 'in this illustrious person's loss. He deserved all that a sincere friend, a brave soldier, a virtuous courtier, a loyal subject, an honest man, a bountiful master and a good Christian could deserve of his prince and country.'

Of Ormond's own share in the additional correspondence under notice not much requires to be said. His letters are

[1] Diary, under date July 26, 1680.

similar in tone and style to the great mass of those which were published by Carte, and are familiar to students of his time; and they convey the same impression of his character. Though a constant and a voluminous correspondent Ormond was not a great letter-writer. His dispatches and State papers are generally clear and to the point; but, though vigorous, they are often cumbrously expressed; and even in his intimate letters Ormond does not often descend to those personal and trivial details which give charm to the correspondence of a great man. But in conversation he had a faculty for pointed and sometimes scathing irony. No rebuke could be more admirable than his retort courteous to the Duchess of Cleveland, who, having in an outburst of feminine temper expressed a wish to see Ormond hanged, was gravely told that the object of her resentment had no worse wish regarding her than that he might live to see her old. Even more stinging is his observation on receiving the condolence of a nobleman whose hostility had constantly embarrassed him, and whose regrets he could not think sincere: 'My loss indeed sits heavy upon me, and nothing else could affect me so much; yet I thank God my case is not quite so deplorable as that nobleman's; for I had much rather have my dead son than his living one.' Still better, perhaps, was his answer to the King when Charles inquired what he thought of the appointment of Shaftesbury to be Chancellor: 'Sire, that lord is a very proper person with whom to entrust the Seals, if your Majesty knows how to get them back again.'

Ormond does not often write in a reflective mood, but to his close friend Southwell he occasionally puts his musings on paper. Thus a year or two before his death he penned this charming sketch of the close of a long life:—

'I am this next week to take a shorter journey and stay away a less time. It is to see a little home in Hampshire; and if I like the situation I am resolved not to make exception to the smallness of the house, because I shall be either able to build to it or I shall not need a bigger. I know the country thereabouts is open, and the way to it good, and I am told the gardens are pleasant and well furnished with good fruit, which is an inducement to an old man that must shortly lay aside the thought of field sports; and the steps downward are very natural from the field to the garden, from a garden to a window, from thence to a bed, and so to the grave.'[1]

The keynote of Ormond's character and policy is the indomitable loyalty which permeated his whole being and animated all his public actions. From his earliest years he was impressed with the feeling that a whole-hearted devotion to the throne and person of the sovereign was necessarily due from the head of that ancient and illustrious house which before his time had already produced as many as eight Viceroys of Ireland, and whose representatives had given unfailing support to the English crown. The harsh treatment his family had received from James the First could not damp his ardour in the service of James's son.

'I confess,' he wrote in a brief fragment of autobiography, 'I confess the undutiful and insolent treatment which King Charles I received from a pack of his ungrateful and ambitious subjects, and the indignation it raised in me to see so good a prince so unworthily used made me resolve to venture all in his cause, though I was very little personally known to him, and not at all obliged by him.'

Loyalty was indeed with Ormond a master passion. Heavy as was his heart at the death of Ossory, it was yet with perfect sincerity that he could say, in reply to the condolences of an acquaintance, that 'since he could bear the death of his great and good master, Charles the First, he could bear anything.' His language on the death of Charles the Second, for whom he had a cordial personal regard, bears the mark of unaffected reality of feeling. After deploring to his friend Southwell the loss of 'the best King, the best master, and (if I may be so saucy as to say so) the best friend that ever man had,' he feelingly gives evidence of his sense of the trying incongruity between private sorrow and public duty :—

'My station, my duty, my allegiance forced me, the very day after I received the stroke, to ride out to proclaim his successor, to put on the habit, and (as well as I could) the countenance of joy and triumph, with dismal sadness at my heart.'[2]

[1] *Manuscripts of the Marquis of Ormonde*, vol. ii. p. 306.
[2] Carte, *op. cit.* vol. v. p. 177.

This passionate devotion to the throne and person of the sovereign was proof against every discouragement, and gave to his career a splendid consistency. 'His whole life,' said Southwell, 'was a straight line, if ever a man's in this world were so.' He was often scandalously treated by his royal master, as, for instance, when Charles the Second, after a pitiable exhibition of vacillating insincerity, recalled him from Ireland in 1669 at the instance of the Cabal. This was an indignity which moved the astonishment of the Court and society, people 'admiring,' with Pepys, that 'the greatest subject of any prince in Christendom, who hath done more for his Prince than ever any yet did,' should be thus disgraced. But Ormond never murmured. He possessed what one of his friends called 'a talent for bearing mortification with courage,' and he never received a slight for which time did not bring the reparation, which was the only revenge that the true nobility of his nature permitted him to take. 'As noble a gentleman as ever the world bred,' he might fall from power, he could never fall from dignity. In Dryden's words—

> 'The Court he practised, not the courtier's art,'

and his services, though never obtruded, were as much at the service of the Crown the day after such a humiliation as they had been at the height of his power. No neglect could induce him to forget his lofty conception of the duty of a subject. Thus it was that his fine patience with the vices of others outwore the courtiers' impatience of his own virtues and won from the careless but not always ignoble Charles, after eight years of studied neglect, that royal *amende* which Carte records :—

> 'Yonder comes Ormond. I have done all I can to disoblige that man, and to make him as discontented as others ; but still he will not be out of humour with me ; he will be loyal in spite of my teeth ; I must even take him in again, and he is the fittest person to govern Ireland.'[1]

The same high sense of loyalty which he evinced for the person of his sovereign Ormond carried into the public service of the Crown. The lengths to which he pushed it were the

[1] Carte, *op. cit.* vol. iv. p. 522.

secret alike of his successes and of his failures. He was the first statesman to act on the principle of an illustrious minister of a later age. With Ormond as with Wellington the first maxim of government was that 'the King's Government must be carried on.' It was this principle that enabled him to display that genius for compromise, that power of working with all sorts of dissimilar persons and parties, which was Ormond's principal characteristic as a statesman. If it sometimes brought him into difficulties, and made him appear, as even his hearty admirer Clarendon said of him, 'unwilling to deny any man what he could not but see it was impossible to grant,' it also enabled him to carry through combinations impossible to men less single-minded, as was shown in the success with which he found means to secure the co-operation of the Irish confederate force towards the end of the Civil War, and in the skill with which, after the Restoration, he conciliated the Cromwellian interests, whose goodwill was the indispensable condition of the maintenance of the restored monarchy. Never too fond of his own opinion, though never slow in tendering it, Ormond was always ready to acquiesce in the decisions of others, and prepared to make the best of them. As Burnet puts it, 'he always gave good advices; but even when bad ones were followed he was not for complaining too much of them.' The master he served may not have been entirely worthy either of the personal devotion with which he was followed, or of the public services which Ormond rendered to his Government. Yet Charles, to do him justice, seems really to have appreciated the zeal of his father's old servant, and the unswerving loyalty to himself, which had been proved through more than ten years of exile and of sacrifice. Though much and often pressed by Court intrigues, he ever afterwards preferred to know that one at least of his kingdoms was in safe keeping by retaining Ormond in the Irish Government.

ARCHBISHOP STONE

It has been justly remarked of Irish history that it embraces periods of political calm as remarkable as those storms, often as sudden in their uprising as destructive in their course, which challenge the attention of the reader at so many stages in the record of the relations between Great Britain and Ireland. If we analyse the Irish chronicle from the Revolution of 1688 to the present day, we shall find periods, sometimes covering a whole generation, which remain almost complete blanks upon the page of history. Thus, in the nineteenth century there are the long silences which intervened between the Union and Catholic Emancipation, between the Repeal and the Home Rule agitations. And in the eighteenth century the pauses are still longer and the silences yet deeper. Between the events that immediately followed the Battle of the Boyne and those that closely preceded the creation of an independent legislature, there intervened a space of something like ninety years. Yet, save for the brief squall that raged over Wood's halfpence, there was, throughout that lengthened period, no popular movement serious enough to threaten gravely the repose of English ministers, much less to engross the attention of the general public of the three kingdoms. To the first sovereigns of the House of Brunswick, Ireland gave little concern through the greater part of their reigns. To them it appeared, to use Horace Walpole's expression, 'no more than a remote part of their dominions which was not accustomed to figure on the theatre of politics.'

This characteristic is best explained by the consideration that in Ireland, though the materials for agitation are never far to seek, the master-spirits capable of giving cohesion and a common purpose to scattered and often antagonistic factions have appeared only at rare intervals. In Ireland, the personal element has always been the dominant factor. Many have aspired to ride the Irish whirlwind, only a very few have proved themselves capable of directing the storm; and the hour of apprehended danger has often passed harmlessly by because it has not brought with it the man who could convert difficulty into disaster. Thus it comes about that Irish history has been characterised by a certain lack of proportion. Swift's brief irruption into Irish politics has been fully explored by historians and exhausted by the biographers of the author of the 'Drapier's Letters.' The story of Grattan and his Parliament is a literature in itself. O'Connell and his triumphs, though still awaiting the final verdict of the impartial historian, are in no danger of being forgotten. But while it is natural the stirring incidents which cluster round strong personalities should concentrate attention on such movements as those which are inspired by the genius of a Grattan or an O'Connell, it is none the less essential to a right understanding of Irish problems that the less conspicuous landmarks of the past should be observed. For it is in the examination of hidden history that the true origin of familiar events is most often revealed. The darker periods of history are not always the least attractive: the obscure is not necessarily the uninteresting. And the investigator is unfortunate who, delving in the dead past, is not occasionally rewarded by the discovery of the secret springs of some long famous but only half-understood event.

Such a period is that which intervened between the age of Swift and the rise of Flood and Grattan. It is a period of which less is known, perhaps, than of any other in the history of Ireland since the Revolution. Yet it forms a chapter which is far from unimportant, and some knowledge of which is requisite to a right conception of the more stirring era which followed. If it is deficient in pre-eminent and dominating personalities, it is not without its share of interesting personalities in politics, literature, and religion. The period which witnessed the rise of a parliamentary Opposition under Anthony Malone at College Green, and of popular agitation under Charles Lucas, has great importance and suggestiveness in relation to the subsequent movement for legislative independence. And the Dublin of Lord Chesterfield's Viceroyalty, and of Mrs. Delany's Letters, is not lacking in social distinction. The importance of such a period cannot be more conveniently indicated than in the form of a notice such as is here attempted of some of its more picturesque figures, and of the once famous controversy over the altered Money Bill which according to Edmund Burke, first showed that the English in Ireland had begun to recollect that they had a country and to transform themselves openly and avowedly into an independent Irish interest.

Perhaps Irish politics have never been so narrowly provincial as during the middle period of the eighteenth century. Scarcely any question of importance then occupied the attention of the statesmen who were responsible for the welfare of the country. This apathy was due in the main to the neglect of their viceregal functions by the noblemen from time to time sent over by English ministers to govern the country. It was the heyday of that extraordinary system of government by Undertakers which prevailed through the earlier part of the century, and was only destroyed by the Octennial Act of 1767. Of this system, by which so many successive Viceroys practically abrogated their functions in favour of certain of the more wealthy and ambitious members of the Irish aristocracy, it is impossible to give a more accurate description than that which has been left us by one of the most eminent of the Lords-Lieutenant who experienced its effects. Writing in 1758, Chesterfield, whose Viceroyalty has been justly praised by Lecky as one of the most successful of the century, gives the following description of his own experience of this curious system :—

'The Lord-Lieutenant may, if he pleases, govern alone, but then he must, as I know by experience, take a great deal more trouble upon himself than most Lord-Lieutenants care to do, and he must not be afraid. But as they commonly prefer *otium cum dignitate*, their guards, their battleaxes, and their trumpets, not to mention perhaps the profits of their post, to a laborious execution of it, they must necessarily rule by a faction, of which faction for the time being they are only the first slaves. The condition of the obligation is this. "Your Excellency or Your Grace wants to carry on His Majesty's business smoothly, and to have it to say when you go back that you met with no difficulties. This we have sufficient strength in Parliament to engage for, provided we appear to have the favour and countenance of the Government. The money, be it what it will, shall be cheerfully voted. As for the public, you shall do what you will, or nothing at all, for we care for that no more than we suppose Your Grace or Your Excellency does. But we repeat it again, our recommendations to places, pensions, &c., must prevail, or we shall not be able to keep our people in order." These are always the expressed, or at least the implied, conditions of these treaties, which either the indulgence or the insufficiency of the Governors ratify. Thus from that moment these Undertakers bury the Governor alive, but indeed pompously.' [1]

Much too self-confident and, indeed, too honest to acquiesce in such an effacement of his office, and chafing throughout his government under the control of a plebeian oligarchy, for which, though unable to withstand it, he felt a most patrician contempt, Chesterfield appears to have conceived an intense disgust for the whole system of Irish government. The references to Ireland in his subsequent correspondence are permeated with a contemptuous cynicism which never varies. Thus, in a letter to his friend Chenevix, Bishop of Waterford, a prelate who owed to Chesterfield's patronage a mitre which he adorned by a life of the simplest piety, he expressed his opinion with uncompromising frankness. Parties in Ireland, he did not scruple to say, thought no more of the public good than they did of the squaring of the circle. The question with them was by no means how Ireland should be governed, but by whom; and whoever prevailed, the difference to the country would be 'no more than that between a cat in a hole and a cat out of a hole.'

If it be urged that the impressions of an Englishman and a stranger like Chesterfield, notwithstanding that his position gave him so full an opportunity of judging at first hand of the political system he was appointed to preside over, were jaundiced by his unsympathetic temperament, no such objection can be urged against the estimate formed of the

[1] *Letters of the Earl of Chesterfield*, edited by John Bradshaw, p. 1222.

Undertakers by an Irish politician whose honesty and sagacity were so conspicuous as to win him the reputation of a statesman, even under a system which hardly left room for statesmanship. Edmond Sexton Pery, who, for a score of years prior to his elevation to the Speakership in 1771, held a seat in the Irish House of Commons, has left us, in a masterly review of the state of parties in Ireland, addressed in 1757 to the Duke of Bedford, a succinct account of the state of parties in Ireland, as it appeared to one who had the best means of judging of its operation from within. It is precisely to the same effect as Chesterfield's, though, being addressed to a Viceroy, the language of condemnation is more decorous. According to this candid observer, the one point on which men of all parties were agreed was that the Chief Governor should not be permitted to interfere in the domestic administration of the kingdom. And the same authority averred that the Undertakers' notion of 'doing the King's business' in each biennial Session consisted in 'procuring the supplies which were thought proper to be demanded by the English Minister, and in preventing the Parliament from examining into the accounts of the previous years.'[1]

For some years prior to the period with which we are now concerned, the principal Undertaker had been Henry Boyle, the Speaker of the House of Commons, a scion of that remarkable house which had been founded more than a century earlier by the great Earl of Cork. Down to the death of Primate Boulter, Boyle had held only the subordinate place in the triumvirate of Lords Justices to whom the authority of the Lord-Lieutenant was commonly delegated. But Archbishop Hoadly, though nominated to the same position which his predecessor had filled so vigorously, had little taste for statecraft, and was content to leave the direction of civil politics and patronage in the hands of his lay colleagues. On Hoadly's death, however, after a primacy of little more than four years, the chief place at the head of Church and State was placed in the hands of a very different prelate. Archbishop Stone united to Boulter's capacity for affairs a love

[1] *Historical Manuscripts Commission Report*, viii. App. p. 175.

of power and a talent for intrigue which have seldom been surpassed in any Minister: qualities which speedily made him the most powerful subject of the Crown in Ireland, and for some time threatened to eclipse all other influences in the State.

Unlike the letters of Archbishop Boulter, which form perhaps the principal authority for the affairs of Ireland for the first twelve years of George the Second, little of the correspondence of Archbishop Stone has been printed. A few letters belonging to his latter years are to be found in the correspondence of the fourth Duke of Bedford, and some others have been made available in the Stopford-Sackville Papers, published by the Historical Manuscripts Commission. But many more survive among the papers of the Duke of Newcastle, which are now among the Additional Manuscripts at the British Museum. They range from the year 1739 to 1762. But by far the greater number of them belong to the years 1752 to 1755, and cover the period of the conflict between the Irish Government and the Irish House of Commons on the subject of the disposal of the unappropriated surplus of the Irish Exchequer.[1] Though the question at issue in this controversy was a comparatively small one, the dispute is one of serious interest in the development of Irish politics, marking, as it does, the first concerted attempt by the Irish Parliament in the eighteenth century to assert its independence of ministerial dictation. It is an incident which has hitherto been little attended to and only half-understood, for the materials available for forming a judgment on the real state of parties in Ireland at the time have been curiously scanty till just recently.

Remembering how little tolerant England has been since the days of the Stuarts of the interference of ecclesiastics in the affairs of state, it may seem strange to illustrate the civil politics of Ireland in the eighteenth century in the person of an archbishop. But the retention by the heads of the Irish Establishment of a large share of civil authority, for almost a century after such a combination of political with

[1] These letters have lately been printed, with an introduction by Mr. Falkiner, in the *English Historical Review*, vol. xx. pp. 508, 735.

ecclesiastical authority had ceased to be possible in Great Britain, is not the only instance of the survival in Ireland of practices from which the British Constitution had, in theory, long been purged. The peculiar condition of Irish politics and society in the eighteenth century naturally tended to throw civil power into the hands of the rulers of the Church. No religious system was ever more thoroughly Erastian than the Irish Establishment in the eighteenth century. The Church of Ireland of that age, and especially of the earlier half of the century, was a religious organisation imposed from necessities of state upon a people who rejected its doctrines. In an institution so circumstanced, it was inevitable that at a period which witnessed the enactment of the Penal Laws, and was marked by the elaborate educational policy of which the Charter Schools were the instrument, such an organisation should lean heavily towards England. It was equally natural that its rulers should become in civil, as well as in ecclesiastical affairs, the instruments of the Government by which it had been constituted, and by whose authority alone it had been sustained. Recruited almost exclusively from England, the Irish episcopal bench became a stronghold of English ideas. The practice by which the Irish Primate, as the subject of highest rank in Ireland, was invariably placed at the head of the commission of Lords Justices in the absence of the Viceroy, provided numerous opportunities for the assumption of a political *rôle* which might easily lead to the absorption of almost the whole executive authority in the hands of an ambitious ecclesiastic. It is no exaggeration to say that during the entire reign of George the Second, and for some years before and after it, the true Lord-Lieutenant of Ireland was the Archbishop of Armagh. A succession of prelates, of whom Boulter's is the best known name, took full advantage of the opportunities thus afforded them. But it was reserved for Stone to prove to the world that the ambitions of a Wolsey and not a little of his power might still be displayed by a Protestant prelate in the Ireland of George the Second.

The Primacy to which Stone was called at the early age of thirty-nine was thus a Primacy much more political than ecclesiastical. Always prone to dependence on the Crown, the concern of the higher ecclesiastics in Ireland under the first sovereigns of the House of Hanover was rather for the State than for the Church. In the choice of such prelates as Boulter and Stone, political considerations predominated over all others. The Prime Ministers by whom the Primates of Ireland were recommended, and in effect appointed, were more solicitous for the effective management of the Irish Parliament than for the episcopal supervision of the Irish Church. Accordingly, the preference given to Stone over his principal rivals for one of the most splendid prizes in the gift of the Crown was due to his known aptitude for the management of affairs, and to the confidence felt by the Premier, Henry Pelham, in the loyal support which he could rely on receiving in Irish business from the old friend and *protégé* of his brother Newcastle. It is, however, no more than justice to the much-maligned eighteenth century to observe that this political conception of a great ecclesiastical position had prevailed in Ireland even in an age when the interests of religion were more particularly regarded. A long succession of sixteenth-century Chancellors, who were politicians rather than Churchmen, had created a tradition that civil rather than religious qualifications were to be looked to in the filling of the higher places on the episcopal bench in Ireland. To such a degree had this become an accepted rule, that as early as James the First's time so experienced an official as Sir Henry Harington did not scruple to apply to Cecil for the succession to Archbishop Adam Loftus; and, as he frankly avowed to Cecil, his 'offer and desire' was to be the Chancellor's successor 'as well to his sperytuall office as to his temporall.' The Irish Chancellorship and the Archbishopric of Dublin were frequently, though not invariably, vested in the same person in the seventeenth century, and this association was not finally terminated till after the Restoration.[1] In the reigns of William the Third and George the First the

[1] Even in England the association of the heads of the Establishment with civil statecraft lasted into the reign of Charles II. Archbishop Sheldon was a member of the Cabinet in 1664, and again in 1673. See Pepys' *Diary*, and *Letters to Sir Joseph Williamson.*

traditional union of the offices was sustained by the frequent nomination of the Archbishops of Dublin to be Commissioners of the Great Seal, while the political preoccupation of the Primates was emphasised by their continual nomination as Lords Justices in the frequent absences of the Viceroys.

The letters of Primate Stone shed a flood of clear and fresh light on the obscure politics of the time. They enable us to understand the process by which the Irish House of Commons was moulded to be the instrument upon which, as was said of Peel in the case of the English one, Grattan could play as on an old fiddle. And they are also valuable for their references to the state of political society at the time they were written, as well as for the illustration they give of the personal idiosyncrasies of the writer. Filled with the chicane of negotiation, with singularly penetrating and able criticisms of the men he had to deal with, with projects for combinations by which this politician might be checkmated or that other utilised, they are the letters of an adroit and able statesman, thoroughly cognisant of every move on the political chessboard which it was his business to watch so attentively. But they are not the letters of a churchman or divine. Not once in Stone's long and familiar confidences to his patron and political chief is religion mentioned, nor is the Church spoken of except as the nomination to vacant bishoprics might affect ministerial interests in the House of Lords. Occasionally the incompatibility of such pursuits with the sacred character of his profession is alluded to, but the topic is never long dwelt on, and the pen of the churchman returns readily to the concerns of the statesman. Nor are we left in any doubt as to the means by which the health of the chief pastor of the Irish Church might become impaired in 'doing the business of Government.' Horace Walpole, in noticing the Primate's death, describes the Archbishop as having 'ruined his constitution by indulgence in the style of luxury and drinking established in Ireland, and by conforming to which he had found the means of preventing the most grievous prejudices, and of gaining popularity, ascendent, power, an instance of abilities not to be matched.' And it is related that when, being threatened with mortal illness, Stone had recourse to his physician, he warned this adviser not to treat his case as that of an average clerical patient. 'Look on me,' he said, 'not as an ordinary clergyman, or as subject to the diseases of the clerical profession, but as one who has impaired his constitution by sitting up late and rising early to do the business of Government.' Stone's letters fully support both Walpole's statement and his own.

The convivial excesses which were still common among the Irish country gentry in the last quarter of the eighteenth century have been described by Sir Jonah Barrington, and there is no doubt that such orgies as those which Sir Walter Scott describes in his account of the Osbaldistones were common in the Ireland of a generation earlier, and remained so for long after they had ceased to be general in English society. From these letters we learn that intemperance equally gross prevailed in the highest ranks of society in the early part of the century. It is indeed hardly an exaggeration to say that wine was the medium through which the King's government was carried on. Chesterfield, whose letters disclose a wholesome disgust with the system, which for a couple of years it had been his business to administer, expressed himself very pointedly on this feature of Irish politics. 'It is a maxim that business is best done over a bottle, and that people are never so fit for it as when they are fit for nothing else. I make no doubt that there has been more claret drunk over the barracks than will be drunk in them in ten years; and I wonder the bridge was not agreed to, considering the national aversion to water.' Elsewhere the same statesman remarked that the five thousand tons of wine annually imported into Ireland were chiefly employed 'in destroying the constitution, and too often the fortunes, of those of superior rank, who ought to take care of all the others.' Cumberland, the dramatist, who had excellent opportunities of observing the manners of Dublin society, and was a frequent guest at the Primate's house, was astonished at the magnificence displayed in the great houses, and at the degree in which 'in several prelatical houses the gravity of demeanour maintained by our English dignitaries was laid aside, and the mitre was mingled with the cockade.' Stone's own testimony is to the like effect. Criticising the conduct of affairs by the Viceroys prior to the Duke of Dorset, he observes that the King's business was indeed carried on, 'that is, the money bills were passed, and the chief governor gave wine to the men and fiddles to the women as usual.' The use made of wine in promoting political ends is yet more candidly avowed in another letter, in which the Primate, felicitating himself on his success so far, expresses his confidence that in future the Government may be carried on 'without trusting entirely to the influence of wine, and the exacting of intemperate promises at the end of a debauch.'

Nor was this use of wine confined to the Government. Intemperance was equally the weapon of the opponents of the administration. 'Satires and claret,' as Walpole puts it, 'were useful weapons even against corruption.' The sheriff of Dublin is described as having died in 1754 of a violent fever, 'occasioned by a very hard drinking bout at a late meeting of patriots in the Tholsel.' The 'Orrery Papers' contain several amusing letters descriptive of the doings of the Opposition. At one of their gatherings—a meeting of the 'gentlemen of the Province of Ulster'—no fewer than thirty toasts appear to have been drunk. Henry Pelham writes with indignation at Speaker Boyle's attendance at the 'drunken and mobbish assemblies' of the popular party; and, not to confine the evidence to English sources, Edmond Pery, in his 'Letters from an Armenian in Ireland,' written in 1756, observes with scarcely extravagant exaggeration that 'their people go to such excesses in their intoxicating liquors that it would be no difficult task to take any city of their kingdom by surprise two hours after the time of dining, as half of the people are at that time usually mad.' Chesterfield is not exactly the man we expect to find in the *rôle* of temperance reformer, but even he was moved to express the pious aspiration that 'it would please God to blast all the vines in the world, and by His thunder to turn all the wines in Ireland sour.'

Of the actual course of the proceedings which so disturbed the ease of the Duke of Dorset's second administration, by far the best account yet available is to be gleaned from the passages relating to Ireland in Horace Walpole's 'Memoirs of the Reign of George II.' That most scandalous of political chroniclers knew little of the internal condition of Ireland, and probably cared still less. But he was keenly interested in the administrative changes in that country under the Cabinets of George the Second, as they affected the careers of the great personages of English politics. Whatever else may be said of the Government of Ireland in that reign, it is at least certain that the Viceroyalty was continuously held, not merely by great noblemen, but by noblemen who held great positions in the actual governing circle. The Dukes of Dorset, Devonshire, and Bedford, the Earls of Chesterfield and Harrington, were all of them important members of the Pelham and Newcastle Cabinets, whose removal to or from Ireland sensibly affected the combinations of the political kaleidoscope. It was from this point of view that Walpole was interested in Irish affairs, and it is manifest from his account of them that he contrived to get information regarding what went on in Dublin which was both accurate and minute, enabling him to draw several excellent and characteristic portraits of persons whose fame was purely Irish. And as, in dealing with Ireland, Walpole departed for the sake of convenience from the chronological order of his narrative, and grouped his Irish information into connected summaries of events running through a considerable period, it is possible to obtain from his pages a clearer account of affairs in Ireland, in the last years of George the Second, than has been left by any other writer. But Horace Walpole, although he knew almost everything that went on in political circles in London, and contrived to know much about the leading personages in College Green, knew very little, if anything, of Ireland itself. To him, contemporary history was little more than the record of political tittle-tattle and the ups and downs of Court favourites. Admirable from the point of view of English politics, it is necessary to correct Walpole's narrative at many points by a reference to conditions of Irish politics and society which, lying a little below the surface, were hidden to this acute and sagacious, but somewhat superficial, observer. And on these points the correspondence of Archbishop Stone with the Duke of Newcastle, and of Lord George Sackville with both, supplement Walpole's narrative in many important particulars.

Prior to the accession of the Duke of Dorset to the Lord Lieutenancy in 1751, a dead calm had prevailed for many years. In the language of one of the numerous Opposition pamphlets which within a twelvemonth were everywhere disseminated, 'everything was happy here and agreeable to England.' Speaker Boyle, who, as already mentioned, was the principal Undertaker, had conducted for many years the little business there was to do in Parliament, and in return for that service had been allowed, by a succession of Chief Governors, complete control of the much more important business of dispensing the Government patronage among his own adherents. Dorset had already served for above six years, from 1730–37, in the same great office, and had seen and realised the degradation of the Viceroy's position in the hands of the Undertakers. Chesterfield, as we have seen, had felt acutely the insignificance of his position, and had revolted against the notion that the great English nobles deputed to represent the Crown should become the puppets of a knot of provincial place-hunters. He had imbued Pelham and Newcastle with a sense of the danger of surrendering authority over Ireland in the fashion which had prevailed for a generation. On Chesterfield's retirement a resolution seems to have been taken to reform the system. It was at first intended that Dorset should directly succeed him. But the Earl of Harrington, who had been obliged by the King to resign the seal of the Secretary of State, insisted on his title to the Lord-Lieutenancy. He was accordingly nominated, and held the post for four years. His administration was undistinguished by a single act of importance, other than the advancement of Stone to the Primacy. But on the resignation of Harrington, the opportunity for which Pelham had been waiting was provided. Dorset returned to Dublin Castle. He brought with him instructions, which were certainly not disagreeable to him, to assert the authority of the Crown and 'to bring back administration to the Castle.'

The task was obviously difficult, but Dorset was favourably circumstanced for its performance. He had been popular in his former tenure of office, and had earned the goodwill of Swift. Several letters from the great Dean, whose friendship was at that period essential to the peace of any Irish administration, are extant in the Stopford-Sackville Papers. He had also the assured support of his superiors in England. The Duke of Newcastle was the Minister through whom the communications between the English and Irish Privy Councils were carried on under his brother's government, and Newcastle, Dorset, and Stone were all three of them on terms of personal and intimate friendship. With Lord George Sackville, the Viceroy's son, as secretary to the Lord-Lieutenant, and with Stone at the head of the Commission of Lords Justices, circumstances were more than ordinarily favourable to an attempt to reassert the paramount authority of the English Ministry over the self-seeking place-hunters, so graphically described by Chesterfield, who monopolised both the honours and the emoluments of Irish administration. Admirably persuasive and adroit, and skilled in the management of men, Stone was from the outset of Dorset's government at the elbow of the Viceroy, and in his absence took the lead in the triumvirate of Lords Justices by whom the business of the State was carried on. The Primate had thus at first no difficulty in carrying on affairs to the satisfaction of his patron. Confining himself in the first instance to the control of the House of Lords, and the disposal of ecclesiastical patronage—the latter at that time an important element in the scheme of English government—he at first aroused no hostile feeling. In the first year of Dorset's government, and before that nobleman came over, he carried on the business of administration with marked success. Amongst other measures he negotiated a plan for improving the currency, which had become so debased that, according to a letter of Lord Orrery, the 'guinea was clipt in such a manner as to want six or eight shillings of its full weight, so that no money is current except at the card tables. There the gentlemen are obliged to produce their purses, out of which the ladies choose the broadest guinea they can find.' Stone withdrew the proclamation under which Spanish pistoles had been recognised as legal tender, and allowed English money to be imported into Ireland.

But when, on the opening of the parliamentary session, the Primate proceeded to consolidate his power by the formation of a separate party in the House of Commons, the friends of the old system took alarm. Henry Boyle, who had filled the Speaker's chair for eighteen years, had unquestioned control of the assembly over which he presided. He had influential connexions among the Irish aristocracy, and commanded immense influence as an owner of Irish boroughs. He was not a man of striking abilities, and at critical moments was always fond of leaning on the advice of others rather than deciding for himself. But he was affable and popular and knew how to make things smooth for the Viceroys who governed through him. According to the compendious character given of him by Horace Walpole, he was 'vain and popular, and, as the idols of the people and of themselves generally are, a man of moderate capacity.' At the outset of Dorset's Viceroyalty, and down to the opening of the Session of Parliament, the best relations were maintained between Boyle and Stone. But the moment that the Primate's adroit diplomacy threatened to establish a strong Court interest in the House of Commons, their friendship was speedily dissolved. The result of the conflict of interest between the Primate and the Speaker was to precipitate a conflict of principle between the English and Irish elements in the Irish Parliament. Factions were created which, in Walpole's phrase, soon imbibed all the inveteracy of party except disaffection. For the first time since the Restoration, an Opposition was formed in the Lower House, in which, oddly enough, not a few of the most vigorous members were placemen and servants of the Crown.

That a definite attempt would be made to assert viceregal authority was known before Dorset's arrival. Lord Orrery, writing from England, was quick to inform his relative, the Speaker, of what was in store. 'There are various struggles and great workings within our mountain of state. When it bursts, some people will be knocked on the head. But, thank Heaven, I am out of this Vesuvius.' No sooner was the Lord-Lieutenant arrived than the issue was quickly joined between the two interests. The Government were anxious to get rid of the Speaker on decent terms, and thought to allay his opposition by the usual panacea. He was offered a peerage and a pension of £1500 a year, but rejected the proposed accommodation in language which, if correctly reported by Walpole, was dignified and to the point. 'If I had a peerage,' he said, 'I should not think myself greater than now that I am Mr. Boyle; for the other thing, I despise it as much as the person who offers it.'

Open war was at once declared, and a struggle immediately ensued. The Speaker started with the initial advantage of a great majority in the House of Commons, which he had consolidated during his long tenure of power by a skilful use of the vast patronage in his hands. The Primate, on the other hand, was supported both by the Viceroy and by the English Ministry, and, as 'the Governor of the Governor,' had acquired the control of all future patronage.

The House of Commons, which thus became the scene of a struggle so important that within a twelvemonth of its commencement, Pelham, the Prime Minister, wrote to Dorset that if a proper stand were not made by the Government the dependency of Ireland upon England might be regarded as over, was a peculiarly constituted body. It consisted of three hundred members, representing half as many constituencies, of whom above two-thirds were returned by boroughs of which the great majority were rotten. Most of the members either belonged to good county families and were the nominees of great peers, or they held positions of emolument in the military, legal, or civil services of the country, and were thus at the service of the Government. Many of the former class had seats in the English House of Commons at Westminster, and but seldom occupied the benches at College Green. But the latter were constantly present and made the normal House. At the beginning of Dorset's administration, the House was already a quarter of a century in being, having been summoned at the accession of George the Second, and it endured throughout the entire reign of that sovereign. Its sessions, which were biennial, were usually but thinly attended, and but that they furnished the sole occasion for the visit of the Viceroy, whose presence brought the territorial magnates to the capital, the assembly would have been still smaller. The Opposition, in so far as one existed, numbered less than thirty, and had hitherto always been powerless to resist the Administration. The Primate Stone in his letters notes that the attendance in the House of Commons on the Money Bill on November 16, 1753, which amounted to 239, was 'the greatest ever remembered'; and, as appears from the Charlemont Papers, it included members who, though elected at the first summons of Parliament in 1727, had not previously taken their seats. Its debates were held in the dignified edifice which had been opened by the Duke of Dorset in his first Viceroyalty, and which the great parliamentary period inaugurated by Grattan was ere long to render famous.

At the outset of the first session of Dorset's government the parties of which the House was constituted, in so far at least as party system can be said to have prevailed, were three in number. The Primate controlled the large official party directly dependent on the immediate favour of the Court. John Ponsonby, afterwards Speaker of the Irish House of Commons, and father of a future Whig leader of Opposition in the English one, controlled a large Whig vote which he placed at the service of the Primate. The Speaker commanded the remainder. This consisted mainly of the friends and adherents of the great family of Boyle, which for above a century had enjoyed so large a share of political and ecclesiastical patronage, but it also included not a few of the place-holders who abounded at College Green.

Before relating the progress of the dissensions between the Primate and the Speaker, it may be convenient to give some account of the leading parliamentary personages.

Considering that the long period of dull, though not unprosperous, quiescence which had remained unbroken since the accession of the House of Hanover was little favourable to the display of great parliamentary qualities, it is remarkable how large a proportion of members of capacity the House of Commons contained. The rank and file were of course provided by the great territorial interest and its nominees. On its roll appear the names of all the great territorial families whose names, since the Act of Settlement at all events, have been continuously associated with the Irish counties. Among the Knights of the Shire were to be found representatives of the Fitzmaurices of Kerry, and the Fortescues of Louth; of the Binghams of Mayo, and the Caulfeilds of Tyrone; of the Skeffingtons of Antrim, and the St. Legers of Cork; of the Wynnes of Sligo, and the Wesleys of Meath. But while the territorial interest of course predominated, some corrective to its power was supplied by the mercantile interest in the representatives of large towns, and by the considerable admixture of the legal element among the members of the smaller boroughs. The great banking houses were honourably represented by La Touches and Burtons, while the Bar, which was afterwards to have so large a part in the glories of Grattan's Parliament, provided the House with its greatest orator in the person of the Prime Serjeant, Anthony Malone.

There was a further feature which, whatever its drawbacks in other respects, was not without its compensations in adding to the variety of the House of Commons. The large number of placemen made a company in themselves. Reflecting of course the predominance for the time being of one or other of the great county families, there was at every period in the history of the Irish Legislature a family group, which proved by its numbers the almost boundless possibilities of family aggrandisement under the eighteenth-century system of placemen and pensioners. In the latest era of the Irish Parliament, the Beresfords were the most conspicuous illustration of this characteristic. In the Parliament of George the Second, the same phenomenon was witnessed in the perhaps unparalleled achievement of the powerful family of the Gores. In 1750, no fewer than nine gentlemen of this name, known as the 'nine Gores,' sat together in the House of Commons, of which one of them had, for a time, been Speaker. Of the nine there was not one who was not in receipt in one form or another of the sweets of Government patronage; no fewer than four among them were eventually advanced to the peerage. One, rising to eminence as a lawyer, attained to the great office of Lord Chief Justice of Ireland and the dignity of Earl of Annaly. And the noble houses of Arran and Harlech derive from this singularly capable family coterie, which, always voting solidly together, engrossed a large proportion of the honours and emoluments at the disposal of those in power.

The official spokesman of the Government in the House of Commons was the Chief Secretary to the Lord-Lieutenant, a title, by the way, which has survived from times when the Viceroy had more than one parliamentary secretary. Under the Dorset *régime*, the post was filled by the Duke's son, Lord George Sackville, who was to win a few years later an unenviable notoriety as the inglorious hero of Minden. Though his conduct on that occasion subjected him to imputations of cowardice, the charge does not appear to have been deserved. His daring had been the redeeming feature in the display of the British on the unfortunate field of Fontenoy, and much later in his career his spirited conduct in a duel evoked the encomiums of his adversary and the reluctant applause of Horace Walpole. But whatever his physical courage, there was no doubt of Sackville's intrepidity in conference and his vigour in debate. There he was audacious to the point of insolence. For though he understood business and was a man of unquestionable capacity, he was deficient in tact and in consideration for other men's feelings; and the difficulties which arose from the very outset of his official career in Ireland were attributed by capable observers in a great measure to his lack of temper and his greed for power. Horace Walpole, in noting Sackville's death, which did not occur till 1785, recalled the provocative character of his Irish career in his comment on him as 'the man who first taught Ireland to think.'

Less conspicuous in debate, but not less important in his

influence in the House, was the leader of the extra-official wing of the ministerial party. John Ponsonby, the second son of the Earl of Bessborough, came of a Cumberland family, which had been settled for about a century in Ireland. Having had considerable grants of land confirmed to them by the Act of Settlement, the Ponsonbys had, by fortunate matrimonial alliances, acquired a leading position in the country, and had founded early in the reign of George the First the Earldom of Bessborough. Supporters of the Cromwellian and extreme Protestant interest in the seventeenth century, they were ardent supporters of Revolution principles; and the future Speaker of the Irish House of Commons further strengthened the Whig connexions of the family by his marriage with Lady Elizabeth Cavendish, daughter of the third Duke of Devonshire. At the moment when Dorset arrived, Ponsonby, who had been for many years in Parliament but was only just turned forty, was at the head of the Revenue Board, a position which, as the case of John Beresford was to prove forty years later, was one of immense influence in the official hierarchy of eighteenth-century Ireland. That influence Ponsonby's connexion with the Cavendishs disposed him to place at the service of a government of which his father-in-law was a member. Accordingly he joined forces with the Primate, and thus enabled the latter to commence operations against the Speaker with a slight majority in his favour.

While the power of the Primate in the House of Commons depended on the support of Ponsonby, the position of Boyle in the same assembly mainly rested on the Prime Serjeant, Anthony Malone. The eulogies cited by Grattan, in his pamphlet in reply to Lord Clare, have rescued from oblivion the name of this remarkable man, and preserved his reputation as a great orator. 'A great sea in a calm,' he appeared to those who knew him in his latter years; 'a great sea in a storm' was the verdict of those who had known him in his prime. And, as Grattan finely added, 'like the sea, whether in calm or in storm, he was a great production of nature.' Of an old Westmeath family, educated at Christ Church, Malone had, on his admission to the Irish Bar, quickly reached eminence in his profession, and had been appointed Prime Serjeant at an early age. In the House of Commons, which he entered in 1727, he was to attain a double fame. It is the distinction of Anthony Malone to have been the first to form at College Green that school of Attic oratory which was to reach its zenith in the sonorous rhetoric of Grattan, though his own eloquence probably came nearer to the stately periods of Plunket. It is also his distinction to have been the inventor of a patriotic opposition in the Irish Parliament. Of Malone's great parliamentary abilities many testimonies survive. But none are more convincing than the frankness with which Stone, who felt their power, admits his superiority to all other antagonists. 'I will be so candid as to own,' he wrote to Newcastle in December 1753, 'that the Prime Serjeant, Mr. Malone, is by far the most able man in the House; and if his dispositions were as good as his talents, the Government could not pay too much for his support. He must bring strong debating support to any side.'

Though Malone's father had been a member of the English Bar, who had a large practice at Westminster and had many English connexions, he came of an Irish stock with strong Irish traditions, and he married a Roman Catholic. These circumstances give a strong national leaning to Anthony Malone's opinions, and though there does not seem to be any warranty for Stone's statement that he was actually born a Roman Catholic, his 'popish connexion' certainly created some suspicion of the sincerity of his devotion to the Revolution principles so strenuously professed by his political allies. Thus while many zealous Protestants in consequence felt averse to the thought of his arriving at that 'principal possession of power' at which he was known to aim, others were fearful of the effect which talents such as his, influenced by national leanings, might have upon the connexion between the two kingdoms. Stone early predicted that the opposition organised by Boyle and Malone would assume the appearance and dimensions of a national movement, and this he attributed to Malone's influence: 'The constitutional dependency upon England is the object upon which the Prime Serjeant's eye is constantly fixed. The Speaker is dragged unwillingly by him.'

'The leaders of the Opposition,' he wrote in 1754, 'do not mean disaffection to the King. God forbid that I should say anything that could be so understood. I do not think it. But some of them do certainly mean an emancipation from the English legislature and from English administration.'

Other figures of importance in the House were those of Philip Tisdal, the Solicitor-General, Stone's principal henchman in the Lower House, and afterwards an eminent Attorney-General; Dr. Francis Andrews, Provost of Trinity College, a *bon vivant*, a scholar, and a man of trusted political loyalty; and among the younger men, Edmond Sexton Pery, who, twenty years later, was to succeed Ponsonby in the chair; and Hely Hutchinson, afterwards so well known as Andrews's successor in the Provostship, and the author of a famous work on the commercial relations between England and Ireland.

The Irish House of Lords before 1750 was, of course, even more stagnant than the House of Commons. In the time of Boulter it had been managed entirely by that Primate, with the help of the Bishops. The Spiritual Peers habitually made the quorum, and in the rare divisions helped to swell the majority. But at this period it can hardly be said that they numbered many persons of eminence. The great Berkeley was still Bishop of Cloyne. But he had already fallen into ill-health. He was not far from his end and took little part in politics, though his remarks on patriotism, suggested by the events of the year 1753, show that he was an interested spectator of what went on. For a long period the deliberations of the peers had been presided over by a series of English Chancellors, and although at the time of which we are now writing its Speaker, Lord Newport, was so far distinguished from his predecessors that his professional career had been passed in Ireland, the whole atmosphere of the place was much more English than Irish. At the head of the Irish peers, in rank and political importance, stood James Fitzgerald, twentieth Earl of Kildare, later and better known as the first Duke of Leinster, and father of Lord Edward Fitzgerald. From the eclipse of the great rival house of Butler, which followed the attainder of the second Duke of Ormond, the head of the Geraldines was *facile princeps* among the Irish nobility. Traditionally connected with the national party of earlier days, his adherence to the Speaker and Malone emphasised the patriotic leanings of the latter, and added to their popularity ; while his connexion with Henry Fox, through his marriage to the daughter of the Duke of Richmond, gave the Opposition a support among the Whig adherents of the Pelham Ministry which proved of great service in the struggle.

Besides these conspicuous personages, two others of less eminence, but of much importance in the Irish capital, require some notice. Thomas Carter had for twenty years held the sinecure office of Master of the Rolls, the reversion of which he had previously acquired by purchase from the Earl of Berkeley, according to a pernicious practice severely condemned by Swift in one of the 'Drapier's Letters.' He had, all his life, taken a prominent part in political business, usually in opposition to the Government. Archbishop Boulter had, as early as 1726, found occasion to censure his conduct as lacking in respect to the English Government. And Horace Walpole describes him as an able, intriguing man, who had always been a Whig, but had constantly fomented every discontent against the Lords-Lieutenant in order to be bought off. He had been closely associated with Boyle throughout the latter's long tenure of the Speakership, notwithstanding that he had himself been a candidate for the chair. He shared to the full the convivial habits of the time, contributing much by a lively wit to the vivacity of the Opposition dinners ; and, according to Pery, he was the author of the ingenious invention of conveying libels in toasts, of which much invidious use was then made in Dublin.

Less eminent at this period than the Master of the Rolls, but even more powerful in the parliamentary interest he exerted, was Nathaniel Clements, the Teller of the Exchequer. He was without the slightest pretension to parliamentary talents, and, according to Stone, incapable of speaking three sentences in public. But his position at the Treasury, where important employment had become hereditary in his family, gave him an influence which in that age of corruption it was scarcely deemed dishonourable to turn to political purposes, and which he was not slow to use. His almost uncontrolled power gave him at once the means of corrupting individuals and of embarrassing the State. At this period the Bank of Ireland had not yet been formed. The Government finances were entirely in the hands of the individuals controlling the Exchequer—so much so, that it was possible for one of the Lords Justices of Ireland to assert that 'the whole stock of the nation is now in the hands of a single person. And how and where vested is known to him only.' This extraordinary state of affairs arose from the fact that the Teller, whose nominal salary was only £250, was really remunerated by the profits of the manipulation of the Treasury balances. And these profits were said to amount in Clements's hands to no less than £8000 a year. Connected by marriage with the great interest of the Gores, Clements belonged, like Carter, to that section of placemen who were disaffected towards the Court set; and, like Carter, he had long been in close alliance with Boyle. Of the methods by which he made his power felt no details are given in the correspondence relating to the controversies of this period, and there is no suggestion that he used his public position for his own private gain, otherwise than as just mentioned, and as the recognised system allowed. But at a later date Clements was roundly accused by Hely Hutchinson of augmenting the Treasury receipts at the expense of his political opponents, by making undue deductions from their salaries in respect of income tax. He even carried this novel system to the point of reducing the salary of the Chancellor of the Exchequer himself. Clements, who preserved his political influence to the close of a long life, and a year before his death procured the elevation of his son to the peerage as Lord Leitrim, enjoyed for thirty years the dignified office of Ranger of Phœnix Park, and in that capacity built the mansion which, for more than a century, has been familiar to the people of Dublin as the Viceregal Lodge.

The Parliament in which the persons just noticed were the leading figures had, throughout the first twenty years of George the Second, remained in a state of passive and even somnolent acquiescence in the policy dictated by the English and administered through the Irish Privy Council. But a question was now to be mooted which in a moment aroused its dormant energies, and brought it into alarming collision with the prerogatives of the Crown. Under the government of the Earl of Harrington a question had arisen on a constitutional point of some delicacy which, at the beginning of Dorset's administration, still remained undetermined. The commercial prosperity which followed the Peace of Aix-la-Chapelle had considerably benefited the trade of Ireland, and at the end of the year 1749 it was found that a considerable surplus out of the moneys voted by Parliament for the service of the Crown remained in the Treasury. The Irish House of Commons proposed to apply this surplus to the discharge of the National Debt, which had been largely increased in the late war, and a Bill was prepared to that effect. No controversy arose on the question of prerogative under Harrington, and the Bill, which contained an acknowledgment of the sovereign's right to direct how much of the surplus could be spared to the purpose assigned by Parliament, was passed in that form. The English Government, however, took the view that this was an interference with the prerogative, and that moneys due to the Crown, being in the absolute control of the sovereign, any surplus could only be dealt with as he might direct or consent. Accordingly, there being again a surplus in 1751, the Duke of Dorset was instructed, while not refusing to sanction the proposed application of the funds, to assert the prerogative explicitly. In his speech at the opening of the session the Viceroy accordingly declared that His Majesty 'would consent and graciously recommend' that so much of the surplus as could be so applied consistently with the public service should be devoted to the reduction of the debt. The House of Commons, under the guidance of Boyle and Malone, took no notice of the Viceroy's phraseology, and omitted all reference to the prerogative in the Bill they sent over to England for approval. It was, however, too soon for an Opposition which relied on the votes of a number of placemen nominally subservient to the Government to press matters to extremities, and the Bill, having been amended in England by the insertion in the preamble of a recital of the King's consent and recommendation, was passed without further protest. Postponing for the present matters of government, the leaders determined to fight for the moment on the safer ground of personalities. The Primate being justly regarded as the chief agent of the English Ministry, they resolved to show their power by attacking one of his known favourites and subordinates, rightly judging that in such an enterprise they would have the support of many whose personal pique was stronger than their zeal for constitutional privileges. The Surveyor-General, Nevill Jones, a *protégé* of the Primate's and the member for Wexford, had been for some years engaged in the erection of barracks through the country. Having been called on by the Lord-Lieutenant to vote more money for this work, the Commons readily complied. But having at the same time been invited to inquire into the alleged malversation of money destined for that service, an invitation intended by the Viceroy as an oblique reflection on the conduct of his predecessor Harrington, the House took advantage of the opportunity to arraign Nevill Jones. They accordingly passed a resolution condemning the contractor for deficiencies in carrying out the work, and calling on him to make good the defects at his own expense, and at the close of the session they declined to present the usual address of thanks to the Viceroy which had hitherto been a matter of course. Having thus given a foretaste of their intentions, and an indication of their power, the Opposition desisted for the present from further measures. The session coming to an end in May, the Viceroy returned to England and matters were left to simmer quietly for eighteen months. The interval was occupied by the Primate in endeavouring to consolidate his forces, and by the Opposition in appeals to the Whig members of the Government. Lord Kildare betook himself to England to present to the King a rather vainglorious memorial against Dorset and the Primate. It had, however, but little effect. 'No facts,' says Walpole, 'were alleged against the Lord-Lieutenant, nor any crime pretended in the Primate but that he was a Churchman,' and the King, who had a high idea of his prerogative, concurred with his Ministry in supporting the Viceroy.

Immediately on the reopening of Parliament in October of the succeeding year, the duel was resumed. There is a gap in the Stone and Newcastle correspondence during the period of the recess, but it is evident from other sources that the Viceroy returned to Ireland fully determined to assert the prerogative in the matter of the disposal of the surplus, while endeavouring to smooth over the personal difficulties which had arisen. Dorset had apparently been so much upset by the troubles in which he had found himself involved that he had designed to throw up his place. But the embarrassments which threatened to follow in choosing a successor made it important to the Ministry that he should remain. 'The thoughts of a successor,' wrote Newcastle from Hanover to his brother the Premier, 'make Dorset's stay in Ireland absolutely necessary.' The Duke of Cumberland seems to have had a hankering for the Irish Government, and the prospect filled Newcastle with dismay. 'I conclude you know the fat, little, round great man would like it,' he wrote. 'We have now nothing to do in the English army; we should then have as little in the Irish one.' It was accordingly arranged that Dorset should return, and that while no surrender should be made on the point of prerogative, the Primate and Lord George Sackville, on the latter of whom Newcastle threw the chief blame, should make it up with the Speaker. Proposals for an accommodation were accordingly made by the Primate, and at first seemed likely to be successful. But matters had gone too far. The Opposition had organised its forces and was confident of its power. Boyle, who was much in the hands of Malone, after taking time to consult his friends, rejected the Primate's overtures, and the battle was resumed with more vehemence than ever.

Parliament met at College Green on October 9. On the 10th an indication of the heat of party spirit was given in the robbery of the Armagh mail, which carried the writ for a new election in county Armagh, with a view to delaying the filling up of a vacancy in a constituency largely dominated by the Primate's influence. In November, a resolution directly aimed at Nevill Jones, and preliminary to a motion for his expulsion from the House, was carried by three votes. Matters were thus ripe for a fight on the larger constitutional issue. The procedure of the former session had been adopted, but on the Bill coming back from England with the words as to consent and recommendation inserted, it was rejected, after a debate of nine hours, by a majority of five, in the largest House that had yet been seen in College Green.

'Whoever,' wrote Horace Walpole, 'has seen the tide first turn in favour of an Opposition may judge of the riotous triumphs occasioned by this victory. The ladies made balls, the mobs bonfires, the poets joyous odes.' Dublin went mad with joy. The 'Patriots,' as the Opposition now began to be called, were toasted as saviours of their country all over the island. A list of the members who voted in the division was printed, in which the supporters of the Government appeared in black and their opponents in red letters, under the title *Insula Sacra et Libera.* Medals were struck which showed the view entertained by the popular party of the real essence of the struggle in which they had been engaged. On one of them, Hibernia with a harp in her hand, and the Speaker with a cap of liberty on his head, were represented together, with Fame blowing a trumpet, and a banner displaying the figures of the majority. Another showed on the obverse 'The Speaker and Liberty'; on the reverse 'The 124 Patriots of Ireland.' Lord Kildare took an hour to pass from College Green to his house not five minutes distant, so cordial were the greetings of the mob. The Dublin chairmen distinguished their patriotism by refusing to carry any fare to the Castle. Finally, Sheridan, the manager of the Smock Alley Theatre, had his stage wrecked and the house reduced to a shell for refusing to comply with a call of the audience for a repetition of some lines in Voltaire's 'Mahomet,' which were applauded as applicable to the defeated partisans of the Court in the House of Commons.

The news of these unexpected and disquieting proceedings

caused no little astonishment in London, where all capable observers were quick to note the significance of this outburst of independence in the hitherto subservient Parliament of Ireland. To so old a parliamentary hand as Bubb Dodington, whose easy indifference to every interest save his own was not easily disturbed, the rejection of the Money Bill appeared a 'dangerous event, and productive of more mischiefs than I shall live to see remedied.' To Chesterfield it seemed equally serious, though it was rather the harm to Ireland than the annoyance to England that this acute and experienced critic deplored. Among the members of the Cabinet, the Duke of Newcastle, always alarmed and ready to temporise, was for conciliation and moderate courses. But to his brother, the Prime Minister, the affair seemed much more grave. 'If a proper stand is not now made,' he wrote to the Primate, 'the dependency of Ireland on this country is over'; and he assured Dorset and Stone of his support in any measures which they might think necessary to mark the displeasure with which the conduct of the Patriots was viewed. Carter, Malone, and Dilkes, the Barracks-Master General, and Sir Richard Cox—a man of some mark, who had taken an active part in developing the linen industry, and had given offence by writing a violent attack on the Administration in a pamphlet called the 'True Life of Betty Ireland'—were accordingly dismissed summarily from their posts. Bellingham Boyle, a near relative of the Speaker, had his pension stopped, and the Speaker himself was threatened with removal from his office of Chancellor of the Exchequer. With these steps, the matter was allowed to rest pending authoritative directions from London, whither two emissaries at once proceeded: Maxwell, the Under-Secretary, to report to the Premier and his brother; and the Marquis of Kildare, as the ambassador of the Opposition, to lay the grievances of the Patriots before the King. Of the two, Kildare's was the harder task. George the Second had notions of prerogative little less pronounced than his grandson's. As Lord Chesterfield put it, abilities greater than Kildare's were needed to convince the King that the surplus of his own revenue was not his own. The King flatly refused to see Kildare, with whom he was, as Henry Fox reported, as angry as it was possible for a man to be. And the views of the sovereign were reinforced by the powerful counsels of Murray, the future Lord Mansfield. The disgrace of Boyle was therefore sanctioned, and he was removed from office. A touch of absurdity was imparted to the whole controversy by the resolution of the Ministry to appropriate the surplus which had been the nominal bone of contention, thus illustrating the real powerlessness of the Irish Parliament. The money was applied by the Crown at its own discretion, and not another word was ever heard about it. But Parliament, to obviate the risk of any future embarrassments, took care by voting every sort of unnecessary expenditure to prevent the possibility of a surplus.

For the moment the Castle had triumphed. The Patriots were indeed more than ever heroes in Dublin, and the displaced officials were *fêted* everywhere. But the agitation must soon have died a natural death had the energetic measures of Pelham and Murray been persevered in. This was the opinion of so competent an observer as Lord Macartney, who was afterwards Chief Secretary under Lord Townshend, and who reviewed the history of these events in his 'Account of Ireland in 1773.' 'Why the Duke of Dorset did not return to Ireland, and why the system then laid down was not pursued, I do not know. But I know that the not pursuing it has been the cause of all the distractions and disturbances in Ireland since that time.' The explanation, however, was not far to seek. The death of Pelham, and the construction of a Newcastle Cabinet, in which Henry Fox had a place which he seems to have mainly valued as a means of thwarting the policy of his chief, had a marked effect on the course of Irish affairs. Fox was closely connected, through Kildare, with the Irish Opposition; and although Murray, who was now Attorney-General and the principal figure in the House of Commons, helped to sustain the Primate in his place, the Dorset influence henceforward declined. Matters slept quietly enough during the twelve months following the prorogation of Parliament. But in the autumn of 1754 it became necessary to consider affairs with a view to the approaching session. Dorset and the Primate had recommended, as a further means of showing the power of the Crown and overawing those members of the House of Commons whose defection had caused the difficulties of the preceding year, that Clements should be dismissed from his post. The latter, however, had his friends at Court, and contrived to postpone a decision till the imminent meeting of Parliament rendered a decision imperative. The matter was referred to the King, who was averse to the removal, if avoidable, but ready to sanction it if deemed an indispensable measure; and the Primate was asked to state explicitly whether the turning out of Clements would ensure a majority in the House of Commons. But while affairs were in this doubtful state the Cabinet underwent another shuffle, as a consequence of which the influence of Fox, who became Secretary of State, both with Newcastle and with the King, was materially strengthened. After much irresolution, the Fox party carried the day. It was resolved to supersede Dorset, who became Master of the Horse, and the Marquis of Hartington, shortly to become the fourth Duke of Devonshire, was sent over as Lord-Lieutenant. Boyle and his friends had thus carried the day. 'The triumph of the Patriots is complete,' wrote Chesterfield, 'and the power is now theirs. With all my heart; let them but use it well.' The measures recommended by Chesterfield to the Patriots in 1775, for this end, were such as to a modern patriot would appear sufficiently extraordinary, and show the limitations of the views of even the most enlightened statesman of that age. 'Let them encourage the extension and improvement of their manufactures, the cultivation of their lands, and, above all, the Protestant Charter Schools. Let them people and civilise the country by establishing a fund to invite and provide for Protestant strangers. Let them make Connaught and Kerry know that there is a God, a King, and a Government—three things to which they are at present utter strangers.' Chesterfield strongly deprecated any further revival of the constitutional disputes. The discussion of 'national points,' he considered, could never be of advantage to Ireland. The people, he thought, had liberty enough, and the Crown had prerogative enough. Those appeared to him the real enemies of Ireland who would enlarge either at the expense of the other.

The new arrangement was intended as a pacification. But it was not efficient for the purpose. The new Viceroy was brother-in-law to Bessborough, the promotion of whose son to the Speakership had been a principal object in the game of faction. Bessborough and Stone had been left as joint Lords Justices, and the former had no notion of giving up the prize for which he had contended. A battle now ensued between the Primate, supported by Lord Bessborough, and the Speaker, backed by Kildare and Fox, for the possession of power in the next recess. Of this contest Horace Walpole gives an amusing account. Boyle demanded the dismissal of the Primate: the Primate was professedly willing to resign his place in the Commission provided the Speaker would resign too. In the end this arrangement was adopted, to the equal disappointment of both aspirants for power. The Patriots, in the language of Walpole, dismissed the woes of their country, for which they had no longer occasion. The Opposition was placated by the reinstatement of Boyle as Chancellor of the Exchequer, and the finding of fresh places for Malone and Carter. At the end of the session, Boyle, accepting an earldom and a pension of £2000 a year, made way for Ponsonby in the Speaker's chair, and Kildare and Bessborough were named Lords Justices on the Lord-Lieutenant's departure from the kingdom. But, before he went, there was time for an object-lesson in the sincerity of patriotism. A motion, made by Pery, to take into consideration the heads of a Bill to secure the freedom of Parliament, by vacating the seats of members accepting pensions or offices of profit under the Crown, was opposed by the full strength of the disinterested Patriots who had refused the Money Bill. The motion was rejected, and among the majority were Malone, Clements, Dilkes, and the whole troop of Gores.

It would serve no useful purpose to recall the petty intrigues which followed these events. The first result, naturally, was to draw down on the 'Patriots' the not undeserved opprobrium of the Dublin mob. Boyle was burnt in effigy, and Malone was hooted; and the Duke of Devonshire was probably not sorry when, on the collapse of Newcastle's Government, he was summoned to construct his own short-lived Ministry and relieved of immediate responsibility for Ireland. A further result of this unprincipled conduct on the part of those who, a short time before, had so successfully posed as the saviours of their country, was to produce a revulsion of feeling in favour of the discredited, but consistent, director of English interests in the minds of English statesmen. Even in his temporary discredit under the Hartington Government, the sagacious Chesterfield had predicted the ultimate triumph of the Primate, as being the ablest of all the competitors for power. 'I am bewildered at your Irish politics,' he wrote in the autumn of 1757, 'but upon the whole, take my word for it, the Primate will be too hard for them all at the last.' Although the new Viceroy, the Duke of Bedford, struggled to maintain his independence of the Undertakers, he was soon driven into an alliance with the only member of the governing group who really understood the management of men. Even while out of the Government, the Primate had shown the extent of his influence in the highest places by managing with equal acceptance to both statesmen, as Dodington's Diary informs us, the delicate negotiations between Pitt and the Duke of Newcastle, which resulted in the alliance that terminated the Duke of Devonshire's Government, and substituted for it the Administration under which Pitt's greatest triumphs were achieved. If he had lost power by attempting to grasp too much, Stone now showed his adaptability to circumstances by coming to terms with his former adversary. Absolutely devoid of rancour and resentment, Stone had no difficulty in acting with those he had formerly opposed. He now entered into a close alliance with his former foe, the ex-Speaker, now become Lord Shannon. The two great Undertakers, together with Speaker Ponsonby, became the joint depositories of power, and for the next six years, till their deaths, which happened in the same month at the close of 1764, their power was undisturbed. Under the successive viceroyalties of Bedford, Halifax, and

Northumberland, the triumvirate were continually appointed Lords Justices, and the influence of the Undertakers was greater than ever before.

Such a result seems a lame and impotent conclusion to the controversy so long and so energetically sustained by the Opposition, and may perhaps appear to contradict what has been said above of the importance of that controversy as a stage in the evolution of parliamentary institutions. Yet it is certain that the struggle over the altered Money Bill marks the first definite appearance in the eighteenth-century politics of Ireland of a patriotic party, professedly actuated by a national spirit. However interested and even venal the conduct and motives of those who masqueraded in the garb of patriotism, their action had enduring effects on the character of the Irish House of Commons. For the first time in its history the territorial oligarchy, which had governed Ireland since the Restoration, became identified in the public mind with the principle of the constitutional independence of the Irish Parliament; and, despite the backsliding of individuals, it continued to be so identified even after the Undertakers had recovered power. The notion of the national identity of Ireland took firm hold of the public mind, and was eagerly adopted by the opponents of the Administration as a means of strengthening the power of the Opposition, and checking the hitherto uncontrolled power of the Undertakers. And for the first time, too, the control of the purse began to be effectively asserted by the House of Commons as an unquestionable constitutional right.

To two observers of great eminence these aspects of the 'Patriot' struggles of 1755 were clearly apparent. Both Edmund Burke, from the point of view of English Whiggism, and Lord Clare, from that of Irish Unionism in its most militant form, have left, in striking passages, their impressions of the immense significance of these events. It was at this period, as the great orator observed in his well-known letter to Sir Hercules Langrishe, that the English in Ireland 'began to be domiciliated, began to recollect that they had a country.' The English interest, at first by faint and almost imperceptible

I 2

degrees, but at length openly and avowedly, became an independent Irish interest fully as independent as it could ever have been 'if it had continued in the persons of the natural Irish.' The clear-sighted and uncompromising champion of English interests in Ireland at the end of the century put the same point in another form, and in his great speech upon the Union referred to the struggle as the fatal precedent on which 'a system had been gradually built which would beat down the most powerful nation of the earth.'

ROBERT EMMET

ALTHOUGH but little respect has been paid to the dying request of Robert Emmet, his reputation has certainly not suffered from the world's persistent refusal to bestow upon it 'the charity of its silence.' Emmet's admirers have not waited for that distant day to which he would fain have adjourned the writing of his epitaph, the day 'when my country takes her place among the nations of the earth.' Thanks to the loyalty to Emmet's memory consistently shown by a most eminent Irish man of letters of the nineteenth century, as well as to the graceful sentiment evoked by Emmet's fate and the sorrows of his love from one of the most gifted of American writers, the name and character of the chief figure in the insurrection of 1803 have been, almost from the first, invested with the glamour of romance. It is not given to many to unite such suffrages as those of Thomas Moore and Washington Irving; and their touching tributes have combined to render the figure of Robert Emmet, even to those who disapprove his ideals and abhor his methods, among the most picturesque in the portrait gallery of Irish patriots.

Nothing, indeed, in the career of the somewhat worldly-minded author of 'Lalla Rookh' is more honourable than his constant zeal for the fame of his earliest friends. For Moore's prose tributes to Robert Emmet are not less touching than the well-known lines which begin

> She is far from the land where her young hero sleeps,

which embalm the memory of the young patriot's attachment to Sarah Curran. In his 'Life of Lord Edward FitzGerald' Moore pronounced a glowing eulogy on his old college comrade as 'among the highest of the few among all I have ever known who appeared to me to combine in the highest degree pure moral worth with intellectual power.' And the poet records in his diary a conversation with Sir Arthur Wellesley at a dinner at Dublin Castle at which he was 'afforded an opportunity within those memorable walls of speaking of Emmet as he deserved.' The merit, says Moore, was far less in the speaker than in the great listener; for 'such a flight of daring at an Irish Chief Secretary's table was at that time little less than a portent, and even the most ordinary of Irish Secretaries could, from his very position, have consigned me to silence with a look.' But Moore found in Wellington an attentive and interested auditor, and was able, as he tells us, 'to thank God as he went to bed that he had lived to pronounce an eulogium on Robert Emmet at the Chief Secretary's table.'

Such enthusiasm as Moore's, coupled with such compassion as Washington Irving expressed in his touching story of 'The Broken Heart'[1] for one 'so young, so intelligent, so generous, so brave—so everything that we are apt to like in a young man,' is more than sufficient to mitigate the untempered harshness of the less favourable criticisms passed by Grattan and O'Connell. For, curiously enough, the least sympathetic appreciations of Emmet have come from the lips of those two most eminent of Irish patriots. Grattan, who, as an old Whig disgusted at the wreck of Liberalism wrought by the excesses of the enthusiasts of democracy, was perhaps scarcely capable of discriminating criticism in such a case, had none but hard words for Emmet and his associates. And O'Connell was still more uncompromising in his disapprobation. 'Never,' he is reported to have said, 'was there a more rash or foolish enthusiast. At the head of eighty men, armed only with pikes, he waged war on the most powerful government in the world, and the end of the mad fiasco was the murder of one of the best of the then Irish judges, Lord Kilwarden.' For this murder Emmet, in O'Connell's opinion, deserved to be hanged, and he considered that but for the romance which his

[1] See Washington Irving's *Sketch-Book*.

attachment to Miss Curran had thrown around him, his memory would long ago have been forgotten. The judgment of the great Liberator is certainly not generous, and perhaps it is hardly just. But, though a sympathy with the too sanguine enthusiasms of youth, and compassion for the errors of a temperament exceptionally ardent, may dispose us to qualify O'Connell's verdict, it cannot be denied that it comes nearer the mark than the preposterous exaggerations of some undiscriminating eulogists, for the charity of whose silence Emmet had every reason to plead. With all respect to such extraordinary and, in a sense, admirable devotion as that exhibited by the author of the 'Lives of the United Irishmen,' Dr. Madden's persistent attribution to his heroes of impossible perfection of character, and to their opponents of equally unattainable depravity, produces an inevitable repulsion on all fair-minded readers. Emmet's title to the remembrance of his fellow-countrymen is safer in the gracious keeping of the great men of letters to whose affecting tributes we have referred, and in the vivid impression created by his own impassioned vindication of his motives, than in the perfervid eulogies of indiscriminate partisans.

The dissent which Dr. Madden's exaggerated apologetics tend to provoke even in those whose approval of the aims and ideals of the men of '98 is cordial and unreserved appears plainly enough in the tone of Mr. O'Donoghue's attempt[1] to give an unrhetorical account of the life of Robert Emmet. Widely as we differ from Mr. O'Donoghue in many of his estimates, his book seems to us to merit the encomium applied by its author to one of the authorities on which he draws, as containing much sane and thoughtful writing, and 'showing an excellent acquaintance with Emmet's time and a thorough appreciation of Emmet's position and ideas.' It is impossible, unhappily, to accord the same praise to Dr. T. A. Emmet's monumental 'Memoirs of the Emmet Family.'[2] Students of the literature of the United Irish Movement will

[1] *Life of Robert Emmet*, by D. J. O'Donoghue, Dublin, 1902.

[2] *The Emmet Family, with some incidents relating to Irish History*, by Thomas Addis Emmet, New York, 1898.

indeed be grateful for the fresh matter derived from authentic and original sources which the book contains. The hitherto unknown and unpublished diary of Thomas Addis Emmet, Robert's elder brother, during his stay in Paris in 1803–04, throws an entirely fresh light on the origin of the insurrection of 1803 and its relation to French projects for an invasion of Ireland. But the point of view of the compiler, as is natural and indeed excusable in the principal representative of the descendants of the Emmet family, is as persistently laudatory as Dr. Madden's; and the readiness with which Dr. Emmet imputes every kind of villainy, possible and impossible, to Pitt and to the Irish Government produces the same undesired effect upon the candid reader.

Whatever opinion may be formed upon the works we have been discussing, it is unquestionable that Dr. Madden and Dr. Emmet have between them supplied the public with every possible material for forming a judgment on their hero. Their united industry has explored practically every document which is now procurable outside the State Paper Office. And it seems unlikely that the State Paper Office can contain anything which may not also be found among the personal papers of the statesmen responsible for the government of Ireland in 1803. In one form or another everything of real importance which can throw light on the circumstances of Emmet's plot or the motives of its chief contrivers has now been made available. For notwithstanding an extraordinary and inherently incredible hallucination of Dr. Emmet as to the destruction of certain papers in Dublin Castle, there is good reason to believe that every State paper of importance relating to the subject is now accessible to the public. Although the records for 1803 at the Home Office and at Dublin Castle are only accessible by special permission, and have never, so far as we are aware, been utilised by any writer, the acquisition by the British Museum of the Hardwicke collection has placed at the disposal of the public either the originals or official copies of practically every paper in the possession of the Government bearing on the Emmet insurrection. The Earl of Hardwicke was at the head of the Irish Government as

Lord-Lieutenant for the five years succeeding the Union, and that part of his papers which covers this episode is particularly complete. In addition to the originals, or office copies of the originals, of many important State papers already published in such collections as the 'Castlereagh Correspondence' and the 'Diary and Correspondence of Lord Colchester,' Lord Hardwicke's collection contains many other documents of an intimate and confidential kind; and it is unlikely that the hitherto unexplored archives of State departments contain anything of consequence which is not covered by the Viceroy's correspondence.

Besides the family documents disclosed in the memoirs of the Emmet family and the State papers in the Hardwicke collection and elsewhere, only one other possible source of information has till recently remained unexplored—the archives, namely, of the French Government bearing on the projects of the Directorate and the Consulate for the invasion of England, and on the negotiations known to have taken place between Napoleon and the United Irishmen. The publication of these archives by the Historical Section of the French Staff, under the title of 'Projets et Tentatives de Débarquement aux Iles Britanniques, 1793–1805,'[1] has now been completed, and the chapters devoted to the negotiations with the Irish leaders from the very inception of the French plans of invasion to their overthrow at Trafalgar supply a hitherto missing link in the chain of historical evidence on the subject. Taken in connexion with the invaluable diary of Thomas Emmet, already referred to, these archives demonstrate the practically continuous character of the negotiations between the French Government and the emissaries of the United Irishmen for the invasion of Ireland during a space of a dozen years. They show that at every step in the development of the conspiracy for the overthrow of the British Government in Ireland, French gold, French weapons, and French soldiers were deemed the indispensable conditions of a successful attempt. And they prove that if the premature

[1] Par Edouard Desbrière, Paris, 1900–02.

outbreak of July 23, 1803, appears at first sight to have been an independent and self-contained movement, it is only because, too impatient to await the tardy development of the plans of the French Government for sending assistance to Ireland, the eager spirit of an uncalculating enthusiast precipitated a rising with which France had designed to co-operate. A careful study of all the information abundantly demonstrates what the bare facts of themselves suggest—that the rising had no real roots in the active discontent of the Irish people, but was due entirely to the promptings of the survivors of the United Irish movement, to the restless activity of a few outlawed conspirators, and to the enthusiasm of a few speculative reformers, of whom the Emmet brothers were the chief.

The theory that Robert Emmet was the sole contriver of the insurrection which will always be associated with his name, that it was devised in Ireland independently of all idea of foreign assistance, and that in his wild project he was acting simply on the impulse of a raw and inexperienced youth, is one which, in spite of his own disavowal, has been sedulously fostered by his friends and apologists. That disavowal was surely explicit enough to have entitled his assertion to credence: 'I have been charged with that importance in the efforts to emancipate my country as to be considered the keystone of the combination of Irishmen, or, as it has been expressed, "the life and blood of the conspiracy." You do honour me over-much; you have given to the subaltern all the credit of his superior.' Yet this disavowal has not prevented his admirers—not less anxious to cover the British Government with obloquy than to vindicate the memory of their hero—from seriously putting forward a theory which, if it could be established, must deprive Emmet of a large part of his title to the praises they bestow upon him. To Dr. Madden must be ascribed the honour of first formulating the extraordinary proposition that the Emmet rising was organised by a Government taking advantage of Emmet's youth, enthusiasm, and inexperience, and acting through the medium of traitors among the United Irishmen who had betrayed their cause and their comrades.

Such extravagant and unsupported hypotheses as those which Dr. Madden advanced are really enough to capsize for the moment the intellect of any candid reader of the history of the times, so utterly inconsistent are they with the known facts of the case. But the confidence with which they are put forward, and the readiness with which they are accepted, have given a wide currency to those fables of a too sympathetic imagination. And as, prior to Mr. O'Donoghue's, no attempt has been made to examine the facts from any less partial standpoint, it is scarcely surprising that Dr. Madden's version of the Emmet insurrection has won a ready credence from the ignorant or half-informed. It was time to make some attempt to exhibit the facts in a fuller and fairer light, and, while doing every justice to all that was attractive in the character of its youthful leader, to indicate plainly the true bearings of the insurrection of 1803. Mr. O'Donoghue's lucid narrative is a considerable step in the right direction, though even he has fallen more than once into the error he deprecates in his predecessors of adopting as facts statements which are 'not borne out by sufficient evidence to justify their inclusion.'

The far-reaching effect of the ferment of revolutionary ideas, which in every corner of the civilised world marked the last decades of the eighteenth century, was nowhere more apparent than in Ireland, and in no instance was the power of those ideas more strikingly shown than in the careers of the men to whom the revolutionary movement in that island owed its chief inspirations. The three leaders of the United Irishmen, whose names have most powerfully impressed themselves on the memory and imagination of the Irish people, are Lord Edward FitzGerald, Wolfe Tone, and Robert Emmet. The names of all three are those of men essentially unlikely, from their origin, to have had any connexion with Irish treason, and in all probability in ordinary times not one of them would have ever been heard of in connexion with popular politics. The first-named, a cadet of the oldest of Irish Whig families, and closely connected, through his mother, with one of the greatest titles in the roll of English nobility, began his career as a British soldier fighting the battles of

England in the American War of Independence, against a people 'rightly struggling to be free.' The second came of a family of Protestant yeomanry of the kind least likely to catch the contagion of anti-British feeling. And neither in the case of FitzGerald nor in that of Tone did the early career of those patriots indicate the slightest affinity to the cause for which both died. Within two years of his adoption of republican principles FitzGerald was on the point of accepting at the hands of Pitt the command of an expedition to Cadiz; and only a few months before he founded the United Irish Society Tone was negotiating with the same minister for the formation of a British colony in the South Seas. The third and youngest of the patriots we have named was in point of race and religion equally unconnected with popular politics.

Robert Emmet was born at 110 St. Stephen's Green, Dublin,[1] in 1776. He was the youngest of seventeen children born to Dr. Robert Emmet, M.D., and his wife Elizabeth Mason. The striking qualities of remarkable men are often imputed to their mothers; but in the case of Emmet there is no doubt that the bent of his character and the turn of his opinions were formed by his father. Dr. Robert Emmet came of a family of English descent, which had settled in the south of Ireland in the seventeenth century. Born in Tipperary, he had, after embracing the medical profession, migrated to Cork, whence he moved to the capital about the year 1770. In that year he was appointed to the position of State physician to the Lord Lieutenant, a post which, though involving attendance at the Viceregal Court, he retained to the day of his death in 1802, notwithstanding the known connexion of two of his children with the treasonable organisation of the United Irishmen. Dr. Emmet appears to have been a man of considerable ability and original views, but too doctrinaire, and even eccentric, in the application of his ideas to life to attract the confidence of practical men. He took a

[1] The exact birthplace of Emmet has been the subject of some controversy. His biographers state that he was born in Molesworth Street. The point has been decisively settled in favour of 110 St. Stephen's Green (the house is now numbered 124) by Mr. David A. Quaid, of Dublin, in a brochure entitled *Robert Emmet: his Birthplace and Burial*, Dublin, 1902.

keen interest in politics, and stimulated the same taste in his children. But Grattan, whose family physician he was, had a very poor opinion of the doctor's political capacity. 'Emmet,' he used to say, 'had his pill and his plan, and he mixed so much politics with his prescription that he would kill the patient who took the one and ruin the country that listened to the other.' Of the peculiarity of Dr. Emmet's political nostrums only one instance is recorded—a novel scheme of proportional representation, according to which the votes of members of the House of Commons were to be multiplied in the ratio of their eminence and capacity; Grattan's vote, for example, counting as five, as against the single voice of an undistinguished member.

Most of the children of Dr. Emmet inherited much of his ability with some of his eccentricity. Their views were coloured from childhood by the extravagance of their father's speculative political philosophy. According to the younger Grattan, the education he gave them was singular and ill-advised; while Curran used to describe him interrogating his sons at the family table: 'Would you kill your brother for your country?' 'Would you kill your sister?' 'Would you kill me?' It is scarcely wonderful that lads so trained should have been apt recipients of the revolutionary ideas which were rife in their early manhood, and have eagerly embraced the philosophy of Tom Paine. To this, however, there was one exception. Temple Emmet, the eldest son, though possessed of an imagination which enriched the natural eloquence he displayed during a brief but brilliant career at the Irish Bar, appears to have been unaffected by his father's oddities of opinion. He died at twenty-eight; but not before he had earned an extraordinary reputation and shown a brilliant promise—he was created a King's Counsel within six years of his call to the Bar—and Lord Norbury, in the course of Robert Emmet's trial, took occasion to pronounce a eulogy, which was manifestly sincere, on the character of his eldest brother as one of the greatest ornaments of the Irish Bar.

Dr. Emmet's second and better-known son, Thomas Addis Emmet, more closely resembled his father, and, like the latter, had much influence on the opinions of young Robert, who was fourteen years his brother's junior. Indeed, it is no exaggeration to say that the insurrection known as Robert Emmet's was much more than half the work of Thomas Addis; and to explain the disciple we must first describe the teacher. Thomas Emmet began life in the medical profession, and was actually associated for some time with his father, according to the practice of those days, in the patent of appointment as State physician. But on the death of his elder brother, Temple, he abandoned medicine for the law; and, called to the Bar in 1790, he at once stepped into considerable practice. In the cases—always tolerably numerous in Ireland—which had any relation to politics, he was constantly retained on the popular side. In this way he became acquainted with Wolfe Tone, then at the beginning of his extraordinary career as a politician. He was a member of Tone's political club, in which connexion he is described in his friend's journal as 'a man completely after my own heart, of a great and comprehensive mind; of the warmest and sincerest affection for his friends; and of a firm and steady adherence to his principles, to which he has sacrificed much, as I know, and would, I am sure, if necessary, sacrifice his life.' Mr. O'Donoghue observes in his preface that, while Robert Emmet's career has appealed more strongly to the Irish people in general than any figure in Irish history since Owen Roe O'Neill, and Sarsfield, it would be absurd to pretend that he had the genius of Wolfe Tone. It may be added that he showed little trace of the speculative powers of his brother Thomas.

Though Lord Edward FitzGerald's and Robert Emmet's are by far the most romantic names in the United Irish movement, Wolfe Tone's and Thomas Addis Emmet's are incomparably the most important in relation both to the genesis of the ideas in which that movement originated and to the history of developments. For the story of its intrigues and stratagems, in the conduct of which he took so keen a delight, Tone's Journal is by far the fullest and best authority; while as an exposition of the views and motives which guided the more thoughtful among those connected with it, the narrative published by Thomas Addis Emmet in 'Pieces of Irish History' is by far the most instructive of extant documents. This unfinished 'Essay towards the History of Ireland,' composed by Thomas Addis Emmet during his confinement as a State prisoner at Fort St. George after the failure of the rebellion of 1798, only carries the history of the United Irish movement down to the year 1796; but as an exposition of the ideas which pervaded the minds of the authors of the insurrection, and especially of those with whom Robert Emmet was brought up, it is abundantly complete. Taken in connexion with the author's own examination before the Secret Committees of the Lords and Commons of Ireland, as printed in the same volume, together with certain letters on Irish politics contributed to the press by Thomas Addis Emmet under the pseudonym of 'Montanus,' it leaves no sort of doubt as to the character of this mild apostle of revolution. The impression thus conveyed unquestionably confirms the justice of Grattan's estimate. Thomas Emmet's writings illustrate in a striking way the influence of the French Revolution on a mind already engrossed with political speculations, and exhibit the rapidity of his advance from the limited object of parliamentary reform, which was the original goal of his aspirations, to the severance of Ireland from Great Britain and the establishment of an independent Irish Republic.

The comparatively limited grievances for the redress of which, according to Thomas Addis Emmet, the reform of the Irish Parliament was desired in the first instance are stated very succinctly in an answer given to the Lord Chancellor in the course of Emmet's examination before the Committee of the House of Lords. Asked what grievances a reformed legislature would remove, he replied, 'In the first place, it would cause a complete abolition of tithes; in the next, by giving the people an increased value in the democracy, it would better their situation and make them more respected by their superiors; the condition of the poor would be ameliorated, and, what is perhaps of more consequence than all the rest, a system of national education would be established.' But with the advent of the French Revolution the horizon of Thomas Emmet and his friends was enormously widened.

'The French Revolution paved the way for the entire accomplishment of what the volunteer institution had begun. A Catholic country had by its conduct contradicted the frequently repeated dogma that Catholics are unfit for liberty; and the waning glory of the British Constitution seemed to fade before the regenerated government of France.'

One other article in the creed of the United Irishmen which Thomas Addis Emmet's essay and other documents in 'Pieces of Irish History' make clear is the sincerity of the majority of the Irish leaders in their belief in the possibility of maintaining Ireland, once separated, in a position of independence not only of Great Britain, but of France and all other powers. This point is of special interest in relation to Robert Emmet, the chief burden of whose speech at his trial was less a vindication of his separatist opinions than a protest against the supposition of his being ready to place his country under French rule. Thomas Addis Emmet constantly averred that he would never have attempted to effect a separation had he entertained a shadow of doubt of the ability of Ireland 'to defy the combined efforts of France and England.' His reliance, he said, was more on Irish prowess than on French promises; and he had persuaded himself that an Irish army, when once organised by foreign assistance, would be powerful enough to withstand a hundred thousand Frenchmen. That Thomas Addis Emmet held tenaciously to this belief to the end is evident from his part in the negotiations carried on with Napoleon in 1803–04 for an invasion of Ireland. He was then the leader of a party among the Irish refugees in Paris who constantly objected to the notion of a French protectorate, which Arthur O'Connor and other refugees were willing to encourage, and he actually secured from the First Consul a promise not to make peace with England without stipulating for the independence of Ireland, and for her treatment by France in every way on the same footing as the United States.

That the views of the elder Emmet were from the first the views of his younger brother there is no room to doubt. Predisposed from the first by his father's precepts to adopt the philosophy of revolution in its extremest form, Robert Emmet's development from boyhood to manhood took place at the very period when his brother was giving practical effect to the doctrines of his father. He had barely reached his twentieth year when the rebellion of 1798 broke out, and when his brother and his brother's friends were made to pay the penalty of their revolutionary principles in a prolonged imprisonment.

No authentic narrative of Robert Emmet's movements in the period of preparation for the rising has ever been written. At any rate no such narrative survives. It is consequently difficult to trace with certainty the sequence of the young conspirator's proceedings. The precise degree in which, at certain stages of his enterprise, he acted upon his own initiative, without direction from those associated with him, must ever remain unexplained. But enough can be gleaned from an analysis of the scattered scraps of information bearing directly on the subject to enable us to form a clear view, not only of the general plan upon which his movement was organised, but of the close connexion which subsisted between the ideas of Emmet and the plans of those chiefs of the United Irishmen by whom the rebellion of 1798 had been organised. Taken in conjunction with the diary of Thomas Emmet, the ascertainable facts demonstrate abundantly the organised character of the conspiracy known as Robert Emmet's. They prove it to have been devised in close conjunction with the exiled leaders of the United Irishmen, to have been modelled in the essentials of its organisation upon the United Irish plan, and to have been based from its inception, like the earlier and more formidable rising, on the expectation of French co-operation.

That young Emmet had early imbibed the revolutionary principles which his elder brother had been so active in translating into action is clear from his connexion with the treasonable movement among certain undergraduates at Trinity College, Dublin. This movement was the subject of a memorable visitation by Lord Clare in his capacity of Vice-Chancellor of the University, an inquisition of which striking accounts have been left in a volume called 'Ireland Sixty

Years Ago,' and in Moore's 'Memoirs.' On that occasion Emmet anticipated his expected inclusion in the sentence of expulsion from the University, which was pronounced against nineteen of his associates, by withdrawing his name from the college books. His remarkable rhetorical ability, frequently displayed in the College Historical Society, had given him, as Moore notes, a wide influence within the college walls, and there is no doubt that he acted as secretary to one of the committees of United Irishmen in the University. There is no evidence as to Emmet's intentions at this period with regard to his future, and most probably he was too deeply absorbed in revolutionary projects to bestow much serious thought on the subject; but if, as was natural to a youth of his special aptitudes, he had thoughts of the Bar, his ambitions in that direction must have been closed by the abrupt conclusion of his academic career. His proceedings from the date of the college visitation in 1798 to the close of the following year are an almost complete blank. Ireland was at the time under martial law, and a person of Emmet's antecedents was sure to be closely watched. There is some reason to believe that he was concerned in an attempt made to rescue the State prisoners who had been arrested in '98, and it may have been a suspicion of this that caused Castlereagh to issue a warrant for his arrest as a person charged with treasonable practices. But this warrant, though issued on April 3, 1799, was never executed, and it may therefore be concluded that he had been guilty of no overt act at this time. Early in 1800 he is known to have visited Fort St. George, where his brother, with other State prisoners, was confined. The elder brother had formed the intention of settling in America on his release, and Robert appears to have arranged to accompany him. But subsequently to this interview Robert's plans were changed, and he determined to remain in Europe. Pending the release of the prisoners, which was deferred in the case of most of them till after the Peace of Amiens, he undertook a tour on the Continent, and travelled extensively in Southern France, Switzerland, and Spain, ultimately settling in Paris. Whether he was at this time actually engaged in furthering plans for insurrection does not appear from any direct source. But there is every reason to accept the statement made in a secret memorandum drawn up by Wickham, the Chief Secretary, in the autumn of 1803, that when Emmet left Ireland for the Continent, early in 1801, he did so with a mission to the French Government from the Executive Directory of the United Irishmen. Wickham's memorandum is based on the secret examinations in Dublin Castle of several of the accomplices in the insurrection, and on secret documents, letters, and papers either found on their persons or intercepted by Government. Though not, perhaps, accurate in every detail, it presents a remarkably clear narrative of the whole business as known to the Government after the failure of the outbreak.

The account given of Robert Emmet's movements tallies with other information in so far as other information is available, and Thomas Addis Emmet in his diary refers more than once to the existence at this time of a United Irish Executive. According to Wickham, Robert Emmet left for Hamburg early in 1801, and, arriving after some delay in Paris, held communication with the heads of the French Government. This probably refers to the interview which Emmet himself states that he had with Bonaparte, an interview which profoundly disappointed him. But even had Bonaparte's views been more favourable, any expectation of immediate French assistance must have been disappointed by the conclusion, in May 1801, of the Peace of Amiens, though the evidently precarious nature of the truce doubtless encouraged hopes for the future. On the release of the State prisoners Robert at once proceeded to Brussels, where he met his brother, and, returning to Paris, seems to have fallen in with Thomas Russell, Wolfe Tone's closest friend, and perhaps the most thoroughgoing and enthusiastic of the survivors of the men of 1798. Russell, who was also intimate with Thomas Addis Emmet, had travelled with the latter from Fort St. George. He arrived at Amsterdam early in August 1802, and proceeded at once to Paris, where he fell in with Robert. Here, it seems probable, is to be found the genesis of the actual design which cost the lives of both Emmet and Russell. In the autumn Robert Emmet returned to Ireland. Before doing so he appears to have confided to some sympathisers the purpose of his journey. According to Lord Cloncurry, he stated in a personal interview that a plan had been formed for a renewed effort to free Ireland, and expressed the most sanguine hopes of a successful issue.

No sort of record exists of the plans that were concerted at this time for a renewal of the attempt to subvert British rule in Ireland. But whatever the precise nature of the scheme formed between the Emmets and Russell, it is clear that a secret committee was at once formed with the object of perfecting the arrangement for a fresh rising. Of these the chief members, in addition to the two leaders, were William Henry Hamilton, a relative of Russell's (who had been concerned from the first in the United Irish movement, and had been among the Irish on board the *Hoche*, in 1798, when he narrowly escaped, disguised as a Frenchman), one Michael Quigley, a bricklayer and small building contractor, and William Dowdall. The last-named was the first of the party to leave France. Going over to London, he appears to have entered into communication with Edward Marcus Despard, a circumstance which suggests that the outward similarity between the attempt of that unfortunate officer to seize the person of King George the Third, and Emmet's notion of capturing Dublin Castle and the chief functionaries there, was more than a chance resemblance. That Emmet was actually concerned in Despard's plot has never been proved; but Despard's supporters were mostly Irish, and the fact that Dowdall was connected with both conspiracies is certain. Despard, however, was arrested as early as November 10, and any plans which may have been based on his co-operation were thus upset. Hamilton, who had come to Ireland with Emmet about November, was soon back in France to report progress to Russell, by whom he was a little later accompanied on his return to Ireland. Measures were at once taken to test the feelings of the country. A provisional government was formed on the '98 model, Russell proceeding to the north to organise Ulster, while other emissaries visited the south. And in February, 1803, as appears from his diary, Thomas Addis Emmet, then residing in Brussels, received fresh credentials as agent in France of the Irish executive, and came to Paris to invoke the aid of the Government of the Consulate.

That such an envoy should have been sent on such a mission at a moment when peace still existed between France and England may appear extraordinary. It is certain, however, that the Irish leaders were well informed as to the secret trend of French policy in regard to a resumption of hostilities. They held the opinion, which events were so soon to confirm, that Napoleon had no intention of maintaining the Peace of Amiens, and they believed that, pending any actual breach of friendly relations, the French Government would be ready to assist with something more than sympathy any movement likely to embarrass an enemy with whom they considered the struggle must sooner or later be renewed. That the Government of France, both before and after the Peace of Amiens, still looked on an Irish expedition as an important move in their own game is clear from the papers from the French archives published in the 'Projets et Tentatives.' As early as 1799, Humbert, the leader of the French expedition to Mayo, had been the author of a proposal for an invasion of Ireland by a force of 12,000 men, which, taking advantage of the prevalent discontent at the impending Union, would, he thought, be amply sufficient to sever Ireland from Great Britain. And, though no definite step had been taken prior to the Peace of Amiens, the ears of the French War Office were never closed to Irish solicitations. That nothing decisive was determined, either then or later, was due solely to Napoleon's disbelief in the ability of Ireland to take an effective share in any programme for her deliverance, and to his resolution to do nothing in Ireland except in relation to his larger project for the invasion of England. In 1798 he had deliberately turned his face from Ireland; and, though he listened from time to time to the solicitations of Irish disaffection, he could never again be induced to seriously consider Ireland as an important factor in his plans.

Robert Emmet himself, as has been mentioned, had an interview with the First Consul in 1802, from which, though he derived the impression that hostilities between England and France would recommence before the autumn of 1803, he came away dissatisfied. Bonaparte, he clearly saw, cared for Ireland only in so far as her fate was involved in his own designs, and had no particular sympathy with her aspirations for independence. However willing he might have been to undertake the conquest of Ireland with a view to making her a French province, which he might utilise as an additional point of attack on England, he had nothing to gain by giving her the independence which alone would satisfy the Emmets.

But whatever the real reasons of his apathy in regard to Ireland, there is no doubt that the disbelief in Irish capacity, which Bonaparte expressed more than once at St. Helena, had much justification at this juncture in the divided counsels of the Irish leaders. The diary of Thomas Addis Emmet, who arrived in Paris from Brussels in February 1803, as the emissary of the United Irish leaders, for the purpose of pressing France to render assistance, shows how pitiably his mission was marred by the jealousies which were rife among the refugees, and by his own refusal to co-operate with rival leaders. Among the political prisoners who, on being released from Fort St. George, had come to Paris, was Arthur O'Connor, perhaps the most distinguished, with the exception of Lord Edward FitzGerald, of the aristocratic adherents of the United Irish cause. Six years earlier O'Connor had had an important share in the negotiations which resulted in Hoche's expedition, and he was thus well known in Paris. Though undoubtedly whole-hearted in his patriotism, his views of the means for attaining independence differed considerably from Thomas Addis Emmet's. With the latter he had quarrelled while in confinement at Fort St. George, and the two men had ceased to be on speaking terms. O'Connor was in favour of a French protectorate in Ireland, while Emmet would hear of nothing but absolute independence. It was thus the fortune of the United Irishmen to be represented officially by an uncompromising envoy, who was without the ear of the authorities in Paris, while a distinguished member of their original body, much better fitted than Thomas Addis Emmet to conduct a negotiation of this kind, was busily engaged in discrediting his old colleague, and denying his claims to act in a representative character. Napoleon appears to have done his best to bring the two factions together, and suggested, through a subordinate, that he would be glad to learn the joint views of Emmet and O'Connor, as ascertained in conference; but though O'Connor would have been glad to adopt this course, the other obstinately refused to meet him, averring that, in addition to personal grievances which he might have been willing to overlook, he objected to O'Connor on 'moral and political grounds.' The real merits of their original quarrel are unknown to us, though it is probable that it originated in the divergence of their views on the eve of the rising in '98 as to the proper time for action; but it is impossiblo not to censure Emmet, even on his own showing, for his refusal to co-operate with O'Connor at a moment when it was manifest that the cordial union of all Irishmen in Paris was the essential condition of success. So far as can be gathered from Emmet's diary, the essence of the disagreement in point of policy between the two parties was that O'Connor was willing to defer the French views of the time and mode in which assistance was to be rendered in Ireland, and was prepared to assent to a temporary French protectorate: an arrangement to which Emmet, who apparently paid no attention to the necessity of giving France some interest of a practical kind in return for her assistance, was vehemently opposed. In the spring of 1803 an expedition to Ireland of 30,000 men, under the leadership of Masséna, appears to have been in contemplation; and Emmet was given satisfactory assurances as to the independence which France was prepared to secure to Ireland. But it was stipulated that no movement should be made in Ireland pending the dispatch of this expedition, which would take six months to prepare. Emmet asked for a passport to enable him to send news of the proposed expedition to his associates. But this passport, applied for as early as May, was not provided until the close of July, by which time the fatal precipitancy of Robert Emmet had already led to the abortive insurrection of 1803.

It is evident that to the neglect or inability of the leaders of the movement to maintain effective communications between their emissaries in France and their active agents in Ireland the failure of the whole scheme of insurrection was largely due. The measures taken by Robert Emmet and Russell for preparing their own people for a rising were framed entirely with a view to early action and the immediate arrival of French assistance. In the absence of any communication from Paris they were not only unaware that the French desired to postpone all action till the late autumn of 1803, but they seem to have counted, with a confidence for which they were entirely without warrant, on the arrival of assistance in the form of arms and ammunition, if not of men, at the time which their own plans required. This too implicit reliance on the expectation of French assistance was not the only example of the rashness and over-confidence of the leaders of this enterprise. They miscalculated most strangely the state of feeling among their own people, and grossly overestimated the degree in which their fellow-countrymen were animated by their own hostility to the British connexion.

Abundant as are the surprises of Irish history, few are more curious or more striking than the completeness of the change which was wrought in Ireland by the incidents of the rebellion of 1798, and, oddly as it may sound, by the operation of the Act of Union. Within a space of less than five years, and despite the embittering experiences of a rudely enforced martial law on the one hand, and the destruction of legislative independence on the other, whole districts, which prior to the rebellion had been seething with discontent and had ardently applauded the doctrines of pronounced Separatists, had become completely reconciled to the Government. Of the change in the sentiments of the erstwhile republicans of Ulster no better illustration can be given than the statement of Thomas Russell that of the jurors empanelled to try him for his share in the insurrection of 1803 as many as six were men who, but a few years before, had taken the United Irish oath; and the evidences of reaction were numerous everywhere. This altered state of public sentiment is chiefly to be ascribed to the manifestation of the depth of racial and religious rancour in the course of the rebellion, which had revealed to the Protestant and English element in the ranks of the United Irishmen the lengths to which their allies had been prepared to go in a policy of proscription. But it must in part also be set down to the effects of the wise lenity of the Addington Administration, which, satisfied with the suppression of overt treason, and with the removal of what they had deemed a rallying point of disaffection in the suppression of the Irish Parliament, had been careful to refrain from provoking hostility by needless harshness.

No doubt there was much exaggeration in the complacency with which the Government of Lord Hardwicke contemplated the effects of its policy of clemency and conciliation. John Wilson Croker gives an account of the condition of the country in a pamphlet on the state of Ireland, published in 1808, which is little flattering to the administration. 'By his public and private gentleness, some ostentatious charity, and the universal purchase of the press, the shadow of popularity was acquired; but this shadow, with which he was contented, deceived England and darkened Ireland.' Undoubtedly Lord Hardwicke and his colleagues underestimated the power of the old leaders of the United Irishmen to foment disorder below the surface. But their confidence that the Irish temperament would respond to the mollifying influences of a kindly conciliation was not altogether ill-founded. Irish disorder is never formidable so long as it is inarticulate; and from banished leaders and a muzzled press little was to be feared.

Against Croker's disapprobation may well be set the evidence of Robert Emmet. According to Wickham, the Chief Secretary, Emmet, in the private examination at Dublin Castle after his arrest, admitted that when he sat down to write his proclamation, his conscience would not allow him to assign an existing grievance, and he was obliged to have recourse to the crimes and follies of preceding times. In a remarkable letter, first made public in the Colchester Correspondence, Emmet has borne striking testimony to the lenity of the Irish administration under the Addington Ministry. This letter, addressed to Wickham, the Chief Secretary, within an hour of Emmet's execution, indicates, according to Mr. O'Donoghue, 'the lamentable weakness of Emmet's character.' It is difficult to follow the biographer's point of view in this remark, for certainly the letter must redound in the judgment of most fair-minded persons to the reputation of Emmet for nobility of character. But at any rate it is a remarkable proof that while the anti-English spirit which animated the authors of the rebellion of 1798, and which was at the root of Emmet's own insurrection, was not to be allayed by moderation on the part of the Government, the people themselves were far less irreconcilable. In it the writer states that, had he been permitted to proceed uninterrupted in his speech at his trial, it had been his intention 'to have done the most public justice to the mildness of the present administration of this country,' and to have stated 'why such an *administration* did not prevent, but, under the peculiar situation of this country, perhaps rather accelerated, my determination to make an effort for the overthrow of a *government* of which I do not think equally highly.' Emmet concluded by averring that he felt it right to make this acknowledgment 'which justice requires from me as a man, and which I do not feel to be in the least derogatory from my decided principles as an Irishman.'

Emmet probably exaggerated the effects of the policy of the Addington Administration in producing a condition of permanent contentment with the Union; but unquestionably under the direction of the Viceroy, Lord Hardwicke, and his successive Chief Secretaries, Abbot and Wickham, a tone of unexampled conciliation was infused into the Irish Government. In its dealings with the Roman Catholics and with the Dissenters of the North of Ireland, the new ministry had been remarkably successful. The goodwill of the hierarchy was earned by the patronage extended by the Government to the lately formed College of Maynooth. The establishment of that institution, quite as much as any expectation of an early fulfilment of their hopes of emancipation, had been a powerful motive with Archbishop Troy and his fellows in extending their approval to the Act of Union. The clerical horror at the principles of the French Revolution is an element which can never be left out of sight in considering the attitude of the Roman Catholic hierarchy towards the problems of Irish politics at the beginning of the nineteenth century. Quite as great as the anxiety of the Government to prevent the young Irish priests from acquiring anti-British sentiments in the course of a foreign education was the solicitude of the bishops to preserve the recruits to the priesthood from the contamination of republican influences. Such views as those which animated the two Emmets were as alien to the leaders of Roman Catholicism in Ireland as they were to the British Government, and in this temper of the hierarchy a conciliatory policy was likely to achieve at least a temporary success.

Concurrently with the conciliation of the Roman Catholic leaders a serious and more durably successful endeavour was made to cultivate the goodwill of the Presbyterians by establishing close relations between the Government and the Assembly, through a constituted agent, by grants in aid of the Presbyterian ministers. The moment was more favourable for such a connexion than at any former time. The republican views of Ulster, so strongly manifested in the preceding decade, had been first modified by the attitude of the Roman Catholics during the rebellion in Wexford. They received a further discouragement in the singular evolution of republican principles which had made Napoleon First Consul for life. Of this policy of conciliating Nonconformity the principal agent, Alexander Knox (the well-known private secretary of Castlereagh), whose knowledge of the North of Ireland was remarkable, wrote that a happier policy had never been resorted to. 'Never before,' he wrote in a remarkable letter, 'was Ulster under the dominion of the British Crown. It had a distinct moral existence before, of which all that we could certainly know was that they were not with the State; therefore, when any tempting occasion occurred, ready to act against it; whereas now the Presbyterian ministers would henceforth be a subordinate ecclesiastical aristocracy,' whose feeling would be one of zealous loyalty.

These considerations are sufficient to account for the fact that, despite the exertions of Emmet and Russell to revive the old resentment of the Roman Catholics and the Presbyterians against the Government, no sort of sympathy was manifested by the people at the moment of the outbreak of July 23, 1803. Neither North nor South displayed the smallest interest in the movement. And in Dublin failure must have been inevitable, even had popular sympathy been greater, from the fantastically unpractical and inadequate nature of Emmet's preparations. It is not our purpose to describe afresh the oft-told story of the Emmet insurrection. The plot to seize Dublin Castle and the defensive positions of Dublin, making hostages of the chief officers of state when captured, was no doubt originally a part of a larger plan for a combined rising in several counties, concerted in co-operation with France and aided by French arms; but the portion of this plan actually carried out was almost childishly impracticable, and certainly justifies Mr. O'Donoghue's judicious verdict that Robert Emmet's qualities were those of a 'romantic but hardly great leader.' No doubt his plans had been confused and defeated, and his judgment unsettled by the premature though partial discovery of his preparations, through an explosion at his arsenal in Patrick Street a week before the rising. But for the inadequacy of these preparations Emmet was solely responsible, since it was by his orders alone that the attempt was made in conditions that to any practical mind precluded the possibility of success. Mr. O'Donoghue censures Emmet's 'astoundingly childlike ignorance and implicit faith in his associates' as inviting serious and damaging criticism. But in truth, as regards the military aspect of the rising, serious criticism is impossible. The insurrection, in so far as it was Robert Emmet's, was the wild adventure of a fanatical enthusiast, and its claims to be regarded as a serious military attempt may be sufficiently judged from the wild rhapsody penned by its contriver within a few hours of embarking on the final stages of his enterprise:

> 'I have little time to look at the thousand difficulties which still lie between me and the completion of my wishes; that those difficulties will likewise disappear I have ardent, and I trust, rational hopes; but if it is not to be the case, I thank God for having gifted me with a sanguine disposition. To that disposition I run from reflection; and if my hopes are without foundation—if a precipice is open under my feet from which duty will not suffer me to run back, I am grateful for that sanguine disposition which leads me to the brink and throws me down, while my eyes are still raised to the visions of happiness that my fancy formed in the air.'

In the foregoing attempt to analyse the causes of the insurrection of 1803, we have been concerned with the character of its chief figure only in so far as it directly affected the movement, and have not sought to dwell upon those purely personal passages in the brief career of Robert Emmet which have done so much to give him a peculiar place in the affections of the Irish people. Emmet's attachment to Sarah Curran is an episode which has no real relation to his political schemes; and it is even doubtful whether it had been formed prior to his return to Ireland in the autumn of 1802, at which period his political purpose was already matured. He has himself stated that when he first addressed Miss Curran he had expected that 'in another week his own fate would have been decided,' and there is no foundation for Mr. O'Donoghue's assertion that a considerable correspondence passed between the two lovers and fell into the hands of the Government. That there was some correspondence is certain, but the letters which were seized by the Government appear to have been limited to two from the young lady and one from her lover. As the subject is one which, quite apart from the political aspects of Emmet's career, has a strong personal interest, and as the facts have not hitherto been correctly represented, it may be interesting to give here some extracts from the Hardwicke Papers, now preserved at the British Museum. These include

Emmet's last letter, and tell us all that can now be known of a pathetic episode.

Lord Hardwicke to the Hon. Charles Yorke

'Sept. 9, 1803.

'A curious discovery has been made respecting Emmet, the particulars of which I have not time to detail to you fully. There were found upon him two letters from a woman, written with a knowledge of the transactions in which he had been engaged, and with good wishes for the success of any future attempts. He has been very anxious to prevent these letters being brought forward, and has been apprehensive that the writer was arrested as well as himself. Till yesterday, however, we were entirely ignorant of the person who had written these letters, which were very clever and striking. The discovery was made last night, by a letter from Emmet intercepted in its passage from Kilmainham prison to Miss Sarah Curran, youngest daughter of Curran the lawyer. Wickham has seen him (Curran), and he professes entire ignorance of the connexion; but I think he must decline being counsel for Emmet, in a case in which his daughter may be implicated.'

Robert Emmet to Thomas and Jane Emmet, written on the day of the writer's execution, and probably his last letter

'My dearest Tom and Jane,—I am just going to do my last duty to my country; it can be done as well on the scaffold as in the field. Do not give way to any weak feelings on my account, but rather encourage proud ones that I have possessed fortitude and tranquillity of mind to the last.

'God bless you and the young hopes that are growing up about you. May they be more fortunate than their uncle, but may they preserve as pure and ardent an attachment to their country as he has done. Give the watch to little Robert. He will not prize it the less for having been in the possession of two Roberts before him.

'I have one dying request to make to you. I was attached to Sarah Curran, the youngest daughter of your friend. I did hope to have had her for my companion for life. I did hope that she would not only have constituted my happiness, but that her heart and understanding would have made her one of Jane's dearest friends. I know that Jane would have loved her on my account, and I feel that had they been acquainted she must have loved her on her own.

'No one knew of the attachment till now, nor is it now generally known, therefore do not speak of it to others[1] . . . her father and brother, but if these protectors should fall off, and that no other should replace them, take (or treat) her as my wife, and love her as a sister.

'God Almighty bless you all. Give my love to all dear friends,

'ROBERT EMMET.'

The passage in this letter relating to Sarah Curran was communicated by the Lord Lieutenant's direction to the young lady's father. Curran, in his letter of acknowledgment, dated September 21, 1803, offers to His Excellency his 'more than gratitude, the feelings of the strongest attachment and respect for this new mark of considerate condescension'; and expresses his wish for the suppression of this extract, if no particular occasion should have arisen for forwarding it to its destination.

[1] Three or four words are obliterated here.

II

ILLUSTRATIONS OF IRISH TOPOGRAPHY

DUBLIN

It is a curious circumstance which has often been noted that the story of the Irish capital does not become the story of the capital of the Irish people until a period long subsequent to the first foundation of Dublin. Although the Irish annalists make occasional mention of the site of the future city of Dublin by its earliest name of Ath Cliath, it is not until the eighth century that vague tradition and unauthenticated legend begin to crystallise into history with the coming of the Norse invader. Owing its origin to Danish auspices, Dublin was neither first built by Irish hands, nor originally peopled by men of Irish race. To the Ireland of the ages before the advent of the Vikings, the spot round which the city was to rise had no doubt always been a place of some importance. For its maritime situation must from the earliest times have necessitated some sort of assemblage of dwellings near the junction of the River Liffey with the Irish Sea. But there is nothing to indicate that either in pre-Christian or early Christian times the ancient Ath Cliath had reached a position of consequence. Until the Danes had fixed their seat in the immediate neighbourhood, no Leinster chieftain or Irish king appears to have chosen the place for stronghold or for residence. Even during the first hundred years of its Norse ownership, it is improbable that any considerable town can have grown up. Indeed, both the name originally given to the place by the native Irish and the later one, likewise of Gaelic origin, which the Scandinavian invaders adopted, indicate that the early importance of the spot was geographical rather than political, and arose less from any settlement of which it had become the site than from the different uses, appropriate to the physical features of the locality, to which the Celt and the Norseman respectively put it. To the former it was Ath Cliath, the ford bridged by hurdles, which formed the most direct means of communication between the ancient kingdoms of Meath and Leinster; and as such it is said, but without any sufficient authority, to have been utilised by St. Patrick when making his way from Wicklow to Armagh. To the latter it was Dubhlinn, the dark pool or haven lying eastward of the ford, a little further down the river, in which the warships of the Viking might find safe harbourage in the course of his marauding visits to the Irish coast.

The earliest ravages of the Danes in Ireland commenced towards the close of the eighth century; but it was not until the year 837 that the Vikings paid their first recorded visit to Dublin. In that year there came 'three score and five ships and landed at Dubhlinn of Ath Cliath' to plunder the adjacent territory. This was the prelude to the incursions of the Finn Gaill or Fair Strangers, the memory of whose settlement in the district north-west of Dublin is embalmed in its name of Fingal. Their advent seems to have been followed within a year or two by the erection of the first recorded building in Dublin, a fortress or fixed encampment which, ten years later, was destroyed by a fresh horde of Northmen. The newcomers represented a different branch of the Scandinavian stock, and are called by the annalists Dubh Gaill, or the Dark Strangers. For some time after their arrival the story of Ireland is a succession of struggles between the two opposite elements in the Scandinavian immigration; but about the middle of the ninth century this antagonism terminated in the general recognition of Aulaf or Olaf the White by all sections of the invaders. It was by this coalition that the Scandinavian power in Ireland was permanently consolidated; and it is in King Aulaf that we are to recognise the true founder of Dublin. In 852, according to the 'Annals of Ulster,' 'Aulaiv, son of the king of Laihlinn, came into Ireland, and all the foreigners submitted to him, and had rent from the Irish.'

For above a century and a half from the establishment of Aulaf's authority, Dublin was the centre of that important Viking confederacy, stretching from Carlingford to Waterford, to which the name of Scandinavian Kingdom of Dublin has been applied. But it is not to be supposed that the Danish supremacy was left unchallenged throughout this long period. The story of the early wars of Ireland after the coming of the Norsemen contains the record of more than one struggle between the native and the alien race for the possession of that fortress by means of which the Danish kings of Dublin sought to buttress their power, and which was to form the nucleus of the future capital. In these contests there were many vicissitudes, and fortune was fickle with her favours. But, though the Irish had their triumphs, they were, for a long period, temporary and barren; whereas from the date of the great battle, fought on September 15, 919, on the banks of the Liffey, within a mile or so of the very site of the original Ath Cliath,[1] until that of the still greater Battle of Clontarf, fought close on a century later, the Danish supremacy in Dublin was complete and unbroken. And although the famous victory of Brian Borumha in 1014 effected the expulsion of the foreigner from Meath and Leinster, it did not effectually achieve the deliverance of Dublin from foreign rule. For above half a century after Clontarf the city remained in Danish hands. Down to the time of the coming of the Normans Dublin continued to be, predominantly at least, the city of the Ostmen, as the Norse inhabitants had come to be known. It was by a garrison of Ostmen that in 1170 it was stoutly, though ineffectually, held against Strongbow and his followers. Thus it is that the oldest memorials which Dublin has to boast are those of its early Norse owners, and that its pre-Norman remains are of Scandinavian rather than of Gaelic origin. Its oldest cathedral—Christ Church—was founded almost a quarter of a century after the Battle of Clontarf by Sitric, its Danish king. Its oldest church, St. Michan's, recalls a Danish saint. And an important quarter of the

[1] The scene of this battle has been hitherto wrongly placed. See *Proceedings of the Royal Irish Academy*, vol. xxvi. sec. C. p. 281.

modern city, on the north bank of the Liffey, has but lately lost its long-preserved name of Oxmantown or Ostmanstown.

But if the earliest traditions of Dublin are undoubtedly those which connect the city with its Norse founders, its earliest authenticated records are as unquestionably Norman. Beyond the associations just mentioned, there is little, if anything, to identify the Dublin of to-day with the capital of the Scandinavian kingdom; or to indicate what manner of city it was that on St. Matthew's Day, September 21, 1170, after its abandonment by the Danish king, Hasculf McTorkil, surrendered to Strongbow and his valiant lieutenant, Miles de Cogan; and which, after the abortive attempt at recapture by a Danish squadron under the dispossessed sovereign, was to become the central stronghold of Norman authority in Ireland. It is impossible to affirm decisively that the fortress of king Aulaf once stood on or near the site of the 'royal palace roofed with wattles after the fashion of the country,' which Henry the Second, on his first arrival in Dublin in 1174, erected for the accommodation of his Court at Christmas-tide. But it is at least extremely probable that it was so. For the physical configuration of the rising ground to the south-east of the city walls must at all times have suggested the eminence on which Dublin Castle now stands as the most appropriate site for a fortress. Thus it may well have been that the battlements of the watch-tower from which king Sitric had followed the varying fortunes of the fight at Clontarf rose from the self-same spot on which for seven centuries His Majesty's Castle of Dublin has been the citadel of the governing authority in Ireland. But however that may be, no trace of the Danish fortress survived the final overthrow of Scandinavian power; and it is really with King John's order for the construction of 'a strong fortress in Dublin, suitable both for the administration of justice and, if need be, for the defence of the city,' that the history of Dublin, considered as a metropolis, must be said to begin.

The Norman captors of the Danish town had received from Henry the Second the charter under which Dublin was to remain, during the long Plantagenet era, the one secure stronghold of English power in an island only half subdued. After the expulsion of the Norsemen, the sovereign 'granted to his men of Bristol his City of Dublin to inhabit and to hold of him, and of his heirs for ever, with all the liberties and free customs which his men of Bristol then enjoyed at Bristol, and through all England.' This charter, subsequently confirmed by King John and others of Henry's successors, gave to the city and its inhabitants an impress which lasted down to Stuart times. 'It is resembled to Bristol, but falleth short,' was the verdict of an English visitor in the time of James the First. The people of Dublin long retained the mercantile characteristics of the great capital of the West of England; and the parish church of St. Werburgh's, dedicated to the patron saint of one of the earliest of Bristol churches, still bears witness to the connoxion between the two cities. The essentially alien character of Dublin, as thus colonised, is well illustrated by the fact that its citizens were long a prey to the depredations of the Irish septs who dwelt within its neighbourhood. Easter Monday of the year 1209 was marked by a memorable raid by the O'Byrnes and O'Tooles, who, descending unexpectedly on the holiday-making citizens, drove them within the city walls, after a slaughter which caused the day long to be remembered in the capital as Black Monday. And Stanihurst, the sixteenth-century chronicler, has recorded how, at a somewhat later date, the Irish enemy carried their raids on one occasion even into the precincts of the Court of Exchequer, 'where, surprising the unweaponed multitude, they committed terrible slaughter by sparing none that came under their dint, and withal, as far as their Scarborough leisure would serve them, they ransacked the prince's treasure.'

It was doubtless upon some such provocation as this that the work of building the castle and raising the walls of Dublin was ordered and enforced by King John. To that monarch, who as Lord of Ireland had a peculiar interest in his father's conquest long before he succeeded to the English Crown, Dublin was perfectly familiar, and he thoroughly understood its needs. The first instructions for the building of the castle were issued to the Justiciary, Meiller FitzHenry;

but it is to a Norman Archbishop of Dublin, Henri de Londres, that the honour of its erection is really due. The fortress appears to have been completed about the year 1220, and the city walls a few years later. But both castle and city underwent considerable expansion at the hands of the Viceroys of the early Plantagenet sovereigns. Henry the Third gave orders for the erection of a great hall, one hundred and twenty feet in length and eighty in breadth, 'with glazed windows after the manner of the Hall of Canterbury,' a building which in later days appears to have served as the place of meeting for the earlier Irish Parliaments; and it was at the behest of the same monarch that a splendid chapel was raised within the castle precincts to the honour of Edward the Confessor. There is not much of external splendour about Dublin Castle as it exists to-day; but there can be little doubt that, as conceived by its Plantagenet founders, it was intended to be a pile worthy to be the principal edifice of a stately capital.

The limits of the medieval city, as encompassed by the walls and turrets designed to defend it, were far from extensive. From the date of its first origin, as the seat of a settled political system, Dublin has a history of over seven centuries, in the course of which the metropolis has from time to time been extended, until at the present day its limits have come to embrace an area of close on eight thousand acres, and to contain a population of nearly three hundred thousand. But these imposing figures have only recently been attained by the inclusion within the city boundaries of several of what until recently were deemed its northern and western suburbs; and down to the year 1900 the city of Dublin had long been understood to mean the area within the North and South Circular Roads, a circumference of about nine miles. But the walls of the medieval city were much less extensive, and can hardly have measured more than an Irish mile, or encompassed an area much larger than that now enclosed in St. Stephen's Green. Its dimensions can be gauged with fair accuracy from Mr. Leonard Strangways' map,[1] by which it will be

[1] See *Illustrations of Irish History and Topography*, by C. Litton Falkiner, p. 3.

seen that the city lay along the south bank of the Liffey, whose waters at high tide ran right up to the walls from a point just below the castle, at which Grattan Bridge now spans the river, to the Old Bridge; the whole forming an irregular quadrangle, near the middle of which stood Christ Church Cathedral. Although portions of the ancient walls are still discernible, their traces are of the faintest, only St. Audoen's Arch surviving to show the precise situation of one of the eight city gates. But no substantial change in the boundaries of the capital having taken place between the thirteenth and seventeenth centuries, a late Elizabethan description of 'the whole circuit of the city walls' enables us to gain a fair notion of the character of the medieval town. The walls were about seventeen feet high, with a breadth of four or five feet, and the numerous towers by which they were defended varied from sixteen to forty feet in height. Within was a rampart, fifteen feet thick, and the walls were stoutly buttressed at various points without. The gates, of which the chief was Newgate, were of imposing dimensions.

Few studies in historical topography can have more real interest than the analysis of the process by which so many of the great cities of modern Europe have been gradually developed from the walled enclosures, which were indispensable conditions of a medieval town, into the spacious and unrestricted amplitude of a twentieth-century metropolis. In the case of Dublin the process is peculiarly well marked and easy to trace, and is the work in the main of three great periods of expansive growth. As late as the era of the Commonwealth, Dublin still remained a walled town, within the ambit of whose fortifications few changes affecting its general aspect had taken place for a couple of centuries. From the days of the later Plantagenets to those of the later Stuarts, it may be said with little exaggeration that no changes on a scale large enough to affect its general configuration were wrought in the appearance of the capital or in its geographical outline. Some extensions of the residential quarter had indeed taken place in the closing years of the sixteenth century, the erection of Trinity College on the site of the old monastery of All Hallows naturally leading to the occupation of the intervening area between College Green and Dublin Castle, now traversed by the spacious thoroughfare of Dame Street. Thus, almost contemporaneously with the foundation of the University, the site on which the Parliament Buildings in College Green —now the Bank of Ireland—were subsequently raised was utilised for the first time by the well-known statesman and soldier, Sir George Carew, for the building at first called Cary's Hospital, but afterwards known as Chichester House, from the name of its owner under James the First, the celebrated Lord Deputy, Sir Arthur Chichester. But no attempt had as yet been made to enlarge the metropolis, either to the north, where the ancient Oxmantown still sufficed for all the inhabitants of Dublin on that side of the river, or to the south-east, where the modern enclosure of St. Stephen's Green was still a common. And along the line of the southern quays, already antiquated to our twentieth-century eyes, fresh meadows ran from the river banks to the old Priory of Kilmainham.

But the Restoration was to change all that. Under the auspices of that illustrious Irishman, the first Duke of Ormond, who held office as Lord Lieutenant for fifteen of the last twenty-five years of the *de facto* reign of Charles the Second, a remarkable transformation was effected. Ormond, and those who with him constituted the Viceregal Court, had, like so many of the followers of his sovereign, passed more than ten years in an enforced exile in the cities of the Continent. The experience was not without a marked educational influence on the exiled cavaliers, who returned from abroad with new and liberal ideas of what a capital ought to be. The walled medieval city which, as late as 1649, had endured a siege in much the same form in which an attack might have been conducted two centuries earlier, speedily vanished before the more advanced notions of the returned Royalists. Houses everywhere sprang up without the walls of Dublin. The space from Cork Hill to College Green, previously but sparsely occupied, was speedily filled up; and the quays began to be formed. On the north bank of the river, Oxmantown Green was so largely encroached upon that St. Stephen's Green, which was first walled in about this time, had to be requisitioned as an exercise-ground for the garrison. The capital grew so quickly that it was noted in 1673 by Lord Essex, one of the Restoration Viceroys, that 'the city of Dublin is now very near, if not altogether, twice as big as it was at His Majesty's Restoration, and did till the Dutch war began every day increase in building.' So rapid was the extension that some of the old-fashioned citizens, accustomed to rely for security on the protection of the city walls, were filled with alarm, and felt obliged to warn the Lord-Lieutenant of the dangers likely to be occasioned in time of war by the large number of dwellings which had sprung up outside the defences of the city.[1] But, apart from the actual extension of streets and buildings throughout this period, the era of the Restoration was marked in Dublin by two great and abiding memorials of the public spirit and enterprise of its seventeenth-century rulers and citizens. The formation of the splendid recreation-grounds of the Phœnix Park, and the enclosure of the spacious area of St. Stephen's Green, at opposite sides of the city, produced a marked effect on the conditions of the further development of Dublin. The Phœnix Park, from the moment it was provided, enormously enhanced the amenities of residence in Dublin. And, although a full century was to elapse before residential Dublin transgressed beyond the eastern limits of St. Stephen's Green, the permanent dedication of so large an area as an open-air space has had an abiding effect on the aspect and atmosphere of the modern city.

Of these two improvements, the first was the work of the Viceroy, the second of the municipality. The germ of the Phœnix Park was found in certain Crown lands, which, having originally formed portion of the possessions granted to the Priory of the Knights Hospitallers at Kilmainham, had been resumed by the Crown on the suppression of the monasteries.[2] To this nucleus Ormond added extensively

[1] See Falkiner's *Illustrations of Irish History and Topography*, p. 43.

[2] See 'The Hospital of St. John of Jerusalem in Ireland,' by C. Litton Falkiner, *Proceedings of the Royal Irish Academy*, vol. xxvi. sec. C. pp. 275–317.

by the purchase of adjacent property to the north and west ; so that, as first designed, the Park comprised above two thousand acres, including the area south of the river now forming the grounds of the Royal Hospital—another monument of post-Restoration magnificence. The Park was not designed by Ormond as the seat of the viceregal residence ; and the present Viceregal Lodge became so only by purchase from a private owner, who, towards the close of the eighteenth century, had been permitted to build a residence in connexion with his office of Ranger of the Phœnix Park. But in its present state the Park, as a whole, owes much to the care and interest of a succession of Viceroys, notably of the celebrated Lord Chesterfield, who took a lively interest in its plantations, and by whom the Phœnix Column in the centre of its principal drive was erected.

St. Stephen's Green, on the other hand, owes its origin to municipal auspices, stimulated in part by the pressure of financial exigency, and in part by the spirit of emulation and zeal for improvement which was abroad under the Duke of Ormond's *régime*. The confusion of the Civil War had worked havoc alike with the material prosperity of the general body of the citizens of Dublin and with the municipal finances. The State Papers of the time depict in mournful colours the ruin and indigence wrought in the course of the long struggle, which in Dublin had been marked by all the horrors of a sustained siege and the desolation inevitably produced by the constant apprehensions of military assault. Accordingly the city fathers could find no better means of replenishing an exhausted exchequer than by letting out the lands round the common called St. Stephen's Green as building lots, at the same time providing for the enclosure of the central space. Although the allotments were taken up by persons of wealth and position, it was not until the succeeding century that the building ground was fully utilised. But in the early half of the eighteenth century the Green became the centre of fashionable Dublin, and the Beaux' Walk, along its northern side, was long the chief resort of the leaders of Dublin society. Down to a late period in the nineteenth century St. Stephen's Green was maintained at the expense of the residents. It owes its present splendour as a public park solely to the munificence of Lord Ardilaun, who, in 1880, carried out at a cost of £20,000 the scenic transformation which has converted it from an ordinary city square into one of the handsomest of city parks. Besides these two great alterations in the geographical aspect of the city and its environs, two striking memorials of the reign of Charles the Second survive in Dublin. The first is the stately building near its western boundaries known as the Royal Hospital, an institution similar to Chelsea Hospital, which was built towards the close of the reign from the design of Sir Christopher Wren on the site of the ancient Hospital of the Knights of St. John. The second is the Hospital or Free School of Charles II, better known as the Blue Coat School, founded and endowed by the liberality of the citizens of Dublin, acting under a Royal Charter. But in the latter case the original Caroline building has given place to an eighteenth-century successor.

With the close of Charles the Second's reign and the ensuing political disturbances, a period was put to the development of Dublin under the Stuarts ; and it was not until the reign of George the Second that those extensive additions began to be made which render the latter half of the eighteenth century the grand period in the architectural adornment of the Irish capital. But the interval between the accession of James the Second and the demise of George the First, though unmarked by any striking memorials, was, nevertheless, characterised by a gradual development of certain districts theretofore but sparsely inhabited, or even wholly waste, whose occupation was an essential preliminary to the more imposing additions of the succeeding age. Thus the considerable territory between the enclosure of the College Park and the river had become so thickly populated as to necessitate the erection of a new parish, now known as St. Mark's ; and some progress was made towards the inhabiting of the low-lying lands immediately adjacent to the north-eastern bank of the Liffey. These extensions were in part the effect of the pronounced development of the city along the banks of the river in an easterly direction, which its growing wealth and prosperity rendered necessary. But they were in part also due to the important enlargement of the port of Dublin by the clearing of the river channel for the better accommodation of shipping. This was an improvement which ultimately transformed the neighbourhood from a wilderness of slough and slob into the busy hive of railway and river-side enterprise of which it has more recently become the scene; but its most immediate and most conspicuous effect was the laying out of Sackville Street and its adjacent northerly extensions—thoroughfares which the subsequent construction of Carlisle, now O'Connell, Bridge first brought into direct contact and communication with the centre of the modern capital.

The age of Queen Anne, which in England has left so clear an architectural imprint, has but few memorials in Dublin. No great building of the first rank survives to recall that era, unless it be the fine Library of Trinity College, which, however, though begun in Queen Anne's reign, was not completed till 1732; and, though the period was marked by a good deal of rebuilding on old sites, the houses then erected have given place for the most part to the more spacious residences of a later time. The main importance of this period in the history of Dublin lies not so much in its visible enlargement as in the extension of its local and municipal institutions, more than one of which, such as the Port and Docks Board, date from the beginning of the eighteenth century. The development of the linen trade, and the diffusion throughout the country of a spirit of mercantile enterprise, which, though it has unfortunately not been maintained, was a very marked feature of the early part of the eighteenth century, exercised a direct effect upon the progress of the Irish capital; and to this increased commercial prosperity must be attributed in a great degree that marvellous outburst of architectural enterprise which marked the reign of George the Second and his successors, and which has left such indelible marks on the face of the city.

For, in its essential features, in almost all that attracts the attention of the passing traveller, the Dublin of to-day is still the Dublin of the closing years of the eighteenth century. With the exception of the cathedrals of Christ Church and

St. Patrick's, the only buildings of real antiquity which it contains, almost every structure of interest, and every characteristic feature of the capital, apart from its natural environs, are memorials of that period. Of those public buildings upon which Dublin now prides itself, the Royal Hospital at Kilmainham is almost the only one which existed in the seventeenth century, and curiously few were added in the nineteenth. Of the great distinctive features in the centre of the modern city, the Parliament House, now the Bank of Ireland, was built in the reign of George the Second; and the great façade of Trinity College, erected at the cost of the Irish Parliament, dates from that of his successor. Modern municipalities have often indulged in lavish expenditure for the housing of their civic Councils; but the handsome meeting-place of the Corporation of Dublin has only been adapted from the Royal Exchange of the eighteenth century, whilst the Four Courts and the Custom House, the two chief adornments of the River Liffey as it flows through the city, are monuments of architects of the same period. Nor are the memories of the most vivid period of Irish history in the Dublin of to-day confined to its public buildings. For the residential quarters of Dublin within the old city boundaries still belong as exclusively as its public edifices to the same period. The great squares commemorate in their names the Viceroys and nobility of the Georgian era, and few of the more important streets were unbuilt a hundred years ago. Save the handsome Post-Office in Sackville Street, which dates from very early in the last century; the fine group of buildings round Leinster House, forming the National Gallery, Museum, and Library; and a few of the public statues; there is little in the configuration of the modern streets of Dublin which would be unfamiliar to an eighteenth-century citizen. In the last-named adornment, indeed, Dublin has never been opulent, and it was notably deficient in statues before the erection of those of Burke, Goldsmith, and Grattan, in College Green; of those of Nelson and O'Connell, in Sackville Street; and of the recently erected monument to Queen Victoria at Leinster House.

The best-known of books about Dublin, Sir John Gilbert's 'History of Dublin,' originated in its author's rambles as a young man through the streets of his native city, and in the memories which his well-stored mind enabled him to recognise as enshrined in the street-names affixed to the principal thoroughfares. And as there is no better stimulus to the faculty of historical imagination than the traditions which are preserved in the street-nomenclature of a modern city, so there is perhaps no better key by which a stranger interested in such associations can attempt to unlock the past than that which is afforded by the simple process of noting the names attached to its more important streets. In the case of Dublin this method of investigation is more than ordinarily simple, requiring for the most part no more elaborate equipment of historical lore than a list of the names of the statesmen who have represented the sovereign in Ireland for the last two hundred and fifty years. The succession of the Viceroys of Ireland is embalmed in the names of the principal streets of the Irish capital; and whoever would trace the gradual development of Dublin has only to make himself acquainted with viceregal chronology from the Restoration to the Union. For the order of its municipal development corresponds with curious precision with the order of the viceregal succession, the name of each succeeding Viceroy being stamped on each fresh extension of the streets of the Metropolis. Thus, the earliest development of Dublin after the Restoration consisted, as already noted, in the extension of the quays on the north bank of the Liffey. Accordingly, we find in this extensive thoroughfare memorials of the chief governors of the period—Ormond Quay perpetuating the name of the great Duke of Ormond; Arran Quay that of his son Richard, Earl of Arran, who twice held office as deputy in his father's absence; and Essex—now Grattan—Bridge, preserving until quite recently the memory of another Restoration Viceroy. In the more modern additions to the city the same rule holds good. Grafton Street, Harcourt Street, and Westmoreland Street on the south side of the city; Bolton Street, Dorset Street, and Rutland Square on the north side, exhibit the order of the street extensions of the eighteenth century. The process might be minutely followed in the names of many of the lesser streets. It can be traced in a less noticeable but still remarkable degree in the case of nineteenth-century extensions in Dublin, and in the street-nomenclature of the various townships outside the borough boundary.

It has not been possible in such a sketch as this to attempt to exhibit the many remarkable events in the history of Ireland with which Dublin has direct associations. To do so would be to tell both too much and too little of the larger story of Ireland. For, though in one sense the story of the capital is the story of the country, the chronicle of Dublin can scarcely be said to abound in striking episodes. Since its capture by Strongbow's followers the incidents of its history have not often been exciting. In Plantagenet times its most thrilling experience was the imminence, in the reign of Edward the Second, of a siege at the hands of Edward Bruce, as the result of an invasion from Scotland which had very serious effects on the course of Irish history; but the Scottish commander stopped short of assaulting the city, and turned his arms in a different direction. Under the first of the Tudors the city was the scene of Lambert Simnel's brief masquerade in the character of the rightful king of England; the pretender being crowned with all the pomp and circumstance of royalty in the cathedral of Christ Church. And in the reign of Henry the Eighth the capital witnessed the most serious revolt against English authority of which it has ever been the scene, when, in 1534, Lord Thomas FitzGerald, while governing the country in the absence of his father, the Earl of Kildare, who had been summoned to England on a charge of treason, laid siege to Dublin, and sought to carry Dublin Castle by storm. But the young Geraldine, who is known in history as Silken Thomas, was unable to cover his treasure with the justification of success, and perished with his five uncles at Tyburn. In spite of the general unsettlement of the country, and the prolonged Irish wars which filled the reign of Queen Elizabeth, the close of the Tudor era was unmarked by any very notable event in Dublin history; and the close of Strafford's administration on the eve of the great Civil War was the occasion of the next outbreak by which the peace of the city was menaced. On October 23, 1641, the Irish Rebellion was heralded by the abortive attempt of Sir Phelim O'Neill to surprise Dublin Castle, as the preliminary to the capture of the capital. But the Government of the day was served on this occasion by the treachery, or indiscretion, of one of the conspirators, and Dublin was spared the bloodshed which elsewhere characterised the outbreak of the insurrection. But, though the authority of the English Government was maintained throughout the struggles of the succeeding decade, Dublin was a witness of many vicissitudes of fortune, in the course of which the city and its citizens were severe sufferers. In the earlier part of the conflict between Cavalier and Roundhead, the Duke of Ormond, as Charles the First's vicegerent, had to meet the attack of the generals of the Catholic Confederation; but, though successful in repelling their assault, he was obliged a year or two later to surrender the capital of his sovereign into the hands of foes more formidable than the King's Irish enemies, and to abandon it to the Commissioners of the English Parliament. Two years later, in 1649, the death of the King having produced a temporary union among all factions in Ireland, the same Viceroy, who had formerly defended the city, was called upon to besiege it. But Ormond's attack was foiled and his army completely dispersed by Michael Jones, the Parliamentary Governor of Dublin, at the Battle of Rathmines; and thenceforward the capital remained in Cromwellian hands until the Restoration. That event, however, was greeted with enthusiasm by the citizens; and Charles the Second was proclaimed in the Irish capital in a perfect delirium of loyalty.

Next, and most exciting of all perhaps among the incidents of Dublin history, comes the brief episode of James the Second's visit, when that monarch, exiled from two of his kingdoms, found a temporary refuge in the third, establishing himself in the Irish capital till the decisive defeat at the Boyne obliged him to abandon it. James was followed by another royal visitor in the person of William the Third, whose stay in Dublin is commemorated in Grinling Gibbons' famous equestrian statue of that monarch in College Green. The war of the Revolution was the last occasion on which Dublin experienced the excitement of actual hostilities; and for more than a hundred years the peace of the city remained undisturbed by any formidable civil outbreak. The military disturbances of the seventeenth century gave place to the more peaceful, though scarcely less exciting, political agitations of the succeeding age, in which Swift, in the character of the author of the 'Drapier's Letters,' and Charles Lucas, a noisy but capable politician, whose statue by Edward Smyth still stands in the City Hall, were the central figures. In 1778 the celebrated meeting of the Ulster Volunteers in College Green was the prelude to the triumph of the patriot party in the Irish Parliament, and the restoration of those parliamentary liberties of Ireland which are inseparably associated with the splendid names of Flood and Grattan, but which in less than twenty years were to be extinguished as a consequence of the agitation of the United Irishmen and the rising of 1798. That insurrection, which was planned to commence on May 23 of that year, was precipitated by the arrests in Dublin, two months earlier, of several of the chiefs of the movement, followed after a short interval by the capture and death in melancholy and dramatic circumstances of its principal leader, the ill-fated and picturesque patriot Lord Edward FitzGerald. For some months after this event Dublin was under martial law, and its citizens were enrolled in yeomanry corps for the protection of the capital. An echo of the United Irish movement was heard five years later, when another brilliant apostle of popular principles headed the short-lived insurrection known as Robert Emmet's rising —an outbreak which proved a hopeless fiasco as a menace to the authority of the Government, but which was attended with melancholy results in the murder of Lord Kilwarden, the Irish Lord Chief Justice, and in the death on the scaffold of the romantic but misguided youth whose enthusiasm had hurried him into a foolhardy enterprise.

The history of Dublin during the nineteenth century is

upon the whole a history of municipal prosperity and expansion. None of the great movements of the period can be said to have originated in Dublin. Nor are the chief triumphs of such great leaders of public opinion as O'Connell and Parnell associated in any particularly striking manner with the capital. The great agitations of the nineteenth century—the movement for Catholic Emancipation, the Young Ireland movement, the Fenian rising in 1867, the Land League agitation of more recent years—though all of them enjoyed in a greater or less degree the sympathy of the Dublin populace, were movements which left the surface of Dublin life practically untouched and untroubled. A melancholy exception is to be noted in the tragic crime known as the Phœnix Park murders in 1882, when Lord Frederick Cavendish and Mr. Burke were the victims of the Invincible conspiracy. In recent years Dublin has been happy in having no history, and its chronicles for the last quarter of a century have been fortunately filled with no more notable items than those which testify to the improvement in the appearance of its thoroughfares. The last generation has witnessed the adornment of some of the leading quarters of the city with such architectural successes as the Museum and Library in Kildare Street, and such triumphs of sculpture as the statue of O'Connell in Sackville Street; and last, but not least, the public-spirited munificence of Lord Iveagh in clearing away the dilapidated houses in the neighbourhood of St. Patrick's Cathedral, and the creation of St. Patrick's Park, has effected a striking improvement in the amenities of the poorer quarters of the city.

YOUGHAL

Irish topography is in general deficient in that wealth of historical or literary association which lends so much charm to a summer's ramble in rural England, and invests with so much romantic interest so many of the ancient cities and boroughs of Great Britain. Cathedral cities, in the sense in which the term is understood of England, Ireland may almost be said to be without. A few of the towns contain indeed the remains of ecclesiastical and monastic buildings. But even where these exist they are, with one or two exceptions, sadly deficient in human interest. Historical continuity has been lost in the endless civil distractions of the island, and tradition itself speaks in confused and scarce intelligible accents.

Yet a few places there are which natural charm and historic associations combine to cover with some halo of romance. There is for instance Youghal. Standing at the entrance of the spacious river Blackwater, and thus guarding the approach to the chief waterway of South Munster, the story of Youghal is in its way an epitome of the history of Ireland. It was the strategical base from which, in the ninth century, the piratical Dane conducted the marauding foray which he delighted to direct against the ecclesiastical lords of Lismore and the scene of the conflicts of the Northmen with the old-time Keltic chieftains of Imokelly, as the wooded district west of Youghal was called. And looking diagonally across to the Bristol Channel and the shores of Pembroke and Devon, Youghal was a port easy of access to the invader and adventurer who sought to conquer or to colonise south-eastern Ireland. As such it became the spoil of the Pembrokeshire knight Robert

FitzStephen, who, in the allocation of Ireland among the followers of Strongbow, secured the fair territory of Imokelly, a district which embraced the southern sea-board from the mouth of the Blackwater to the haven of Cork. From Fitz-Stephen the lands of Imokelly passed to his half-brother Maurice FitzGerald, the ancestor of the famous breed of the southern Geraldines with whose fortunes the fate of Youghal was intimately connected from early Plantagenet to late Tudor times. To FitzGerald was due the making of Youghal as a medieval town. By him the place was colonised with citizens of Bristol who gave to it the trading characteristics it long retained. Through him it received from King John the first of several charters which betokened the favour of a succession of the Plantagenet Lords of Ireland. To FitzGerald also it owed in all probability the protecting presence on the summit of its most commanding eminence of one of those cloistered fortalices which were among the surest tokens of the coming of the Norman; and finally to him may perhaps be ascribed the foundation of St. Mary's Church, the first of more than one medieval fane whose remains attest the former dignity of the town.

Thus far the record of Youghal does not differ greatly from that of other towns in the South of Ireland, such as Wexford and Waterford; but it is the distinction of Youghal that, unlike these better-known places, it continuously attracted the favour and attention of the rulers of the country. For centuries after the decay of English power consequent on the Bruce invasion and the gradual shrinkage of English authority within the ever-attenuating margins of the Pale, Youghal appears to have possessed a peculiar importance as the chief means of access to South Munster. The charters of six successive English monarchs from Edward the Third to Edward the Fourth prove the importance attached to the town. Edward the Fourth made Youghal one of the limbs of the Cinque Ports, and Richard the Third continued the tradition of royal favour by confirming his brother's charter. Henry the Seventh, in recognition of the loyalty of the townsmen during the rebellion of Lambert

Simnel, did the like. It was not until the rising of Perkin Warbeck that the traditional devotion of the men of Youghal to the English crown was tarnished by the adherence of the inhabitants to the cause of that pretender. But they soon returned to their allegiance, and the prosperity of Youghal grew without hindrance for another half century or so; till it became involved in the failing fortunes of the Desmond Geraldines. In the middle of Elizabeth's reign it received an almost fatal set-back at the hands of the descendant of its first Geraldine benefactor. Gerald, sixteenth Earl of Desmond, in the course of his rebellion, laid siege to the town, and on its surrender Youghal was given over to five days' sack, in which, as the Four Masters tell the tale, the Geraldines seized upon all the riches they found in the town, levelled its walls, and broke down its courts and castles, so that it was not habitable for long after. Youghal never regained its medieval splendour. For though in Stuart times it witnessed many memorable events, they were not of the kind that make for civic prosperity. After the Desmond sack the town became the alternate prey of contending parties; and though the great Elizabethan Earl of Ormond rebuilt its walls, the revolution of Munster which followed the Desmond rebellion effectually forbade the rebuilding of its fortunes. Whatever the period of calm, which lasted from the accession of James the First to the rebellion of 1641, may have done to repair the damage, its effects must have been completely obliterated by the ensuing ten years of strife, which culminated in the occupation of the town by Cromwell and his army, who spent the winter of 1649–50 in Youghal.

Nevertheless it is to this darkest period of its commercial history that some of the most attractive associations of Youghal belong, and it is to the misfortunes that followed the Geraldine rebellion that it owes the inspiring memories that cluster round the names of Raleigh and of Spenser. It was on the partition of the vast heritage of the Desmond Geraldines that the favourite Raleigh received in 1585 a grant of above forty thousand acres of the confiscated territories of Munster, including the valley of the Blackwater from Lismore to Youghal. The careless courtier took little heed of his Irish property or of the terms upon which it was granted to him. But he did come to Youghal, and it is not the least interesting of the associations of the town that Raleigh was for two years its mayor. For a little while, at all events, he resided in the quaint old Tudor house which is still shown to visitors, with its garden, and the yew tree, actual or mythical, under which he is said to have smoked his Virginia tobacco, and watched the growth of that potato which has been the blessing and the curse of Ireland. Whether or not Raleigh cared a straw for his Irish property, it was certainly a possession which in such times as those in which he lived could scarcely be worth a straw to a mercurial courtier such as he. For its development were needed such qualities as belonged to the strenuous and self-made Richard Boyle, the most opulent plutocrat of the day, who became Earl of Cork and owner of half Munster. The rebellion of 1598 which ruined the poorer fortunes of Edmund Spenser was equally destructive to the once splendid prospects of Raleigh, who was glad enough to get rid of his territories and their responsibilities for a beggarly fifteen hundred pounds. In 1602 Raleigh sold his estate and quitted Youghal for ever, and for the next forty years Youghal was the scene of those ceaseless activities which caused Cromwell to say that had there been more Earls of Cork there had been no rebellion. It is of Lord Cork that such living memorials of its former greatness as Youghal still contains speak most eloquently. The Collegiate Church which he rebuilt is filled with memorials of himself and his family, monuments of the unsightly kind in vogue in the early Stuart days, and though not without a suggestion of the over-elaborate magnificence of a *nouveau riche*, still impressively characteristic.

But besides its visible memorials, its history and its traditions, Youghal possesses one other association of great interest which, though one has to go back three centuries for its origin, has only lately been discovered. Recent literary research has identified the origin and lineage of Spenser's wife, and in doing so has given a new meaning to sundry passages in the 'Epithalamion' and 'Amoretti' of the poet. The

Elizabeth of the Sonnets has been identified with Elizabeth Boyle, a cousin of the Earl of Cork, and daughter of one of the many relatives of the great Munster Undertaker who followed him to Ireland. The famous strand of Youghal, nowadays the favourite summer resort of the holiday makers of Cork, derives a new charm when it is remembered that it was to it that the poet alluded when he wrote in the 'Epithalamion':

> One day I wrote her name upon the strand ;

and that the splendid sea which breaks upon it is the same that ' neighboured near ' to the dwelling of the poet's mistress when the author of the 'Faery Queene' wooed and won his bride in far-off Munster three hundred years ago.

KILKENNY

The morning of Kilkenny's history is a morning without a dawn. No far beginnings of a dim tradition go back to the twilight of the gods. We pass without transition from utter dark to clear day. The city emerges into history only at the period from which it is possible to watch its subsequent course in almost unbroken continuity. For of Kilkenny in the dark ages practically nothing is known or knowable. Unlike Armagh and some other cities, it has no pre-Christian legends; and although from about the sixth century it was probably the seat of a monastery founded by the saint from whom the place takes its name, no record of the primitive community of St. Canice has been preserved for us. An inland town, thirty or forty miles from the sea, Kilkenny escaped the incursions of the Danes, and we are thus without even such negative evidence of its state in the ninth century as the chronicles of Viking raids have preserved for us in the case of many other towns. Thus of civil history prior to Plantagenet times Kilkenny has practically none. All that the annalists record of earlier date is that in 1085 'Ceall-Cainnigh was for the most part burned,' and that sixty years later Gillapatrick, one of the chiefs of the adjacent district, was treacherously killed there by the rival sept of the O'Brenans. There can indeed be little doubt that the site of the Norman castle which for above seven centuries has kept watch and ward over what is called in Ireland 'the marble city' must in yet earlier days have been the fortress of the lords of Ossory. But it is only with the advent of Strongbow that Kilkenny first appears on the stage of history; though a strong argument for the existence of a pre-Norman town is supplied in a couplet in the old French 'Song of Dermot and the Earl,' which describes how Strongbow's followers quartered at Kilkenny returned after holding council of war 'to the hostels where they were before lodged.'

In the story of not a few Irish cities, where the poverty of material forbids any consecutive narrative, it chances that the barrenness of their civil annals is in some degree redressed by the wealth of ecclesiastical records. But in the case of Kilkenny not only its civil but its ecclesiastical history dates from the coming of the Norman. It is true that none of the Irish dioceses has an antiquity older than that of Ossory. Its founder, St. Ciaran, was the contemporary, if not, as some claim, the precursor of St. Patrick. But the monastery of Saighir, which was the earliest capital of the see whose centre is now fixed in Kilkenny, is situate in the King's County, and separated by half the diocese of Killaloe from that of which Seir-Kieran is still a parish. Later the fame of the first Bishop of Ossory became eclipsed by that of St. Cainneach (Kenny), the comrade of St. Columba. But though it is with Kilkenny that the memory of this saint is now connected, the head quarters of the See of Ossory remained for some centuries at Aghabo, where St. Cainneach had founded a monastery. It was not until 1178 that Bishop O'Dullany, transferring both the tomb of this saint and the ancient chair of St. Ciaran to the site of the cathedral of St. Canice, permanently erected Kilkenny into the capital of the diocese. Thus the period of the foundation of the See of Ossory is, like the history of the city, coeval with the English conquest of Ireland. And although the round tower which stands close to the medieval cathedral undoubtedly derives from an older foundation and an earlier age, it is with the settlement of Strongbow in the midst of the territories brought him by his marriage with Eva McMurrough that the story of Kilkenny, ecclesiastical as well as civil, begins. From Strongbow's time to that of the Tudors the history of Kilkenny is an epitome of that of the English in Ireland. It was by his son-in-law William Marshall, Earl of Pembroke, that the foundations were laid of that famous castle which, alone among

Irish residences, can boast a continuous occupation for above seven centuries. On the failure of the male heirs of the Pembroke line and the partition of the vast Strongbow inheritance among five heiresses, Kilkenny passed to the De Clares, Earls of Hertford and Gloucester, and from them to the Despencers. From these last the castle was purchased in 1392 by James, third Earl of Ormond, the head of that illustrious house which already ruled the great palatinate of Tipperary, and with whose fortunes the story of the city has ever since been indissolubly connected.

The importance and interest of Kilkenny in the medieval history of Ireland arises in part from its geographical position, in part from its being continuously in the possession of families closely allied to the Norman or English interest, and devotedly attached to the English connexion. Though lying beyond the Pale, its proximity to Waterford, the strategic key to South Leinster, and its position within eighty miles of Dublin, made it comparatively easy of access from England. On the other hand, its neighbourhood to the wild territories of Ossory and Leix made its possession by friendly hands a matter of serious consequence to the English crown. Hence it was that Kilkenny was called upon to play so conspicuous a part in the political history of Ireland. Down to Tudor times it was the frequent meeting-place of Parliament, including that famous assembly convened by Lionel, Duke of Clarence, which passed the well-known enactment that takes its name from the town. It was by the provisions of the Statute of Kilkenny that the Plantagenet rulers of the country sought to maintain the use of the English language, and to enforce adherence to English modes of civilisation in those territories where the descendants of the Anglo-Norman colonists had become more Irish than the Irish themselves. To this same nearness to the seat of English power Kilkenny owes the first of at least three visits with which it has been honoured by English sovereigns. It was at Kilkenny that, shortly after its acquisition by the Earls of Ormond, Richard the Second fixed his Court for a fortnight in that last and fatal expedition to Ireland which heralded the fall of his fortunes. An episode in his sojourn forms one of the many incidents which gilds Kilkenny history with the romance of the Middle Ages. For it was from the castle of Kilkenny that the English sovereign took the field on the day when he knighted the heir of the rival who was so soon to dethrone him. As the old French chronicler tells the tale, the King 'out of true and entire affection sent for the son of the Duke of Lancaster, a fair, young and handsome bachelor, and knighted him, saying, "My fair cousin, henceforth be preux and valiant, for you have some valiant blood to conquer."'

In later Plantagenet and early Tudor times the story of Kilkenny is involved in the long feuds which the Earls of Ormond maintained with the Desmond Geraldines, their neighbours to the south-west, and the Leinster FitzGeralds, their rivals in that struggle for the possession of administrative power which occupied so much of the fifteenth and sixteenth centuries, and which culminated in the devastating wars of Elizabeth. It was in her reign, and in the time of the celebrated Thomas, tenth Earl of Ormond, cousin to his sovereign through her Boleyn blood, that Kilkenny was raised into a city; and it was on his invitation that Spenser made acquaintance with the place and was able to make familiar mention of it in his enumeration of the Irish rivers:

> the stubborne Newre, whose waters grey
> By faire Kilkenny and Rospontë boord.

But though the traditions of Kilkenny are thus English, the city is very far from being without its patriotic memories. For by an odd irony it was in this very centre of English influence that the only parliamentary assembly which can fairly be termed Irish held independent sway for close on a decade. To Irish patriots Kilkenny is above all else the city of the Confederation. Here from 1642 to 1648 the Irish Catholic Confederation held its meetings, made its laws, and raised its armies, under the very shadow of the castle whose lord was throughout that period the actual Viceroy of Ireland. The story of the Kilkenny Confederation is the most remarkable example in modern history of the existence of a *de facto* government, civil and military, completely armed with all the normal powers of central administration, concurrently with the maintenance of the *de jure* authority in the country. The deliberations of the Confederation were held with all the forms of Parliament, and the Supreme Council which constituted the executive discharged all the offices of Government. It stamped its own coins, set up its own courts of justice, settled the ownership of estates, re-established the Roman form of worship, sent embassies to foreign Courts, and received the Pope's Nuncio in its midst. This last and crowning mark of its sovereign authority contained the elements of disruption. Dissension led the way to the 'Cessation' or understanding with Ormond and the Royalist party which preceded the death of Charles the First; and a year or two later the cannon of Cromwell compelled the surrender of the city. It was doubtless in recognition of the strength of its patriotic instincts and the part played by the Confederation that after the Restoration the Irish town was erected into an independent borough returning, like the city itself, two members to the Irish Parliament. This arrangement lasted until the Union, but was evidently not without its disadvantages: for it is to the bickerings between the rival municipalities that we owe the legend of the Kilkenny cats. The annals of the city under the later Stuarts continued to be filled with interesting incidents. Under the ægis of the first Duke of Ormond, the illustrious personage who was thrice Viceroy of Ireland and earned the envy of contemporary courtiers as the richest subject of the King, Kilkenny became, in the words of an English writer, 'the most pleasant and delightful town of the kingdom of Ireland.' The year after the old Duke's death saw it in the hands of James the Second's army; but the second Duke, adhering to William the Third, soon had the satisfaction of entertaining that monarch in his ancestral castle. Thereafter the prosperity of Kilkenny suffered an eclipse from which it has never wholly recovered, in the temporary ruin of the illustrious house of Ormond, through the attainder and exile of the second Duke. The interest of its modern annals is literary and dramatic rather than legislative or military. Congreve, Swift, and Berkeley received their education in Kilkenny School, and the drama nowhere received greater encouragement in Ireland than in the private theatre which flourished in Kilkenny at the beginning of the last century.

DROGHEDA

THE geographical position of Drogheda in a great degree explains the importance of the part played by the town as well in the racial contentions of medieval Ireland as in the politico-religious strife of later centuries. The wide estuary of the Boyne presents the most obvious of entrances into Ireland from the east, and thus the port of Drogheda, situate near the mouth of the most considerable of the rivers that flow eastward to the Irish Sea, was from early times the key to the most fertile pastures and the most impregnable strongholds of the interior. To the ninth-century Viking the Boyne was an easy avenue to the rich granaries and luxuriant pastures of the ancient kingdom of Meath and its adjacent territories; while the possession of a commanding point of vantage on the southern confines of Ulster gave him control of the most convenient landward approach to the wild fastnesses of the North. To complete its strategical advantages, Drogheda is separated by no more than thirty miles of level country from Dublin, the road passing through the richest wheat-bearing district in Ireland. Thus when Turgesius in the ninth century made Drogheda—the bridge of the ford—the *point d'appui* of his devastating activities, he not only established what proved to be a most valuable connecting link between the Danes of Dublin to the south and Carlingford to the north, but he provided a citadel which was to serve his Anglo-Norman successors for many a century as the sentinel of English power on the frontiers of Ulster. For the territory of Uriel, which embraced the modern country of Louth, though now included in the province of Leinster, was anciently a part of the Ulster kingdom, a connexion which is still maintained in the ecclesiastical sphere by the inclusion of Louth in the archiepiscopal province of Armagh. Thus happily placed within easy reach of the capital both by land and by water, Drogheda was utilised during the Plantagenet and Tudor periods as a military outpost of the first consequence, alternately serving, according to the ebb or flow of English power, as a bulwark for the defence of the Pale, or as a base for offensive operations against the northern septs, which was its main use in the earlier period of English rule in Ireland. Later when Ulster fell back into undisputed Irish control, and the Boyne became the northern boundary of the limits of English authority, Drogheda was utilised as a buttress against the incursions of the O'Neills.

As with most Irish towns, so with Drogheda, the municipal history of the borough begins with the coming of the Norman. To Hugo De Lacy, the first Viceroy of Ireland, who had received from his sovereign the splendid grant of the opulent territories of Meath, the strategical value of the place was at once apparent, and by him was built the first of two castles of Drogheda and Blackagh which long guarded the defences of the town on either side the Boyne. A generation later the castles of Drogheda were excepted from the confirmation of the Palatine grants of Meath to De Lacy's successors, and thenceforward were held by the Crown as royal fortresses under the charge of separate constables. Hence arose a curious administrative feature which, among Irish towns at least, is peculiar to Drogheda. The two castles became the respective seats of independent municipalities. Modern Drogheda sits astride the Boyne, forming a homogeneous town of which the larger portion lies on the north bank of the river. But it is not difficult to trace to-day the indications of that independent existence of its northern and southern sections which was dignified in the Plantagenet days by two charters separately granted to 'the mayor and citizens of Drogheda on the side of Louth' and to 'the seneschal and burgesses of Drogheda on the side of Meath.' The city and borough of Drogheda remained separate municipal entities down to the reign of Henry the Fourth, and it was not until 1412, after many and sometimes sanguinary quarrels, that a sermon by an eloquent Dominican monk having persuaded the inhabitants 'how good and pleasant it is for brethren to dwell together in amity,' the two jurisdictions were amalgamated, and the county of the town of Drogheda was created by charter. The municipality thus constituted long preserved an honourable pre-eminence among the cities and boroughs of Ireland. The common form of the preliminaries to all fresh legislation in the Plantagenet and Tudor Parliaments bracketed Drogheda with Dublin, Waterford, and Limerick in the list of cities whose liberties the sovereign undertook to respect; and the mayors of the town appear even to have asserted a civic superiority over and above the chief magistrate of the capital. Edward the Fourth, in recognition of the services rendered by the citizens in expeditions against the O'Reillys of Cavan, granted to the Mayor the right to wear a sword as the Mayor of London did, and as late as 1552 in a contest for precedence which had arisen between the Mayors of Dublin and Drogheda when taking the field in the Queen's service, it was adjudged that the latter should have pride of place on the homeward march.

Of the numerous stately churches which the medieval town could boast many have long been a prey to dumb forgetfulness, and all trace of them has vanished. Of others the cannonade of Cromwell and the torches of his soldiers have left only the scantiest remnant. Of the Priory of St. John the Baptist, founded by the Knights of St. John, in which King John is reputed to have held a council, scarcely a stone remains; and of a spacious Dominican friary, large enough to accommodate the train of a monarch and permit the assembling of a parliament, only the gaunt fragment called the Magdalen Steeple survives. Yet here it was that Richard the Second in the first of his Irish expeditions received the submissions of the 'four Irish kings,' whose inability to adapt themselves to the usages of a Norman Court is so quaintly described by Froissart. But in late Plantagenet times these buildings, with the Abbey of St. Mary's, whose central tower still presides over some squalid ruins in the dirtiest portion of the modern town, were only a few among many ecclesiastical foundations which easily explain the selection of Drogheda by Edward the Fourth as the seat of an intended medieval university 'with like manner of liberties, privileges, and laudable customs' to those enjoyed by the University of Oxford. Nowadays, unfortunately, only the imposing structure of St. Laurence's Gate still stands in its entirety to help us to an impression of the appearance of the walled medieval town.

But it is not its early military consequence, nor the splendour of its vanished architecture, nor the stark memories of Cromwell's inhuman massacre, that constitutes Drogheda's chiefest title to eminence in the roll of Irish towns. Among its most memorable historical associations are those which connect it with the early parliamentary history of Ireland. Not only was Drogheda among the earliest boroughs to return burgesses to Parliament, but it was, alike in Plantagenet and Tudor times, the frequent and favourite meeting-place of the Irish legislature. It was here that the early Plantagenet sovereigns held more than one important council, and it was here that under Henry the Sixth, Richard Duke of York held, in 1450, as Viceroy of Ireland, the second session of the first Parliament in which the existence of a House of Commons as a separate and formally constituted assembly can be traced. Here, too, the first recorded Speaker of that assembly made protestation of the privileges of the Commons of Ireland in the form familiar at Westminster.[1] By a statute of the same reign the place of assembly of the Parliament was limited to Dublin and Drogheda, and thenceforward down to Elizabethan times the legislature was summoned to sit in Drogheda as frequently as in the capital. The celebrated Parliament called by Sir Edward Poynings, which settled the constitutional system of Ireland on the footing which substantially remained unaltered for three centuries, was held in the Dominican Abbey; and it was not until as late as 1585 that the town on the Boyne ceased to be resorted to as the seat of the legislature, 'by reason of the inability of that town to bear the train of a Parliament.' Never since has Drogheda come so near as it seems to have done in those Tudor days to the fulfilment of the prophecy recorded in Holinshed's 'Chronicles' that 'Ross was, Dublin is, Drogheda shall be the best of the three.'

[1] See p. 200, *infra*.

ARMAGH

Of Irish cities Armagh is at once the oldest and the newest. No other town in Ireland has so much the air of a cathedral city. Yet the atmosphere is redolent not of the medieval associations that cling to the grey walls of a cathedral, but of the placid restfulness of the eighteenth century. In this modern town may be found an English Street, a Scotch Street, and an Irish Street; and the nomenclature reflects not inaptly the racial variety of the inhabitants. Yet the groundwork is English, for the adjacent rural population is mainly of English stock. But these are comparatively modern characteristics. This English population is of barely three centuries' standing, and the architecture of the city of less than two. Yet to recall the memories that are embalmed in such a history as that of the city of Armagh one must go back not only behind the present, but almost behind the past itself, stepping at one bound from the modern to the medieval, and at another from the medieval to the prehistoric. For nowhere is the contrast more marked between the remote antiquity of Irish historical origins and the long silences which intervene between recorded episodes to destroy all natural continuity and intelligible sequence.

For above fifteen hundred years the ancient city of Armagh has been entitled ecclesiastically to the term long applied to it in bardic literature of 'the Head of Ireland.' An antiquity greater by a full century and a half than that of Canterbury might serve to satisfy the pride even of Milesian antiquaries. And yet the ecclesiastical antiquity of Armagh, great though it be, is very far from exhausting the claims of this oldest of the surviving cities of Ireland to the respectful attention of topographical genealogists. Old as is the history of St. Patrick's settlement, the earliest traditions of Ard Macha are older by at least seven centuries. To no more modern epoch than the fourth century before the Christian era belongs the legend of Macha of the Golden Hair, and the foundation of the fortress whose site the fair and warrior queen is said to have traced out with the pin of her golden brooch. Thenceforward Emania, as Macha's fort was called, became famous in song and legend as the most eminent after Tara of Irish royal residences, and as the scene of the chivalry of the Knight of the Red Branch. Thus it is that the history of Armagh enshrines at once the most venerable traditions of Irish Christianity and the most romantic of Irish pre-Christian legends. But if the early glories of Armagh are ancient, it is long too since they vanished. As far back as 332 A.D. Emania had been already so completely ruined in the warfare of the tribes that all traces of its site had been practically obliterated by St. Patrick's time. Even as early as the fifth century of our era little was left of Macha's fort save the circumvallations that followed the lines drawn by the queen with her brooch-pin. 'Emania's burgh has perished, save that the stones remain,' says the Calendar of Œngus. In St. Patrick's time the lord of the territories once ruled from Emania was a chief of another race, who had shifted the seat of his capital a mile or two to the eastward. Daire, King of Oriel, was the ruler with whom St. Patrick treated for the possession of the height known as the Hill of the Willows, as Macha's height was also called.

But if there be no Irish city more ancient in its traditions than Armagh, it may be doubted whether there is any which is more modern in its aspect, or which is so poor in physical evidences of its historic past. A venerable cathedral still crowns the height of Macha, and occupies the site on which St. Patrick reared his church; and on an adjacent eminence a yet more splendid fane has lately been raised. But the first of these is in essentials no older than the seventeenth century; and the second stands as a fine example of what nineteenth-century cathedral builders could achieve. It may even be doubted whether the city boasts, save in the foundations of the old cathedral, any building which is much more than two hundred years old. For this contrast between the actual modernity and the historical antiquity of Armagh the reasons are unfortunately ample. They began to operate unusually early, and they continued to affect the city unusually late. As early as the seventh and eighth centuries, according to the annalists, Armagh had already been completely destroyed by fire on four separate occasions within a space of one hundred and twenty years. At the close of the ninth it was sacked by the Danes from Dublin. St. Patrick's primitive church, if it had survived the preceding conflagrations, was evidently destroyed on this occasion; for, says the chronicler—

> Pity, O Saint Patrick, that thy prayers did not stay
> The foreigners with their axes, when striking thy oratory.

A little later marauders of the same breed 'took the valuables of the Chamber of Armagh and burned them on the green.' It was an appropriate set-off to these Danish depredations that the sovereign who inflicted the heaviest blow upon the Danish power in Ireland chose for his last resting-place the Cathedral of St. Patrick; and there accordingly Brian Borumha and his son Murrough were laid on the morrow of the fatal victory of Clontarf. But the overthrow of the Dane was insufficient to give peace to Ireland, or rest to Armagh; and the city continued to follow in its history the course of the same unfortunate fate which had hitherto marred its progress. The fame of its connexion with St. Patrick, the renown of its schools, where even the fury of the Northman's onslaught could not quench the zeal of its scholars, of whose learning and piety a remarkable memorial survives in the celebrated 'Book of Armagh,' as well as its position as the Metropolitan See, continued, even after the coming of the English, and the final erection of Dublin as the capital, to give Armagh pre-eminence among Irish cities. Yet viewed as a seat of civil authority and a centre of urban life Armagh may almost be said to have disappeared from history for the four centuries following the English invasion. The province of which it was the centre was the scene of perpetual raids, during which the city was many times destroyed. By the end of the fifteenth century the city had dwindled to the collection of hovels which a century later Camden found it. So insecure was its situation by reason of its position in the unsubdued wilds of Ulster that the Archbishops of Armagh, who as well before as after the Reformation were in a great degree the instruments of English Government, made no attempt to reside in the primatial city, but fixed their seat in Drogheda. To such a condition of desolation and semi-barbarism had the city and its people been reduced at the commencement of the Tudor period that Octavian de Palatio, an Italian prelate who filled the See under Henry the Seventh, is said to have relieved his feelings by stigmatising the civilisation of Armagh in the uncomplimentary doggerel :

> Civitas Armachana,
> Civitas vana,
> Absque bonis moribus ;
> Mulieres nudæ,
> Carnes crudæ,
> Paupertas in ædibus.

In Elizabethan times the city was alternately in the hands of the English Deputies and of its Ulster lords, the O'Neills. And it suffered almost equally under either. Now a Viceroy would fortify the cathedral against the Irish enemy. Next that enemy would burn it to the ground. And anon, when the zeal of some Primate had rebuilt it, the unlucky edifice would fall once more in the crash of some fresh disturbance.

The more modern history of Armagh from the time of the Plantation of Ulster is little more than a history of the Primates of the Established Church. With the restoration of the cathedral by Archbishop Margetson began the practical re-building of Armagh as what was long, and till comparatively recently may be said to have remained, an English town. The Primates of the old Establishment were not only great ecclesiastics, but great political personages ; the Archbishop of Armagh being commonly at the head of the commission of Lords Justices by whom, through a great part of the eighteenth century, Ireland was in effect governed. Under the ægis of these prelates it was that Armagh began to assume that air of comfortable prosperity and neat respectability which still characterises its thoroughfares. Primate Boulter was the first of these great dignitaries to initiate the structural improvements which his successors Stone and Robinson carried through. Of these, the former, whose remarkable comeliness of person earned him the sobriquet, which conflicted so strangely with his avowedly mundane ambitions, of 'The Beauty of Holiness,' superintended a rearrangement of the thoroughfares which practically transformed the city; and it is from his time that the red marble to which Armagh owes its title of the marble city began to be used in the flags of its pavements. But it is to Primate Robinson, Lord Rokeby, that the place owes the characteristic features which still mark this old cathedral town. He it was who resumed the use of Armagh as the residential seat of the primacy; for his predecessors had long preferred the security of Drogheda and its comparative proximity to Dublin to the risks which attended life in the head quarters of their See. Primate Robinson, too, it was who formed the fine demesne and built the spacious mansion in which the last surviving prelate of the Irish Establishment still reigns as Archbishop of Armagh. To him also is due the library which abuts upon the cathedral, and the observatory, a little to the north of the city, which has won for Armagh some share of repute in astronomical discovery. Lord Rokeby was less fortunate in his more strictly ecclesiastical buildings. His work on the cathedral was ill-conceived, and, through no fault of his own, worse executed; and it was reserved to a nineteenth-century Primate of not less splendid munificence, the stately Lord John Beresford, to complete the restoration of that edifice in its present form. The building which occupies the hallowed site of St. Patrick's original church is not and can never be transformed into a temple architecturally worthy of its majestic traditions. In its external proportions it is altogether eclipsed by the splendour of the noble structure which has quite recently been reared to the honour of the apostle of Ireland. Yet it possesses a quiet dignity of its own not unsuited to its story; and its interior memorials are characteristic of the traditions of the Church to which it belongs. Of its statues, which are both numerous and artistically admirable, perhaps the most striking is a representation by Roubiliac of Thomas Molyneux, brother to the first of those Anglo-Irish patriots through whose constancy of purpose the independence of the Anglo-Irish Parliament was achieved. The flags with which the aisles are hung mingle the trophies of the Peninsula with the emblems of the Irish Volunteers. And the stately cenotaphs of two Beresford Primates recall an order of prince-bishops who have vanished for ever, but whose magnificence was not unsuited to their times. And finally it is typical of the immutability of the intercourse between the church of St. Patrick and that of St. Augustine that Edward White Benson, Archbishop of Canterbury, should, as a modest inscription records, have preached his last sermon in the cathedral of Armagh.

GALWAY

Galway is at once the most Irish of cities and the least so. No one can cross the great bridge which spans the Shannon at Athlone on the journey from Dublin to the West of Ireland without feeling something of that atmosphere of freshness and of freedom, of irresponsibility and unconventionality which is the charm of Connaught and of Connaught folk. This sensation, of which it is happily impossible to divest oneself in any of the five counties of the Western province, is most strongly felt in the county of Galway, and most of all in the capital town of that extensive territory. It is in Galway and in the society of Galway people that one best understands that vein of fun and frolic in the Irish temperament which Charles Lever enjoyed so heartily and represented so vividly. And yet Galway, considered historically, can scarcely be called Irish at all. Not only does it owe its origin, like most Irish towns, to the enterprise of the Saxon invader—for town life was little suited to the genius of the pastoral and in great measure nomadic Kelts who stood for the Irish people before the twelfth century—but its inhabitants were for ages mainly of foreign or non-Keltic extraction. Of the thirteen families from whom Galway gets its title of the 'City of the Tribes' scarcely two can be referred to an Irish progenitor. The thirteen 'tribes' enumerated in the rude mnemonic couplet

Athy, Blake, Bodkin, Browne, Deane, Darcy, Lynch,
Joyce, Kirwan, Martin, Morris, Sherrett, French

contain indeed more than one name which we now regard as distinctively Irish. But with the exception of Kirwan there is not one of them which can be shown to have been connected with Galway prior to the fourteenth century. Irish as we deem it now, Galway from the twelfth century to the eighteenth was a stronghold of the invader, a representative of Norman or English rule in the wild places of the West.

History prior to the coming of the Norman, Galway, as a city, has none. Its site was occupied only by the dwellings of a few fishermen, the predecessors of that quaint collection of huts which is now known as the Claddagh, a primitive municipality under the protection of the O'Flaherties, the most powerful of the Connemara septs, and the lords of West or Iar-Connaught. Some faint traces there are of Danish depredations, and there are definite records of the destruction of the O'Flaherty Castle by which the fishermen were dominated on two separate occasions just before the Norman invasion. But, apart from this, history is almost a blank until the thirteenth century, when, the O'Flaherties having been ejected, the town was built by the De Burgo Earls of Ulster, who were likewise lords of Connaught. Then began that strife between the dispossessed O'Flaherties and the new owners of Galway which lasted for at least four centuries: for as long, in fact, as Galway retained the characteristics of a medieval town which were stamped upon it by its founders. Tradition has it that the inhabitants of the city long invoked the protection of Providence from the raids of the 'ferocious O'Flaherties' by the legend, engraved on its Western gate:

From the fury of the O'Flaherties
Good Lord deliver us;

while the undying hostility of the descendants of the ancient sept is embalmed in the imprecation of a seventeenth-century representative of that ancient and combative stock, who was wont to ascend the eminence of Bunowen and there 'declare war against all the potentates of the world, but especially against that pitiful and pettifogging town of Galway.'

Under the ægis of its De Burgo lords Galway expanded from a poor fishing village to a walled town of considerable strength, and the place of chief importance in the Western province. It became an outpost of Norman civilisation and a stronghold of English authority in the Connaught wilderness. But in the general relaxation of English authority which followed the Bruce invasion, Galway, like many other places, fell away from obedience to the Crown. Its defection was hastened by the accidents of the De Burgo family history. The third De Burgo Earl of Ulster was murdered in 1333, when his vast estates passed to a daughter, Elizabeth, whose succession to the Connaught possessions of her father was repudiated by the younger branches of the De Burgo family. Sir William and Sir Edmond Burke, ancestors respectively of the Earls of Clanricarde and Mayo, raised the standard of revolt, threw off their allegiance, and adopted the dress and language of their Irish neighbours. MacWilliam Uachtar and MacWilliam Iochtar, as the Hibernised De Burgos respectively called themselves, divided the territories of Mayo and Galway between them. Galway in this division fell to the ancestors of the Clanricardes, whose descendants were thenceforward lords of the town. The legitimate title to the province and its capital still remained in the daughter of the third earl, through whom it was carried into the Plantagenet line, and in 1369 the manor of Galway was found by inquisition to belong in right of his wife to Lionel Duke of Clarence. But although the interest which the later Plantagenets had thus derived in the chief city of Connaught was of some benefit to Galway in procuring a grant of mercantile privileges from Edward the Fourth, the Connaught De Burgos retained their power and were never afterwards interfered with, though the armorial bearings of the legitimate branch long continued to be used as the arms of Galway.

The town, however, though it could not fail to be dominated by the De Burgo power, was by no means alien to the English connexion. Its commercial interests were much too important to be jeopardised by politics. It soon returned to its allegiance, and its growing value and consequence as a seat of English influence in the midst of both Irish enemies and English rebels was recognised in successive charters. From Richard the Second Galway received a charter, and from 1377 onwards it returned a representative to Parliament. The town ultimately received from Richard the Third the Charter under which it was governed down to the reign of James the First. The first Mayor of Galway dates accordingly from 1485. It was perhaps to the consciousness of the honour thus recently conferred on the city by the English Crown that we owe the unique example of devotion to 'law and order' which a few years later was given by James Lynch FitzStephen, Mayor of the city, who having first participated in the trial and death sentence of his son for the murder of a young Spaniard, defeated the efforts of his friends to procure a reversal of the sentence by himsélf becoming the stoical executioner of the culprit.

Under the Tudors Galway rapidly developed, and attained perhaps to the acme of its prosperity. Its municipal records, which from the date of the Charter of Richard the Third are exceptionally perfect, show the English character of the place, and the extent of its foreign commerce. Its freedom was restricted to such as spoke English and shaved their upper lip once a week; and statutes were made to ensure the credit of the town in its dealings with France and Spain. Thus by 1614 it could properly be described as a town, small but with fair and stately buildings, with houses fronted with hewn stone, and garnished with fair battlements, and as forming 'a commonalty composed of the descendants of the ancient English founders of the town, who rarely admit any new English to have freedom or education among them, and never any Irish.'

The prosperity of Galway continued unabated until the outbreak of the Irish rebellion; but thereafter the city became the shuttlecock of contending parties and its mercantile greatness rapidly declined. Having been fortified by Mountjoy during the war with Tyrone its military importance had become considerable, and during the Civil War it was held for and against the King by a succession of leaders including the Papal Nuncio Rinuccini. After the execution of Charles the First the city became the pivot of a memorable negotiation between the Catholic Royalists and the Duke of Lorraine, to whom the town was offered in pledge as security for the Duke's projected expedition to Ireland and an expenditure of £20,000 in succouring the royal cause. It was in connexion with this project that a remarkable map of Galway was executed which still preserves for us the features of the city as it stood in the middle of the seventeenth century.[1] Shortly after the place was surrendered to the forces of the Parliament, when its ecclesiastical buildings and monuments suffered the usual consequences of a Cromwellian victory. Then began a period of municipal seesaw reflecting the ups and downs of political fortune in the larger world of the Three Kingdoms. These mutations did not make for civic prosperity, and although as late as Queen Anne's time the city was described by an intelligent traveller as still the second town in Ireland after Dublin, the great days of Galway had gone never to return. Ever since 'Ichabod' has been Galway's sufficient motto. To Maria Edgeworth, who visited the town seventy years ago, Galway appeared the dirtiest town she had ever seen, and the most desolate and idle-looking. It is not much better now. Yet still the place preserves in its decay the indelible charm of its associations, and the indefinable attraction inseparable from the sunny temperament of Connaught and its people.

[1] This map has been reproduced by the Galway Archæological and Historical Society.

III

STUDIES IN IRISH HISTORY

IRISH PARLIAMENTARY ANTIQUITIES

MANY writers have treated of the Irish Parliament in its final stages, but little has been done either to elucidate its origin or to follow its constitutional development, as revealed in such information as has come down to us concerning its early constitution and its formal procedure. By what gradual steps the Parliament of Ireland was modelled to the form in which it is familiar to us, by what influence the House at College Green came to be the appropriate area for the majestic eloquence of Flood and Grattan, and what were the views entertained prior to the eighteenth century of the restrictions placed upon the independence of the Irish legislature by the celebrated Act of Sir Edward Poynings, are questions quite as important as others which have been discussed at great length. Though nothing can be more out of place in a serious historical work or more destructive to the true philosophy of history than the pedantry which is the besetting sin of the antiquary, the historian has often much to learn from Dr. Dryasdust. This is true of almost every variety of history, other than contemporary history; but it is especially true of constitutional history. Perhaps there is no department of human progress in which the continuity of the present with the past is more plainly exhibited than in the story of the development of political institutions. Nowhere certainly has the magic power of form and ceremony, or the governing force of precedent, exerted a more striking influence on the course of affairs than in the evolution of our Parliamentary system. Of the power which the necessity for deferring to the unwritten code of Parliamentary practice can exercise over even the most zealous reformers, the history of the British House of Commons, in almost every stage of its progress, offers countless examples; while the mysterious majesty that dwells in the exterior symbols of authority, even in moments of revolutionary triumph, never received a truer homage than was implied in Oliver Cromwell's masterful contempt for the bauble of the mace.

As there is no more instructive guide to the study of a constitutional system than a knowledge of the origin, meaning, and gradual development of the forms and ceremonies which have grown with its growth and strengthened with its strength, so there is no surer key to the correct apprehension of purely Parliamentary history than a knowledge of early Parliamentary forms. Of the value of this aspect of historical research an admirable example is given in Bishop Stubbs's great work on 'The Constitutional History of England,' in that illuminating chapter entitled 'Parliamentary Antiquities,' in which the historian has sought to realise the character of the medieval Parliament of England in what he calls its formal aspects. By describing the method of summoning, choosing, and assembling the members; by tracing the legislative processes of initiation, discussion, and enactments; by examining the time, place, and mode of summons at, for, and by which Parliament was assembled; and by investigating such matters of constitutional form and usage as the arrangement of the two Houses, their rules for transacting business, and the forms employed for prorogation and dissolution, the historian of the 'Constitutional History of England' has thrown a flood of clear light upon many of the larger problems involved in his inquiry. Of the relevance of such formal matters to any fruitful discussion of the growth of the English Constitution no student of the history of institutions is likely to entertain a doubt; and their importance in relation to the development of the legislative powers of the Irish Parliament is equally self-evident.

The materials for such an endeavour are of course very much fewer in the case of the Irish than in that of the English Houses of Parliament; the records of Irish political institutions in early times being vastly less numerous and much more imperfect than those available for Great Britain. Enough, however, exists to justify the attempt to realise at least some features of the 'formal aspect' of an Irish Parliament. The writers who have dwelt most fully on the characteristics of the legislative system which the Union superseded have made but little attempt to trace the successive stages in its development. They have paid practically no attention either to the ceremonial of the Irish Parliament in general or to the procedure of the Irish House of Commons in particular, notwithstanding that the consideration of the formal aspect of the Irish legislature has been the professed object of more than one writer. That these historians should have neglected this part of their function is, however, scarcely to be wondered at, in view of the poverty of the materials available in their time. The earliest printed Journals of the Irish Parliament only commence with the year 1634; and of the difficulty of ascertaining the constitutional forms of the pre-Stuart period no better illustration need be asked than the fact that Sir John Davis, whose business it was, as Speaker of the Parliament of 1613, to examine into the procedure of an assembly which had then been in abeyance for a generation, found it practically impossible, after the most diligent inquiry, to arrive at the facts. Those writers who have essayed even a portion of the task which baffled Davis have not proceeded very far in their inquiry. Thus William Lynch, in his 'View of the Legal Institutions, Honorary Hereditary Offices, and Feudal Baronies of Ireland,' has discussed with much learning and acuteness the character of the legislative institutions introduced into Ireland by its earliest Plantagenet rulers. But though he has thrown a good deal of light on the constitution of those early councils and assemblies of the great men of the realm which for want of a better name have been given the title of Parliaments, however widely they may and must have differed both in their constitution and their powers from what we now call by that name, he has confined himself to one, and that a very limited, branch of his inquiry. The value of Lynch's contribution to the literature of the subject lies in his careful examination of the earliest Parliamentary Writs of Summons, of which many are extant in ancient Close and Patent Rolls of the Plantagenet era.[1] But neither he nor Sir William Betham, whose work on 'The Origin and History of the Constitution of England and the Early Parliaments of Ireland' deals with the earlier councils and Parliaments, has carried the inquiry down to modern times. Betham's investigation closes with the reign of Richard the Third, and Lynch's barely touches upon the Tudor period. The same remark is true of Monck Mason's 'Essay on the Antiquity and Constitution of Parliaments in Ireland,' a work which, like the two first mentioned, was written early in the last century, and is mainly intended to rebut the evidence adduced by Sir John Davis, in his well-known book, to show that there was no separate Parliament for Ireland for one hundred and forty years from the time of Henry the Second. Nor is the student likely to be greatly assisted in this inquiry by an eighteenth-century work which at first sight might appear to offer a fuller contribution to the literature of his subject. Viscount Mountmorres's 'History of the Principal Transactions of the Irish Parliament from 1634 to 1666' is little more than an analysis of the earliest printed Journals. And though it is prefaced by a 'Preliminary Discourse of the Ancient Parliament of that kingdom,' the latter is itself little more than a reprint of John Hooker's account of the 'Order and Usage how to keep a Parliament in England,' which was compiled by the author for the guidance of the Irish Parliament of 1569, and was first printed in the Irish portion of Holinshed's 'Chronicles.' More useful from the point of view of the student of Irish Parliamentary antiquities than any of the works we have enumerated is Hardiman's well-known edition of the Statute of Kilkenny, published more than sixty years ago by the Irish Archæological Society in their 'Tracts Relating to Ireland.' But this work dealt of course only with a frag-

[1] The same author, in his treatise on *The Law of Election in the Ancient Cities and Towns of Ireland*, which was published in 1831, gives a very valuable *conspectus* of the Irish Boroughs returning members to Parliament from 1358 to 1800. But this table does not specify the boroughs returning members to any of the Tudor Parliaments prior to that called by Sussex in 2nd Elizabeth.

ment, though a most important fragment, of the history of early Parliaments in Ireland. A most lucid summary of the earlier constitution of the Irish legislature is, indeed, furnished by Mr. Bagwell in his 'Ireland under the Tudors.' But no adequate attempt has yet been made by any writer to combine with such notices of the primitive Parliamentary system of Ireland as survive in the earliest historical chronicles the information (fragmentary and unsatisfactory, but so far as it goes authentic) which has been disclosed in the various State Paper publications of the last half-century. There is consequently the less occasion to apologise for even so partial an effort as can be undertaken here to collect what can be gathered upon this subject.

In the endeavour to glean such stray grains of information concerning the origins of Irish Parliamentary institutions as have escaped the destroying hand of time it might seem natural to begin with the statutes of the realm. But these unhappily are extremely imperfect. The first attempt at an edition of the statute law of Ireland was not made until as late as 1569, when, at the suggestion of the Speaker of the House of Commons in the Parliament of that year, authority was given to the John Hooker already mentioned to print the statutes at his own charges. But though the patent given to Hooker recited that 'divers Parliaments have been holden in Ireland, and divers laws statutes and acts made in the same, which laws being never put into print have been altogether turned to oblivion,' nothing further was done to give effect to the proposal.[1] Thus it was not until 1621 that Sir Richard Bolton, afterwards Lord Chancellor of Ireland, published in one folio volume the first collected edition of the statutes. Nor, although subsequent statutes were printed regularly enough, was it until the reign of George the Third that anything like an adequate edition of the Irish statutes was provided. In the year 1765 the publication of 'The Statutes at Large passed in the Parliaments held in Ireland from the third year of Edward II, A.D. 1310, to the first year of George III, A.D. 1761, inclusive,' was commenced. The title was, however,

[1] *Calendar of the Carew Manuscripts*, vol. i. p. 387.

very misleading. Had the editor been able to give the statutes in sequence for the whole of that period he would have accomplished much more than is ever likely to be achieved by any successor. But although the edition contains six statutes of Edward the Second, no attempt was made to examine the extant rolls of Parliament from that reign down to the seventh year of Henry the Sixth, a period of more than a century being thus left blank. And although several statutes of the latter monarch and of his successor are given, the legislation of Richard the Third, whose brief reign was marked in Ireland by numerous statutes, is completely omitted,[1] while that of Henry the Seventh is only very imperfectly exhibited.[2] At the end of George the Third's reign propositions were set on foot by the Irish Record Commissioners for supplying the defects of the imperfect edition issued at its commencement, and for editing the statutes, so far as they remained extant, from the original roll of Parliament. But this project remained in abeyance until the beginning of the present century, when the task of producing a complete and

[1] Parliaments were, undoubtedly, called in Ireland with great frequency in the reigns of the Lancastrian and Yorkist sovereigns. At least ten Parliaments were called in Ireland under Henry VI; and it was even found necessary to enact that the Deputy should not summon Parliament more than once in the same year. In the reign of his successor the Legislature met almost annually; while under Richard III two Parliaments were held, the first in 1482, the second in 1483–84. In the first of these Parliaments no less than twenty-seven statutes were enacted, and in the second, eighteen. See transcripts of the statutes made nearly a century ago under the direction of the Irish Record Commissioners, and preserved at the Irish Record Office; and also an annotated copy of the printed statutes in the same repository, which affords much valuable information on the early statutes.

[2] Under Henry VII at least six Parliaments were called. Of these the first was held in 1492 by Walter, Archbishop of Dublin, as deputy for the Lord Lieutenant, Jasper, Duke of Bedford. It passed in the course of its two sessions as many as thirty-two statutes—the last which were drawn in Norman-French. Of the other Parliaments of Henry VII, besides the celebrated one summoned by Sir Edward Poynings, two were held by Robert Preston, Lord Gormanston, the first at Trim, and the second, which was subsequently declared void for want of any formal summons of the Knights of the Shire, at Drogheda. A Parliament was held in 1498 by Gerald, Earl of Kildare, at Castledermot, and another, which may, however, have been no more than a second session of the same Parliament, was held by the same Deputy in Dublin in the following year. Ware laments in his *Annals* that the laws made in this Parliament were not upon record in his time. He mentions that one Nangle was imprisoned in England on a charge of having surreptitiously taken away the Rolls. Henry VII's last Parliament, which was likewise summoned by an Earl of Kildare, held three sessions in Dublin, and one at Castledermot in the last year of the reign. See authorities cited above.

definitive edition of the hitherto unedited Irish statutes was taken up by the present heads of the Irish Public Record Office.[1]

In the attempt to trace the evolution of Parliament, in the modern conception of the institution from the inchoate legislature of the early Plantagenet councils, the most reliable clue is furnished by an examination of the history of the greatest of all Parliamentary offices, the Speakership of the House of Commons. Apart from the great interest of the Speaker's constitutional functions, in which were early crystallised the liberties of the Commons, the creation of the office must manifestly mark the commencement of the separate existence of the Lower House as a distinct branch of the legislature. From what period we are to date this commencement in the case of the English House of Commons has never been precisely determined, but it was certainly not later than 1377, as from that date onwards the Speaker is mentioned in all the records, and the succession of the Speakers is complete. In the case of Ireland unfortunately no such record is available. Until very lately only the names of those Speakers who had been chosen since the Parliament of 1613 had been ascertained, and some competent authorities even appear to have considered that the separation of the two Houses, or at least the separate sitting of the two Houses in Ireland. could not be dated further back than Stuart times. Recent research has, however, shown conclusively that, as might be expected from the practical identity of ceremonial in the two legislatures, the Irish Speakership can boast of much earlier antiquity. Not only has the succession of the Irish Speakers been definitely ascertained from Henry the Eighth's Parliament of 1541, in which the title of King of Ireland was first conferred on the sovereign, but it has been demonstrated that as early as the middle of the fifteenth century the Speaker was a well understood essential of the Irish Parliamentary system. It has been discovered that the Statute Roll for the year 1449, by some curious and fortunate exception to the case of every

[1] The first volume was published in 1907:—*Statutes and Ordinances and Acts of the Parliament of Ireland; King John to Henry V*, edited by Henry F. Berry, D.Litt., I.S.O.

other extant roll, contains a complete record of the formalities attending the opening of the Parliament to which it related, that, namely, which was held in Dublin in that year by Sir Richard Nugent, Lord Delvin, as Deputy for the Lord Lieutenant, Richard Duke of York. The entry is so curious that it is worth extracting in its entirety. It sets forth that on the Tuesday following the opening of Parliament:

'The Commons presented one John Chever for their Speaker, and the said Deputy-Lieutenant graciously agreed and well accepted of him: and hereupon the said John delivered to the said Deputy a schedule of his protestation, supplicating him most humbly that his said protestation be entered of record in the roll of Parliament, which schedule of the said protestation was read in Parliament: And hereupon the said Deputy charged the Clerk of the said Parliament to enter it in the roll of Parliament of record, the tenor of which protestation is as follows:

'"The Commons of the said Parliament have elected John Chever for their Speaker, to show and declare for them in the said Parliament all manner of business which they have to declare in the said Parliament, with the protestation following; that is to say, that if it happen that the said Speaker (which God forbid should be his intention) should show anything or say anything to the displeasure of the said Deputy, prelates, lords and peers of the said Parliament, through ignorance, mistake, or surplusage, without assent or by assent of the said Commons, that it be not recorded or reported; but that at such time as it be perceived or challenged by the said Deputy and the Council of the King, prelates, lords and peers aforesaid, he may, by good advice and much deliberation of the said Commons, reconsider, amend, augment, or abate the business and matters aforesaid, the which protestation is enacted by authority of the said Parliament."'[1]

It will be seen that in this 'protestation,' which is again recorded in the roll of a Parliament held in Drogheda in the succeeding year, the rights of freedom of speech and favourable interpretation were vindicated by the Irish Speaker, as far back as the twenty-sixth year of Henry the Sixth, in strict accordance with the English usage. The fact affords a strong presumption, in spite of the absence of any earlier record of the office,

[1] Transcripts of Irish statutes preserved at the Irish Record Office.

that the Irish Speakership was of practically equal antiquity with its English prototype; and that in other respects the Dublin House of Commons followed the forms and copied the observances of the Second Chamber at Westminster. It is clear, too, from this record that not only was the form of protestation practically identical with that employed in England, but that the conception of the office of Speaker which prevailed in early times was the same in the Irish as in the English House of Commons. Formerly, as is well known, and as his title denotes, the functions of the Speaker were not only those of the spokesman of the Commons: they were those of a nominee of the Crown, and in effect a representative of the Government. One of the earliest writers on the English Constitution, Sir Thomas Smith, writing of the Tudor House of Commons, defines the duties of the Speaker's office, and states that 'the Speaker is he that doth commend and prefer the bills exhibited into the Parliament, and is the mouth of the Parliament. He is commonly appointed by the King or Queen, though accepted by the assent of the House.'[1] The Irish State Papers make it abundantly clear that this was the view of the Speakership entertained in Ireland by the advisers of the Crown throughout the Tudor period. The Speaker was invariably a nominee of the Crown; he had either been a judge, like Sir Thomas Cusake, the first recorded Speaker of Henry the Eighth's reign, or he actually held concurrently with his Parliamentary post a judicial office. Chever, the fifteenth-century Speaker, was while holding that position Master of the Rolls, and probably owed to the favour earned by the discharge of his functions in the House of Commons the Chief Justiceship of the King's Bench to which he ultimately attained. Speaker Cusake, at all events, seems to have thoroughly understood what was expected of him by the power to which he owed his nomination to the Chair of the House of Commons. For while he followed his predecessor's example in addressing to Sir Anthony St. Leger what that Deputy described as 'a right solemn proposition,' vindicating the liberties of his order, he was even more vigorous

[1] *Commonwealth of England*, edition 1633, p. 77.

in his assertion of the authority of the Crown, and the respect due to the royal prerogative.[1]

In Holinshed's 'Chronicles of Ireland' we have, from the pen of one who was himself a member of it, a report of the proceedings at the opening of Sir Henry Sidney's Parliament,[2] which has preserved for us an epitome of the speeches interchanged between the Lord Deputy and the Speaker of the House of Commons. The language of Speaker Stanihurst on that occasion again illustrates the fidelity with which the constitutional forms of Westminster were imitated in Dublin. The Speaker made the customary declaration of unworthiness and incapacity, desiring that some man of more gravity and of better experience, knowledge, and learning might supply his place; and went on to claim the immemorial liberties of the Commons—freedom from arrest and freedom of speech. He did not, however, petition, as was then usual in England, that a favourable construction might be put upon his actions; nor did he, as had been customary in England from the time of Henry the Eighth, require freedom of access to the person of the sovereign, or claim any corresponding privilege in relation to his representative in Ireland; but, in lieu of this, he demanded that in the event of misconduct, the punishment of the offending member should be in the exclusive control of the House of Commons itself.[3]

In general it may be pretty confidently predicated of any institution or usage introduced into Ireland under its Plantagenet or Tudor rulers—or, for the matter of that, by much later governors of the island—that it is likely to present a more or less perfect copy of an English model. This is preeminently true of the Parliamentary institutions of Ireland, which were fashioned with careful regard to English precedent, in almost every particular. Accordingly, although the information which can be collected either from the statutes or

[1] See Appendix A for succession of the Speakers of the Irish House of Commons, with biographical notices of the early Speakers.

[2] This Parliament met on January 17, 1568–69, and holding three sessions did not terminate until December 1570.

[3] Holinshed, vol. vi. pp. 342, 353; Stubbs's *Constitutional History*, vol. iii. p. 472.

from the State Papers touching the formal procedure of early Parliaments in Ireland is slender enough, we find that such indications as are available confirm the evidence which the history of the Speakership affords that the Dublin legislature closely followed the example of the English one in the methods of its arrangements and the order of its sessions. The formal recital prefixed to the statutes of most of the Plantagenet and Tudor Parliaments gives evidence of two features in which this characteristic is exhibited. That in regard to Parliamentary times and seasons the Irish practice corresponded with the English is shown by the coincidence of the dates and periods of the Parliamentary session with the terms of the law courts; while the influence of the early practice in England in determining the place at which Parliaments should be held, is shown in the peripatetic character of the High Court of Parliament, which may be described as having in early times gone on circuit almost as regularly as the judges. The latter fashion, indeed, prevailed even as late as Tudor times, for it was not until Elizabeth's reign that Dublin became the invariable scene of the deliberations of Parliament. The practice on this point varied, indeed, at different periods. In the earliest period of which there is any clear record, the Parliaments of Edward the Second and the Third were certainly without any fixed place of meeting, and were doubtless summoned pretty much in accordance with the political exigencies of the moment or the convenience of the Viceroy for the time being. Kilkenny, Drogheda, and Trim were favourite venues with the Plantagenet Deputies; but Parliament also sat in places now of no importance, such as Castledermot in Kildare, and Baldoyle,[1] within a very short distance of Dublin. Later on, but prior to the Tudor period, it appears to have been enacted that no Parliament should be held elsewhere than in Dublin and Drogheda. Yet in 1541 this limitation, which was probably never very closely observed, was repealed,[2] and the provincial sessions of earlier times again became the

[1] See *Illustrations of Irish History and Topography*, by C. Litton Falkiner, p. 28, note 1.

[2] See Statute 33 Hen. VIII. c. 1, s. 2.

rule rather than the exception in the Parliaments called by the Deputies of Henry the Eighth. Thus Lord Leonard Gray's Parliament [1] sat successively in Dublin, Kilkenny, Cashel, and Limerick. That summoned by Sussex under Queen Mary sat in turn in Dublin, Limerick, and Drogheda; and even as late as 1585 Sir John Perrot's Parliament was prorogued to the last-named town on one occasion, though owing to the want of proper accommodation it never sat there.[2]

It followed from the perambulatory character of its sessions that the Irish Parliament long remained without a definite place of meeting, and Ireland was long without its Westminster. When convened in the country, Parliament usually sat in the great hall of some principal ecclesiastical foundation. Thus the celebrated Parliament of Sir Edward Poynings held its deliberations in the great hall of the Dominican monastery in Drogheda. The earliest Parliaments in Dublin were doubtless held in the long-vanished 'Great Hall' of Dublin Castle, though certain Deputies who happened to be Priors of Kilmainham seem to have summoned the legislators to meet in the equally splendid apartment of the Priory of the Knights Hospitallers at that place. Later, however, and down to post-Restoration times, Christ Church Cathedral was the most usual meeting-place, if not of the whole Parliament, at all events of the House of Commons.[3] Strafford's Parliaments

[1] It held as many as eight sessions between May 1, 1536, and December 20, 1537.

[2] *Calendar of State Papers* (*Ireland*), 1586–88, p. 30, Perrot to Walsingham, February 20, 1585–86.

[3] The Commons most probably sat in Christ Church in the 'Common House.' This building, which is referred to in an Act of Henry VI as 'the Common House within the Cathedral of the Holy Trinity,' may perhaps have been on the site of the 'sumptuous fabric' in the precincts of Christ Church in which the Four Courts were situate in the seventeenth century. See Harris's *History of Dublin*, p. 43; Camden's *Britannia*, p. 1367. As regards the times and hours at which Parliament met, sittings were held every week-day while Parliament was in session, excepting the principal feasts of the Church. The hours, which were from 8 A.M. to 11 A.M. (the afternoons being devoted to Committees), were apparently governed by the difficulty of providing artificial light. Hooker, in his account of the proceedings in Sidney's Parliament, mentions the sitting of the House of Commons till 2 P.M. as quite exceptional. 'The time and day was so far spent above the ordinary hour, being well-nigh two of the clock in the afternoon, that the Speaker and the Court rose up and departed.' This is the nearest approach in Tudor times to an all-night sitting in the Irish House of Commons. Holinshed, vol. vi. p. 345.

were held in Dublin Castle; where, however, the apartments formerly devoted to them had been wrecked thirty years earlier by an accidental explosion of gunpowder, and the Houses of Parliament are described by Sir William Brereton as much meaner than the English House of the same time.[1] The Duke of Ormond was the first Viceroy to hold Parliament in the neighbourhood now associated with the meetings of the Irish legislature. The Restoration Parliament held its sittings in Chichester House, on the site of the famous building erected in 1729; and with the unfortunate exception of James the Second's Parliament, which was held at the King's Inns, College Green was the scene of every meeting of the Irish legislature from the Restoration to the Union.

Except in the case of the entry in the Statute Roll of Henry the Sixth, already cited, there are practically no materials available for a history of the Irish Parliament, from the point of view here contemplated, of earlier date than the sixteenth century. And for the first half of that century the extant documents bearing on the subject are very slight. The State Papers of Henry the Eighth afford, however, a valuable picture of the early constitution of Parliament, and illustrate the manner in which the application of English systems to Ireland is apt to preserve forms and institutions in that country to a date long after that at which they fell into desuetude in England. Thus it was not until the Parliament of 28th Henry VIII, held by Lord Leonard Gray, that the clerical proctors were adjudged to have ceased to possess the right of participating in the legislative functions of the Irish Parliament. In England clerical proctors had originally formed part of the representatives of the spiritual estate; but there is no record of the date at which, if they ever possessed them, the proctors had ceased to exercise legislative rights. Long before the Tudor era they had ceased to be summoned to Parliament, their Parliamentary privileges having merged in those which they possessed as members of Convocation. In Ireland, however, it appears to have been otherwise. 'At every Parliament

[1] See *Illustrations of Irish History and Topography*, by C. Litton Falkiner, p. 380.

begun and holden within this land,' to quote the language of the statute by which the proctorial rights were extinguished, 'two proctors of every diocese within the same land have been used and accustomed to be summoned and warned to be of the same Parliament.' Whether they were present in a purely consultative capacity, or were deemed to possess like legislative powers with the lay members, is a matter of some doubt. It is certain, however, that their rights in this regard were not considered absolutely obsolete and incapable of revival. In the endeavour to defeat the ecclesiastical legislation of Henry the Eighth's Irish Ministers, the opponents of the royal policy were fain to resort to the proctorial vote as a Parliamentary weapon. It was claimed that the proctors had a like status in the House of Commons with that enjoyed by the prelates in the House of Peers, and their complete equality with the Commons was asserted. The spiritual peers in the Upper House even went the length of declining to consider the bills sent up by the Lower until they should be assured that the concurrence of the proctors had been obtained. However extravagant such a claim may have been, it could hardly have been seriously put forward had the Parliamentary functions of the proctors faded to the insignificant and subordinate point which they had reached in England, where the heads of the Church in a like contingency at Westminster had not ventured to do more than mildly petition that the clergy of the Lower House of Convocation might 'be adjoined and associate with the Lower House of Parliament.'[1] It was, however, too late in the day, even in Ireland, to procure the effective revival of the legislative status of the proctors. The Deputy referred the constitutional question to the judges, who reported that the proctors had no voice in Parliament, and that even were it otherwise, their voice might be ignored, since there was abundant evidence of the passing of many Acts of Parliament notwithstanding that, as it was recorded, 'procuratores cleri non consenserunt.'[2] The result of the

[1] Stubbs's *Constitutional History of England*, iii. 462.

[2] Gray and Brabazon to Cromwell, May 18, 1537, *State Papers, Henry VIII*, vol. ii. pt. iii. p. 438.

abortive claim thus put forward was to put a final and formal end to the proctorial vote. For the Deputy, urging that the effect of their interposition would be to give them 'such a pre-eminence in Parliament that though the King, Lords and Commons assent to an Act, the Proctors in Convocation House (though they were but eight or nine in number, as sometimes they be here no more) shall stay the same at their pleasure, be the matter never so good, honest, and reasonable,' at once brought in legislation to put an end to their jurisdiction. A bill 'against proctors to be any members of Parliament' was accordingly passed, which deprived the proctors of any voice in the proceedings of the legislature, declaring that they 'should not be accepted, reputed, deemed or taken as parcel or any member of the said Parliament, but only as counsellors to the same.'[1] The period thus put to the legislative functions of the proctors as representatives of the clergy was no more than the inevitable result of the challenge of the prelates. The latter had attempted to enforce a constitutional anachronism, and Parliament did no more than formulate a declaration of what in England had already become settled constitutional practice. It is difficult to see any warrant for the view put forward recently that the Act against proctors was part of a deliberate scheme to limit the powers of Parliament, and that the abolition of 'the Second Estate of the Realm' constituted the second step in 'the reduction of the Irish Parliament.[2]

It is in connexion with the sessions of the Second Parliament of Elizabeth, which assembled in January 1569, that we meet with the first authentic evidence of Parliamentary manners and customs. Of the first meeting of this legislature several notices survive. The historian Campion chanced to be living in Dublin, in the family of Speaker Stanihurst, at the time of the assembling of the Parliament, which met at Christ Church Cathedral in response to the summons of the Lord Deputy. To Campion accordingly we are indebted for an authentic report of the speech of the Lord Deputy, Sir

[1] Statute 28 Henry VIII. c. 12.
[2] *The Closing of the Irish Parliament*, by John Roche Ardill, LL.D.

Henry Sidney, at the opening of the Parliament, and of the Speaker to the Lord Deputy.[1] But there are much more detailed references to the same Parliament in two documents which were lately found. They contain respectively the evidence of an independent spectator of the ceremonies attending the opening of the Parliament, and the diary of its session kept by one of its members. The first of these documents is a 'List of the Lords Spiritual and Temporal in the Irish Parliament 1568–9,'[2] which not only preserves for us the roll of the peers summoned to that assembly, but includes several interesting particulars of a picturesque and personal kind. The recorder of these details was one Robert le Commaundre, Rector of Tarporley in Cheshire, and a *protégé* apparently of the Lord Deputy.[3] He was, as appears from the other contents of the commonplace book from which this record is taken, an antiquary with heraldic leanings, closely interested in the minutiæ of ceremonial, and his observations

[1] Campion had come over as a tutor to young Richard Stanihurst, the Speaker's son. Residing in the Speaker's house, he was, as he states in the preface to his History, in 'such familiar societie, and daylie table-talke with the worshipfull Esquire, James Stanihurst, Recorder of Dublin,' that he knew everything that went on. Campion was present at the prorogation of Parliament at the close of the first session. His summary of what passed on that occasion is the first conscious attempt at reporting the proceedings of an Irish Parliament, and Campion gives this account of his work as reporter :—'The day of prorogation, when the Knights and Burgesses of the Commonalty resorted to the Lordes of the Upper House, much good matter was there uttered between the Deputy and the Speaker, whereof comming home to my lodging I took notes, and here I will deliver them as neere as I can call them to minde, in the same words and sentences that I heard them.' The principal matter of these orations related to educational topics, Stanihurst felicitating his audience on the passing of the Act for the erection of Free Grammar Schools (12 Elizabeth, cap. 1), while regretting that 'our hap is not to plant yet an University here at home.' Campion's *History of Ireland*.

[2] See Appendix B.

[3] To the compiler's own description of himself as Rector of Tarporley and Chaplain to Sir Henry Sidney, little information can be added. Tarporley is a small town about midway between Chester and Crewe, which lay directly on the road from London to Holyhead, and through which, in the sixteenth century, as Commaundre records in some notes to a list of the Lord Lieutenants and Deputies of Ireland, the Viceroys were in the habit of passing with their retinues on their way to Ireland. Whether or not it was in this way that Commaundre made the acquaintance of Sir Henry Sidney, it is certain that he accompanied that nobleman to Dublin, in 1568, in the capacity of chaplain, and was a witness of the proceedings at the opening of the Parliament in Christ Church, on January 17 of that year. He does not appear to have remained long in Ireland. Unlike a good many viceregal chaplains of that age, he did not reach the Irish Episcopal Bench, but died Rector of Tarporley in 1613. He did, however, profit by the pluralism which was so common in his time,

have the air of careful and accurate notes. The descriptive part of Commaundre's document, presenting the scene in the House of Lords on the opening day, is curious, and is better given in his own words:

'The Lord Deputy of Ireland sat under the cloth of estate in his robes of crimson velvet, representing the Queen's Majesty's most royal person. Item, Robert Weston, doctor of laws, and Dean of the Cathedral Church of St. Patricks Dublin, Lord Chancellor of Ireland, sat on the right of the said Lord Deputy. Item Thomas Butler, Earl of Ormond and Ossory, Viscount Thurles, High Treasurer of Ireland, sat on the left of the said Lord Deputy. Memorandum that these two lords sat severally above by themselves, one either side of the said Lord Deputy, having their seats enrailed about, and hanged or covered with green; and the said Lord Deputy had steps or greeses [stairs] made and covered for the seat of estate, being richly hanged. . . . Memorandum that the Chief Justices of the one bench and the other, the Chief Baron, the Master of the Rolls, and the Queen's Majesty's Attorney-General and her Highness' Solicitor, did sit together at a table in the midst of the Parliament House. Memorandum that Mr. Stanihurst, Recorder of the City of Dublin, was Speaker of the Lower House, and did wear for his upper garment, when the Lord Deputy sat in the higher house under the cloth of estate, a scarlet gown; and this Mr. Stanihurst was a very wise man and a good member of the Commonwealth of Ireland.'

The presence of the Lord Chancellor and the High Treasurer at the opening ceremony as late as Elizabethan times is a fresh illustration of the conservatism of Irish usage. For in the Plantagenet Parliaments these functionaries appear to have enjoyed a similar precedence: the preamble to early Acts of the Irish Parliament commonly reciting that the legislature was constituted of 'the Deputy, the Chancellor and Treasurer,

being appointed Rector and Prebendary of the Parish of Kilmactalway, County Dublin, and Vicar of Bodenstown, County Kildare. But that Commaundre did not account the personal charge of these cures as necessarily obligatory on him, appears from a bond executed on March 14, 1570–71, wherein he acknowledges himself indebted to one John Thomas in the sum of £100, in consideration whereof he made over to Thomas for the term of his own life both the parsonage of Kilmactalway, with its prebend, and the vicarage of Bodenstown 'frank and free, without payment of any rent.'—Morrin's *Calendar of Patent and Close Rolls in Ireland*, ii. 639.

and all the lords spiritual and temporal, and the King's Council in Ireland.' The presence of the chief judges and the law officers of the Crown was in conformity with contemporary practice at Westminster, it being customary in the Parliaments of the Tudor sovereigns for the more eminent legal and judicial functionaries to attend the opening ceremony in their robes.

The second manuscript referred to above is a brief narrative of the proceedings of the same Parliament in the form of a diary kept by John Hooker, the well-known contributor to Holinshed.[1] Like Henry Flood two centuries later, Hooker enjoyed a seat in the English House of Commons as well as in the Irish one, sitting for the city of Exeter in the former and for the ancient borough of Athenry in the latter. His experience in the first capacity was of much value to him in the second, at a period when it was sought to improve upon the previously irregular methods in vogue in Dublin, and to conform more closely to the English method. It was in aid of this endeavour that Hooker, who was not merely a member of the English House of Commons, but a well-known authority on matters of form and procedure, drew up for the information of his fellow-members at Dublin the book of the orders of the Parliaments used in England which, as already mentioned, is printed in Holinshed. But in addition to this service to his contemporaries, Hooker has left for the benefit of posterity a diary of the proceedings of Sir Henry Sidney's Parliament, which, though brief, may be fairly enough described as the first extant Journal of the Irish House of Commons.[2] For though only relating to the doings of the first session of this Parliament, it is a manifestly accurate record of the business transacted, and contains exact particulars of matters not ascertainable in the case of any other of the Tudor Parliaments. The diarist was at pains to set down, for example, the figures of the divisions which took place on the principal questions debated, and thus not only to supply us with particulars of the first recorded divisions of the Irish House of

[1] Hooker, who was an uncle of the eminent theologian, Judicious Hooker, had come to Ireland in connexion with Sir Peter Carew's litigation about his Irish estates.

[2] See Appendix C.

Commons, but to give us some insight into the state of parties at the time. Hooker also throws valuable light upon the functions discharged by the judges in relation to the deliberations of Parliament. It is noteworthy that in Sidney's Parliament, as in that of which Sir John Davis was Speaker nearly half a century later, much of the time of the House was devoted to the discussion of constitutional issues, such as the validity of the sheriff's returns to the writs of summons, and the title of certain members to be returned to Parliament. It was in respect of this topic that the opinion of the judges was required; and it is noticeable that the matter having been referred to the judges' decision, the House declined to accept the account of their judgment returned by the Lord Deputy through the Speaker. Even when the Attorney-General came down to the House with a like announcement of its purport, the majority were still dissatisfied, and required the presence of the judges themselves, who were accordingly obliged to appear and declare their opinions in person.

But by far the most important result of an analysis of the constitutional history of Ireland as disclosed in such fragmentary notices of the Tudor Parliament as have come down to us is the conclusion it enables us to reach as to the true origin of the remarkable enactment known as Poynings' Law, the circumstances which led to the introduction of that measure, and the motives which induced the Irish Parliament not merely to acquiesce in its adoption, but to insist on its retention in the Statute Book. Paradoxical as it may appear, it is nevertheless the case that this celebrated measure, which is commonly adverted to as the first attempt of the English governors of Ireland to shackle the independence of its Parliament, really originated in the desire of that Parliament to limit the authority of the Deputies appointed by the Crown. And not only was this so in relation to the origin of the measure, but it remained the view of its object and effect which continued to be held for many generations and in successive Parliaments by the national party in the Irish legislature. It is worth while to consider the course of events, both as regards the original inception of Poynings' Law and its subsequent operation, in the light of the information which the State Papers and other recently discovered evidence have made available.

The immediate occasion of the limitation which was placed by Poynings' Act on the power of the Irish executive to initiate legislation is to be found in the dissatisfaction engendered in Ireland by the manner in which the Deputies of the later Plantagenet sovereigns had exercised the powers previously vested in them. From the accession of Edward the Fourth —that is, for more than a generation prior to the government of Sir Edward Poynings—none of the eminent personages nominated to the great office of Lord Lieutenant had personally visited the seat of their government. Power had fallen into the hands of the Deputies to whom the executive authority was confided; and these Deputies had been exclusively chosen either from the heads of the Irish nobility of the Pale and its environs, or from the higher ecclesiastics. The government was thus in exclusively Irish hands, and the nominal authority in England made no attempt to control the action of its subordinates. But, as has often happened since, the surrender of English power to Irish instruments was far from giving universal satisfaction in Ireland. Each new Deputy had his own axe to grind, and he usually sharpened it at the expense of his personal enemies. The history of Ireland under the sovereigns of the House of York, as disclosed in the unpublished statutes, is in a great degree the story of the rivalry between the great Houses of Butler and FitzGerald, varied only by the occasionally successful assertion of the ambition of such lesser lords of the Pale as the heads of the Barnewall family. The statutes of Edward the Fourth offer conclusive evidence of the extent to which the Earls of Kildare during the period of their practically uncontrolled rule utilised Parliament for purely personal objects and made it the instrument of family aggrandisement. Accordingly, after the troublesome experience of the Simnel business, and the crowning of 'the ladde,' as one of the Irish statutes terms the impostor, had obliged the English sovereign to turn his attention to Ireland, and take measures to depress the power of the adherents of the House of York in that country, the ministers of Henry the Seventh had no difficulty in procuring the consent of the Irish Parliament to a law which would deprive future Deputies of the power of initiating legislation on their own account.

Not the least curious feature in the history of the subsequent operation of Poynings' Law is the great inconvenience which it occasioned to the English Government and its corresponding popularity with the anti-English element in the Irish legislature. A law which rendered it impossible to propose legislation until its provisions had first been communicated to the English Government was manifestly likely to hamper administration; and this was quickly found to be its effect. The Deputies of Henry the Eighth had of course no difficulty in arranging the preliminaries of Parliamentary business, and in submitting to the English ministers the legislation which in the first instance they proposed to introduce in Parliament. But it was otherwise with measures of urgent necessity, arising out of unforeseen circumstances. At a time when cross-channel communications were slow, tedious, and uncertain, and when the interchange of dispatches between Dublin and London might occupy a month, the necessity for certifying every item of a proposed new enactment to the English Privy Council before submitting it to the Dublin Parliament was extremely irksome to the executive. Accordingly, it is not surprising to find that when in 1533 it became necessary to call the first of Henry the Eighth's Irish Parliaments, the very first preoccupation of ministers was to devise measures for modifying Poynings' Law. A communication addressed by Audeley, the English Chancellor, to Thomas Cromwell, shows clearly that ministers had to count with strong Irish opposition to any attempt to ignore Poynings' legislation. 'I have seen,' Audeley said, 'the Act made in Ireland in Poynings' time. I do not take that Act as they take it in Ireland; nevertheless . . . I have made a short Act that this Parliament and everything to be done by authority thereof, shall be good and effectual, the said Act made in Poynings' time, or any other Act or usage of the land of Ireland notwithstanding.' [1]

[1] *State Papers, Henry VIII*, vol. i. pt. ii. p. 440.

A measure of this scope was accordingly passed by the Irish Parliament [1] providing that the Acts of Lord Leonard Gray's Parliament should be valid, Poynings' Act notwithstanding. But that this was intended by the Parliament which passed it to be no more than a temporary and limited dispensation, is shown by the fact that the statute, though applicable to legislation required for 'the king's honour, the increase of his Grace's revenues and profits, and the commonweal of the land and dominion of Ireland,' did not sanction legislation relating to private property, or to corporate bodies. Even as so limited the dispensing statute was very unpopular in Ireland, and attempts which were made to restrict its operation still further had to be dealt with by a further Act, declaratory of the true intent of the statute.

The legislation of 1533 seems to have sufficed for the remainder of Henry the Eighth's reign, and no difficulty appears to have arisen as to the true construction of Poynings' Act in the Parliament of 1541. But in 1557 the Earl of Sussex, who held the sole Parliament called in Ireland during Mary's reign, found himself confronted with the same difficulties which had embarrassed the advisers of Lord Leonard Gray. An Act which that Deputy was obliged to bring forward 'declaring how Poynings' Act shall be expounded and taken' [2] shows in its terms the exact nature of the practical difficulty involved in a strict adherence to the statute of Henry the Seventh and the expedient adopted to cure it. 'Forasmuch,' it recites, 'as many events and occasions may happen during the time of the Parliament, the which shall be thought meet and necessary to be provided for, and yet at or before the time of the summoning of the Parliament, was not thought nor agreed upon.' Yet Sussex did no more than provide for the extension of Poynings' Act to legislation formulated during the session of Parliament. He made no attempt to suspend the operation of the law itself, as the Act of 1533 had done; and in the first Parliament of Elizabeth, held while Sussex was still Deputy, though many important measures were submitted, no attempt

[1] Statute 28 Henry VIII, cap. iv.
[2] Statute 3 and 4 Philip and Mary, cap. 4.

was made to infringe or limit what was deemed to be the secure charter of the Parliamentary liberties of Ireland.

Of the views of the Irish Parliaments of Henry the Eighth and Mary in reference to the amendments of Poynings' Act, the indications, though clear enough, are mainly those which the terms of the amending measures themselves supply. But in the case of the Parliament of Sir Henry Sidney, called in 1568, we have the accompaniment of the evidence furnished by Hooker in the narrative and diary already referred to, and by several letters and dispatches which survive in the State Papers of Elizabeth. Although this Parliament did not meet till the close of the year 1568–69, it had been intended that it should have met three years earlier, and authority had been given to the Lord Deputy to summon it, notwithstanding that Elizabeth was herself averse from calling it. Sidney, however, was desirous on financial grounds of calling Parliament together, and wrote requiring the royal sanction. In giving it the Queen used language which, having regard to the subsequent course of events, is not a little remarkable. She relied on the provisions of Poynings' Act to safeguard the Crown from reckless legislation.

'Whereas,' she wrote, 'we understand you are desirous to have authority to call a Parliament, the rather for the receiving of our subsidy there . . . before we assented thereunto we could have been contented to have had advertisement from you what other matters you thought most meet to be commended in the same for the benefit of our service. For, except the same might appear very necessary, we have small disposition to assent to any Parliament. Nevertheless when we call to remembrance the ancient manner of that our realm, that no manner of thing ought to be commended or treated upon, but such as we shall first understand from you, and consent thereunto ourself, and consequently return the same under our great seal of this our realm of England, we are the better minded to assent to this your request. And I authorise you to devise with our council there only of such things as may appear beneficial for us and that our realm.'[1]

[1] *Calendar of State Papers (Ireland)*, 1509–73, p. 324, Elizabeth to Lord Deputy Sidney, January 16, 1567.

But though this language not only has the true touch of Tudor absolutism, but shows that Elizabeth's view of the effect of Poynings' Act was the modern one, it is evident that Sidney's knowledge of the practical difficulties in enforcing it disposed him to take the course which had commended itself to his predecessors, Gray, St. Leger, and Sussex. He refrained from using the authority thus given him, preferring to suspend the law of Poynings, and to rely for the prevention of any untoward consequences and the safeguarding of English interests upon the presence of a large number of English members who should be nominated to sit in the Irish House of Commons for such boroughs as were in the control of the Crown. Accordingly, when, two years after the authority to hold a Parliament had been granted by Elizabeth, Parliament was actually summoned, the Deputy, so far from acting in the manner desired by Elizabeth, caused a bill for the repeal of Poynings' Act to be submitted as the first measure of the Government, and as the preliminary to the initiation of such other measures as the Viceroy and the Irish Privy Council had resolved to introduce. But he quickly found that the state of feeling in the House of Commons remained exactly what it had been shown to be in the Parliaments of Henry the Eighth and Mary; and that Irish opinion still looked to the law of Poynings as the one effective weapon of defence against unpopular measures. In spite, therefore, of the presence in the Dublin Parliament of the numerous English members who had been returned in the Government interest, Sidney's bill to enable the Parliament to deal with measures 'concerning the government of the Commonwealth and the augmentation of Her Majesty's revenues' met with an extremely hostile reception. For when after three or four days' wrangling over the validity of the return of the English members—who were objected to as non-resident in their constituencies—during which, according to the account of an eye-witness, 'the lower house was very disquiet . . . and in some disorder,'[1] the House of Commons proceeded to discuss the bill, the Irish Opposition not only proved unexpectedly formidable, but

[1] Holinshed, vol. vi. p. 343.

increased at every day's sitting in Parliamentary strength till finally it proved to be in a majority.

From Hooker's Diary it appears that the bill passed its first reading without a division, that on its second reading there were 'of the one part forty for the negative, and of the other fifty English for the affirmative,' but that on the third reading 'the said byll of poyninges being redd the third tyme was miche debated and dyscoursed but at lengthe overthrowen, for the polls of thenglysche were forty-four, and of the irishe forty-eight.' Lord Chancellor Weston thus reports to Cecil what was evidently deemed by Sir Henry Sidney and his Irish advisers a great Parliamentary catastrophe:

> 'The first bill that was read was touching the suspending of Poynings' Act; a good and profitable bill, and worthy of much favour; and so we thought it would have found. But it was handled as things are used to be that fall into angry men's hands: without good advice and consideration it was with great earnestness and stomach overthrown and dashed.' [1]

Inconvenient as this rebuff must have been to ministers, it soon appeared that a rigid insistence on the letter of the law on the part of the Irish House of Commons would involve an almost complete paralysis of its legislative functions, unless the Parliament were prepared to accept without the alteration of a syllable the measures which had been approved by the English Privy Council. For it was ruled by the judges that no amendments would be in order, since measures altered in Ireland could no longer be deemed to have been approved in England; and consequently that nothing was open to the Dublin legislature but the acceptance or rejection of the Government bills as drafted. Faced with the alternative of being thus reduced to a position of legislative impotence, the Commons gave way, and Parliament having been formally prorogued to enable the rejected bill to be reintroduced in a fresh session, the measure was passed through all its stages in a single day. Hooker's Diary accordingly contains the

[1] Letter of Lord Chancellor Weston to Cecil, dated February 17, 1569, *State Papers* (*Ireland*), vol. 27, No. 25.

triumphant entry: 'Item on moneday the 21 of february the parliament assembled and that day the act for the repeale of ponynges act was passed and then the parlament proroged tyll the wenesday.'

But though thus driven to consent to the suspension of the Act, the Irish Parliament took effective measures to insist upon the principle underlying Poynings' Law, and to mark their belief in its importance as a security against the abuse of viceregal power they passed an Act 'that there be no bill certified into England for the repeal or suspending of the statute passed in Poynings' time before the same bill be first agreed on in a session of a Parliament holden in this realm by the greater number of the lords and commons.'[1] The position thus taken up by the Irish legislature with reference to Poynings' Act, and the determination not to permit any relaxation of its provisions, was still more strongly emphasised when in the last Parliament of Elizabeth—that called by Sir John Perrot in 1585—a bill was introduced for the total repeal of this statute. It was pointed out by ministers that the effect of the original Act, coupled with the further measure of 16th Elizabeth, was that Parliament was 'shut up and forbidden to make any law or statute unless the same be first certified into England.' Yet though the Deputy in proposing the repeal intimated his readiness to confer with Parliament touching the heads of any legislation proposed to be brought in, the measure was rejected by the House of Commons by the large majority of thirty-five.[2] And even when Perrot, following Sidney's precedent, prorogued Parliament and submitted the bill in a second session, his proposals were again rejected. It is a somewhat curious circumstance that the earliest divisions of the Irish House of Commons of which there is any record should be those in which successive Parliaments of the sixteenth century declined on patriotic grounds to abrogate the very statute the repeal of which was to become the greatest triumph of Irish patriotism in the eighteenth century.

[1] Statute 11 Elizabeth, c. 8, s. 3.

[2] Letter dated May 27, 1585, from Sir Nicholas White, Master of the Rolls in Ireland, to Burghley, *State Papers* (*Ireland*), vol. 116, No. 56.

It is plain from this analysis of the dealings of the Tudor Parliaments with Poynings' Law that the view commonly entertained of the famous legislation of Henry the Seventh is in a great degree erroneous. It would, of course, be only a very perverse reading of the facts which would find in the Irish support of Poynings' proposal a proof that its author had no intention to fetter the independence of the legislature, or which would attempt to deny either that it was capable of being used for that purpose, or that the long-accepted view of its ultimate operation was a correct appreciation of its legal and practical effect. Whatever the motives which induced the Irish element in the Dublin Parliament to assent to the measure, it remains true that, in Hallam's language, 'by securing the initiative power to the English Council, a bridle was placed in the mouth of every Irish Parliament'; and this, as we have seen, was Elizabeth's own view of the Act. The Irish Parliament, as Lecky puts it,[1] was undoubtedly 'absolutely precluded from originating any legislative measures, and its sole power was that of accepting or rejecting such measures as were laid before it under the sanction of the Great Seal of England.' But what is not less certain than all this is, not only that the bridle was placed in the mouth of the Irish legislature with its own assent, but that it was so placed by its own desire, and that the Irish Parliament long and strenuously resisted its removal. It is clear that, however true it be that Henry the Seventh's advisers had their own reasons, which were pretty certainly not exclusively Irish reasons, for proposing this legislation, there were strong inducements, of a purely Irish and patriotic kind, to lead Irishmen not merely to acquiesce in but to desire it. If it be true that, as the late Dr. Richey put it,[2] 'this, the most disgraceful Act ever passed by an independent legislature . . . bound future Irish Parliaments for three hundred years,' it is equally certain that the same writer's assertion that the measure was 'wrung from the local assembly of the Pale' is a very great exaggeration of the facts. For, as has been shown, it is abundantly

[1] *History of England in the Eighteenth Century*, 2nd edition, vol. iv. p. 358.
[2] *Short History of the Irish People*, p. 232.

proved that for at least one of those three centuries the powerful and sufficient obstacle to the repeal of the disabling Act was the opposition, repeatedly offered and as often vehemently expressed, of the representatives of the patriotic interest in the Irish Parliament.

APPENDICES

APPENDIX A

The Succession of the Speakers of the Irish House of Commons, with Biographical Notices of the early Speakers

In no publication is there any list of the Speakers of the Irish House of Commons. Lascelles' 'Liber Munerum Publicorum Hiberniæ,' to which one naturally turns for such a record, does not, of course, include any record of an office which does not derive directly from the Crown. And that useful compilation, Haydn's 'Book of Dignities,' will also be consulted in vain for a succession of the Irish Speakers. From the Stuart period onwards the names can be collected without much trouble from the Commons Journals; but prior to that time there is no source of information except the State Papers, and one or two chance references in contemporary histories. From these sources the names of the early Speakers in the following list, of each of whom a brief account is appended, have been taken.

During the period for which the succession is complete, from the year 1541 to 1800, there were in all twenty-five elections to the Chair of the House of Commons; but as several Speakers held office in more than one Parliament, the roll of actual Speakers includes no more than eighteen names. Of these the first thirteen were members of the legal profession. This was in accordance with the early precedents in the English Parliament, where the practice of choosing a lawyer for the Chair doubtless originated in the duty formerly cast upon the Speakers of expounding to the House of Commons the purport of the measures laid before it, and the consequent desirability of some legal training in the persons charged with such a task. The invariable choice of a lawyer had perhaps a further justification by analogy to the practice of the House of Lords, of which the Lord

Chancellor was the immemorial Speaker. In times when, as already noted, the championship of the royal prerogative seems to have been one of the primary functions of the Speaker, it became habitual to select not merely a member of the legal profession, but one directly connected with the Government, or, as we should now say, a law officer. Thus of the Tudor and Stuart Speakers, four held the office of Attorney-General, two that of Solicitor-General, and two that of Prime Serjeant; Sir Thomas Cusake had been a Judge of the Common Pleas before his election to the Chair, and Sir Nicholas Walsh was Chief Justice of the Presidency of Munster and Second Justice of the Queen's Bench. There are three examples of the selection of the Recorder of Dublin—those of Stanihurst, Catelyn, and Forster; and the last-named was also Attorney-General at the same time. All three represented the city of Dublin. From the reign of Henry the Eighth to that of Queen Anne the legal tradition remained unbroken; and although from the accession of the House of Hanover to the Union there is no example of the nomination of a Crown lawyer to the Chair, every one of the eighteenth-century Speakers, with a single exception, had been called to the Bar. The exception is eminently one of those which prove the rule, since the case of Speaker Conolly, who filled the Chair during the reign of George the First, is an example which is unique in the Parliamentary history of the Three Kingdoms, of the selection of the first Commoner from the ranks of the solicitors' profession.

An examination of the careers of the legal Speakers subsequent to their election to the Chair shows that the pursuit of politics as a royal road to professional preferment is no very modern practice. Many of them attained to the highest judicial eminence, and almost all of them ultimately ascended the Bench. Three of them—Sir Thomas Cusake, Sir Maurice Eustace, and Alan Brodrick—reached the Woolsack, thus exchanging the Speakership of the House of Commons for that of the House of Lords; and the first-named was also for a time Master of the Rolls. Three—Sir Nicholas Walsh, Sir Richard Levinge, and John Forster—not Lord Oriel, but the Speaker of Queen Anne's time—presided over the Court of Common Pleas; and one Speaker, Rochfort, became Lord Chief Baron.[1] To Stanihurst and Catelyn, who had earned, respectively, the favour of such powerful Viceroys as Sidney and Strafford, the Speakership would

[1] Rochfort was also named one of the three Commissioners of the Great Seal in 1690.

doubtless have proved no more than an episode in their legal careers, had they lived beyond middle age. But both of these Speakers died prematurely. There is no need to dwell on the causes which interfered with the further promotion of Sir Richard Nagle. The case of Sir Audley Mervyn is a solitary example of the neglect of Government to utilise an opportunity of rewarding a Speaker. There appears to have been abundant ground for this omission, if Mervyn was justly suspected of a plot to overturn the Government. But whether he was not promoted because he plotted against the Government, or whether, as is not impossible, he plotted against Government because he was not promoted, it is impossible now to determine.

Speaker Stanihurst is the first Speaker of whose official utterances any trace remains. As already mentioned, Campion has epitomised his speech at the prorogation of the last Parliament over whose deliberations he presided. Richard Stanihurst mentions three of his father's speeches as existing in his time; but these do not appear to be anywhere extant. They may have perished among the lost manuscripts of Stanihurst's distinguished grandson, Archbishop James Ussher. Speaker Walsh's observations at the dissolution of Perrot's Parliament are very fully summarised in the 'Irish State Papers Calendar,'[1] and the remarkable speech of Sir John Davis before Lord Deputy Chichester, which is, of course, a classic among such utterances, has been more than once published. The speeches of the later occupants of the Chair of the House of Commons are noted in the Journals of that House.

The Succession of the Speakers of the Irish House of Commons

1449 John Chever, Master of the Rolls.
1541 Sir Thomas Cusake, Chancellor of the Exchequer.
1557 James Stanihurst, Recorder of Dublin.
1560 James Stanihurst, again elected.
*1569 James Stanihurst, ,, ,,
1585 Sir Nicholas Walsh, Chief Justice of Munster and Second Justice of the Queen's Bench.
*1613 Sir John Davis, Attorney-General.
1634 Sir Nathaniel Catelyn, Recorder of Dublin.
1639 Sir Maurice Eustace, Prime Serjeant.

[1] *Calendar of State Papers (Ireland)*, 1586–88, p. 55.

1661 Sir Audley Mervyn,[1] Prime Serjeant.

1689 Sir Richard Nagle, Attorney-General.

1692 Sir Richard Levinge, Solicitor-General.
1695 Robert Rochfort, Attorney-General.
1703 Alan Brodrick, Solicitor-General.
1710 Hon. John Forster, Recorder of Dublin and Attorney-General.
1713 Alan Brodrick.[2]
1715 William Conolly.
1727 William Conolly, again elected.
1729 Sir Ralph Gore, Bart., Chancellor of the Exchequer.
1733 Henry Boyle, Chancellor of the Exchequer.
1756 John Ponsonby, First Commissioner of Customs and Excise.
*1761 John Ponsonby, again elected.
1769 John Ponsonby, ,, ,,
*1771 Edmund Sexton Pery, afterwards Viscount Pery.
*1776 Edmund Sexton Pery, again elected.
1783 Edmund Sexton Pery, ,, ,,
1785 John Foster, afterwards Lord Oriel.
*1790 John Foster, again elected.
1798 John Foster, ,, ,,

In the above list the office mentioned after the Speaker's name in each case indicates an office held concurrently with the Speakership.

An asterisk prefixed to the date denotes a contested election to the chair. The Speakers not so marked were elected *nemine contradicente*.

Biographical Notices of the early Speakers

John Chever

John Chever, who was twice elected to the Speaker's Chair, was Master of the Rolls at that time, and is in all probability identical

[1] During Sir Audley Mervyn's absence in England in 1661, Sir John Temple, the Solicitor-General, was temporarily elected Speaker.

Temple was designed by the Duke of Ormond for the Speakership in the intended Parliament of 1678, which, however, was never called, as appears by a letter in the Ormonde papers at Kilkenny.

[2] Brodrick vacated the Chair on his appointment in 1710 to the position of Chief Justice of the Queen's Bench. Being dismissed from that office by Harley in the following year, he re-entered the House of Commons in 1713, and was elected Speaker by a majority of four. Brodrick's re-election is perhaps the first instance of the choice of a Speaker in opposition to the wishes of the Court.

with the John Chever who is mentioned in the 'Chartulary of St. Mary's Abbey' as having been Chief Justice of the Chief Place in 1472.[1] He is probably also identical with the John Chever mentioned in a document printed in the 'Council Book of Richard II,'[2] who is described in the year 1442 as of Lincoln's Inn, and a brother of William Chever who was then Second Justice of the King's Bench, and as concerned in the defence of James, fourth Earl of Ormond, against charges of maladministration which had been brought against that nobleman. Chief Justice Chever died in 1474; and his will, dated June 4 of that year, has been printed in Archbishop Tregury's Register of Dublin Wills, 1457–83,[3] so carefully edited by Dr. Berry. Besides legacies to John, sixth Earl of Ormond, it contains bequests of masses for the soul of the testator, and of James, fifth Earl of Ormond, who was Lord Lieutenant in 1453, which seem to indicate that Chever was a *protégé* of the latter nobleman, and probably owed his promotion to his influence.

Sir Thomas Cusake

Sir Thomas Cusake sprang from a stock which, though not ennobled, was among the most ancient families of the Pale—the Cusacks of Cosyneston, or Cussington, in Meath. It had become connected by marriage with more than one of the oldest houses of that county, and had acquired so much property as justified Sir Anthony St. Leger in describing the Speaker as 'a gentilman of the beste possessions of any man of his degre within this your Inglisshe paale.'[4] Cusake's mother appears to have been a Wesley, and his daughter married Sir Henry Colley; so that, if the pedigree given by Sir Bernard Burke may be relied on, the Duke of Wellington was directly descended from the first Speaker of the Assembly of which Arthur Wellesley was one of the youngest and latest members.

Nothing is known of Cusake's early professional career, but there are many evidences of his success in attaining its prizes. In 1535 he first received important preferment, being appointed a Judge of the Common Pleas. But he held this office for a very short time, his

[1] *Chartularies of St. Mary's Abbey, Dublin*, ii. p. 24.
[2] *Roll Series, Appendix*, p. 287.
[3] *Register of Wills and Inventories of the Diocese of Dublin in the times of Archbishops Tregury and Walton*, 1457–1483: edited, with Translation, Notes, and Introduction, by Henry F. Berry, D.Litt., I.S.O., p. 146.
[4] *State Papers, Henry VIII*, vol. iii. pt. iii. p. 320.

patent being revoked on his nomination a year later to the Chancellorship of the Exchequer. His tenure of that office in 1536–37 renders it certain that Cusake was a member of the House of Commons in Lord Leonard Gray's Parliament; and it is highly probable, though the fact cannot be demonstrated, that he had his first experience of the Speakership in that Parliament. Cusake's election to the Chair in St. Leger's Parliament took place on June 18, 1541, immediately after the formal opening of the session by the Deputy. We have no record of his conduct in the Chair; but at the end of his first session he was dispatched to England to report its proceedings to Henry the Eighth, St. Leger commending him to his sovereign as 'Speaker of your Parliament here, who hathe taken greate paynes in setting forth of your Highnes causis.'[1] That he acquitted himself on this mission to the satisfaction of the King and his advisers appears by the encomium passed upon him in Henry's letter to the Deputy, in which the Speaker, who was charged with the bringing over of the Acts approved of by the English Privy Council for submission at the next session of Parliament, is commended as 'a man of wit, servyce and good actyvyte, and affeccion to travail in our affayres for the benefyte of the lande.' In token of this good opinion, the Deputy was notified of the royal pleasure that 'immediately after his cummyng home' he should 'swere hym of our Pryvye Counsail there, and so use his advise in all occurrentes accordingly.'[2]

In June 1542, on the elevation of Sir John Alen to the Woolsack, Cusake became Master of the Rolls. It does not appear whether his appointment to this office interrupted his discharge of his Parliamentary duties; but as the Mastership of the Rolls in Ireland at this time, and long subsequently, did not involve the discharge of judicial functions, he probably retained his seat in the House of Commons, and continued to preside over its deliberations. Cusake continued in this post for eight or nine years, until in 1551 he in turn succeeded to the Chancellorship. In 1550 he was temporarily appointed to the custody of the Great Seal, in the absence of Sir John Alen, and a year later was confirmed in his office. The patent appointing him recites the King's approval of 'the wisdom, learning, good experience, and grave behaviour' exhibited by Cusake.

Cusake's elevation to the Chancellorship took place in the third year of Edward the Sixth's reign, and was doubtless the reward of his devotion to Reformation principles. He had asserted his

[1] *State Papers, Henry VIII*, vol. iii. pt. iii. p. 320.
[2] *Ibid.* p. 334.

allegiance to Henry the Eighth's views of the ecclesiastical supremacy of the Crown in his address to the Deputy on his appointment as Speaker; and on the dissolution of the monasteries the Abbey of Lismullen had been assigned to him. Under Henry's successor the Chancellor became a principal pillar of the Reformation in Ireland, and in 1552 was nominated a Lord Justice in the absence of the Deputy. In this capacity he became in effect the principal governor of Ireland for the remainder of the reign. On May 8, 1552, he dispatched to the Duke of Northumberland a 'boke of the present state of Ireland,' containing a minute account of the condition of Ireland. This important State Paper, which has been printed in the 'Calendar of Irish State Papers,'[1] gives us perhaps the best account extant of the state of the provinces and the disposition of the septs during Edward's reign. More than one copy was made of it; and being known to Sir James Ware, it earned for its author the distinction of being included among that great antiquary's 'Writers of Ireland.'

On the accession of Mary, Cusake was for a time continued in the Chancellorship. But he had been too closely identified with the policy of Edward the Sixth's advisers to be suffered to remain in power; and in 1555 he had to give place to Sir William Fitzwilliam. Being then stripped of judicial office, Cusake resumed his Parliamentary career, and in the two Parliaments of Sussex, in 1557 and 1559–60, was again a member of the House of Commons. In the latter he was returned for Athenry, and appears to have been thought of as a possible Speaker by Sussex, though Stanihurst was in the end preferred to him.[2] It is curious that, though he survived until 1571, and was much employed in Elizabeth's reign under the Governments of Sussex and Sidney, Cusake never again received legal preferment. Archbishop Curwen, who succeeded Fitzwilliam after a few months, retained the Chancellorship after Mary's death; and although, in view of the Archbishop's expected death or resignation in 1563, Cusake was designated as Lord Chancellor, on the recommendation of Sussex, yet when the vacancy actually occurred three years later his claims were overlooked by Sidney, who

[1] 1509–73, p. 126.

[2] See a document printed in the *Hatfield Papers*, part iii. p. 459, in which it is stated by the writer that 'Cusack or Stanhurst will be fit to be speaker.' This document, which is conjecturally dated by the editor of the Calendar, 1589, manifestly belongs to 1559, and was written by Sussex in view of the approaching session of Parliament. From its mention of Scurlocke as Attorney-General, the document cannot be of later date than 1559, since Scurlocke died in that year.

appointed Robert Weston. The ex-Chancellor remained, however, an active member of the Irish Privy Council, undertaking several expeditions through the country, and reporting his observations to England. He frequently corresponded with Cecil, to whom he wrote in 1566 that his services in Munster would not be forgotten for a hundred years.[1] Cusake died at his seat of Lismullen on April 1, 1571, and was buried in the parish church of Tryvett, Co. Meath. His son Robert became in 1560 a Baron of the Exchequer, but died before his father in 1570.

Some account of Cusake is given in the 'Dictionary of National Biography' (vol. xiii. p. 355), where his birth year is stated as 1490, for which no authority is given, but without any mention of his having been Speaker. A very full biography of him, in which his lineage and antecedents are minutely traced, appears in O'Flanagan's 'Lives of the Lord Chancellors of Ireland' (vol. i. pp. 207–37). The State Papers of Henry the Eighth contain very numerous references to Cusake; and he is also frequently mentioned in the general 'Calendar of Irish State Papers.'

James Stanihurst

In contrast to his predecessor in the Chair of the House of Commons, Stanihurst belonged to a family long settled in the city of Dublin, and closely associated with the commerce of the Irish capital. Both the father of the Speaker, Nicholas, and his grandfather, Richard Stanihurst, held the office of Mayor of Dublin, the latter in 1489, and the former in 1542. Nicholas Stanihurst is described in the list of churchwardens of St. Werburgh's, Dublin, as a public notary; but he seems to have dabbled in medicine, and is counted by Ware in his list of Irish writers as the author of a Latin treatise entitled 'Dieta Medicorum.' One John Stanihurst, who was Archdeacon of Kells early in the fifteenth century, was probably of the same family.

The connexion of his father and family with the city was the means of procuring for Stanihurst his first professional advancement. He was little more than thirty, and cannot have been many years at the Bar, when, in 1554, he was appointed to act as deputy during the illness of the Recorder of Dublin, Thomas FitzSimon, with the reversion of the office so soon as it should become actually vacant. A few months later, on the death of FitzSimon, he was formally

[1] *Calendar of State Papers* (*Ireland*), 1509–73, p. 296.

appointed Recorder.[1] It was, perhaps, fortunate for Stanihurst that the tenure given him was for life, for it would appear from the action of the city assembly when appointing his successor that his absorption in political and other affairs was somewhat resented. This can hardly be deemed surprising, since within a few years, as appears from various Fiants, Stanihurst was appointed successively to the positions of Clerk of the Crown in Chancery, Seneschal of Esker, Master in Chancery, Customer of Dublin, and General Escheator. His successor in the office of Recorder was, therefore, appointed only 'durynge the good wyll and pleasure of the assemblye'; was required to 'be resydent and keape his contynuall dwellinge within the lymyttes and fraunches' of the city; and was enjoined not to 'receave office of the prynce, ne yearelye fee or annuytie.'[2]

It was within three years of his appointment to the Recordership that Stanihurst was first returned to Parliament, where he represented the city with which he was so closely identified. Of his first election to the Parliament of Philip and Mary, called by Sussex in 1557, there is no record. Nor have we any account of the circumstance of his election to the Chair of the House of Commons, for which not merely his legal training, but his association with Dublin, the long connexion of his family with its neighbourhood, and his consequent acquaintance with the principal members from the Pale, doubtless rendered him an appropriate choice. It is curious to find that concurrently with the Speakership Stanihurst also held, in the three Parliaments of 1557, 1559, and 1568, the office of Clerk of the

[1] The terms of the Recorder's oath of office are given in Gilbert's *Dublin Corporation Records*, vol. i. p. 250, from the Dublin Chain Book, and are worth reproducing :—

'The oath yeven by Mr. Patrick Sarsfeld, Maior of this cittye of Dublin, unto James Stanyhurst, the Recorder of the said cittye, the xviiith daye of January, in the first and second yeres of the reignes of our soverain lord King Phillip, and of our soverain lady Queen Mary :

'First you shall sweare to be faithfull and true unto our soveraigne lord, the King, and to our soverain lady, the Queen, King and Queen of England, France and Ireland, their heirs and successours for evermore. You shall geve your faithfull and true counsaill unto the Maior of this cittye for the tyme beinge, as a Recorder should doe, and shall at all tymes annswer hym for counsaill without lawful impediment. You shall justly and truely minister justice unto all the King's and Queen's subjects that shall have to doe before you, and in right and true manner execute all and singular things appertaining and belonging to the office of Recorder of this cittye. These and all other things for the King's majestie and Queene's weale, and the weale of this cittie, to your power you shall keape, doo and execute. Soe God you helpe, and by the holy contents of this book.'

[2] *Ibid.* vol. ii. pp. 85, 86.

Parliaments in the Upper House—a position which his father had filled in St. Leger's Parliament of 1541. Unless the two Houses sat on separate days, it is plain that Stanihurst can only have discharged the duties of this office through a deputy.

Stanihurst died in Dublin on December 27, 1573, in his fifty-first year. His will, dated a week earlier, is in the Dublin Record Office. His son, Richard Stanihurst, the well-known translator of Virgil, and author of the Description of Ireland in Holinshed, who is the chief authority for the facts of the Speaker's career, states that he 'wrote in English the three "orations" which it fell to his lot as Speaker to address to the Lords Deputies Sussex and Sidney.' From the son's language it is to be inferred that these survived the Speaker, either in print or manuscript; but except for Campion's report of the last of them in his History, they have not come down to us. Richard Stanihurst's references to his father are couched in a strain of affectionate admiration; and the Latin verses he composed in his honour will be found in his 'Description of Ireland.'

It would appear, too, from the few independent references to him which survive, that the Speaker's was a very interesting personality. Campion's remarks, too, are couched in a strain which indicates that that very able writer was greatly impressed with the ability and character of the Speaker, in whose house in Dublin the author of the History of Ireland for a time resided. In acknowledging the assistance he received from the Speaker in writing his History, Campion dwells with evident affection on Stanihurst's character:—'Notwithstanding as naked and simple as it [Campion's narrative] is, it could never have grown to any proportion in such post-haste, except I had entered into such familiar societie, and daylie table-talke with the worshipfull esquire James Stanihurst, Recorder of Dublin. Who besides all curtesie of hospitalitie, and a thousand loving turnes not here to be recited, both by word and written monuments, and by the benefit of his owne Library nourished most effectually mine endeavour.' According to his son, Stanihurst, besides being learned in the business of his profession, was 'a good orator and a proper divine.' His claim to the former character is vindicated by his official addresses as Speaker. Two specimens of his writings remain to testify to the extent of his theological learning. But the title of a lost Latin work, 'Piae Orationes,' and his correspondence with O'Heirnan, Dean of Cork, whom Ware describes as a learned divine, suggest that this erudite

Speaker was an appropriate ancestor to the great Archbishop Ussher. A short account of Speaker Stanihurst is prefixed to the notice of his better-known son, Richard, in the 'Dictionary of National Biography' (vol. liv. p. 89).

SIR NICHOLAS WALSH

Of the Speaker of Perrot's Parliament much less is known than of either of his predecessors in the Chair of the House of Commons. No particulars of a personal kind seem to be now recoverable concerning his career; and it does not appear whether he was related to an eminent namesake who became Bishop of Ossory in 1577, and who was murdered at Kilkenny in 1585. Nicholas Walsh was, however, eminently successful in the pursuit of the legal profession, in which he held successively a number of important offices. His first judicial position was that of Second Justice of the Presidency Court of Munster, to which he was appointed in 1571, during Sir John Perrot's administration of that province. Five years later he was raised to the Chief Justiceship of the same Court. In 1585 he was nominated Second Justice of the King's Bench. Three years later he was sworn of the Irish Privy Council. The Queen's letter directing his appointment states that 'Nicholas Walsh, having been here in this realm about such suits and causes as concerned his private estate, now departs hence with our good favour, for that we are not ignorant how long and faithfully he hath served us as our Chief Justice of Munster, and now likewise in the second Justiceship of our bench at Dublin.' But, though the letter does not mention it, the Privy Councillorship must have been intended mainly as the reward of Walsh's services as Speaker in 1585–86; for in that capacity, as the tone of his 'oration' at the dissolution of Perrot's Parliament indicates, he had shown his allegiance to the Tudor view of the Speaker's office, and had steadily vindicated the prerogatives of the Crown. This speech is very fully summarised in the 'Calendar of State Papers.'[1] His 'diligence in Parliament' had, however, been expressly recognised by a grant of £40 in lands. Walsh doubtless owed his selection for the Chair by Perrot to the acquaintance he had previously had with the Deputy when the latter filled the office of President of Munster; and it may have

[1] *Calendar of State Papers* (*Ireland*), 1586–88, pp. 55–58.

been with a view to this selection that Walsh was transferred to the King's Bench the year before the meeting of Parliament.

In 1597 Walsh was appointed to the Chief Justiceship of the Common Pleas, and held this office till his death. In the same year he received the honour of knighthood through the Lord Justice, Sir Thomas Norris. He appears to have been in the confidence of Sir John Davis, and was frequently sent on special commissions to Munster. His report on the circuit of 1606 to the Earl of Salisbury has been printed from the 'State Papers' in the present writer's 'Illustrations of Irish History and Topography,' p. 141. Walsh died in Dublin in April 1615. His will, dated March 9, 1613, is at the Record Office.

APPENDIX B

List of the Lords Spiritual and Temporal in the Irish Parliament, 1568–69 [1]

The Names of all the Noble men as well Spiritual as Temporal, which were summoned to appear at a parliament holden at the City of Dublin within her Majesty's realm of Ireland xvij° die Januarij Anno Dñi 1568 et regni dñe nrẽ Regine Elizabeth undecimo, Sir Henry Sydney, knight of the most noble order of the Garter, Lord President of Wales, then Lord Deputy of the said Realm of Ireland.

The said Lord Deputy of Ireland sat under the Cloth [of] Estate in his robes of crimson velvet, representing the Queen's Majesty's most royal person.

Item, Robertus Weston, Legum Doctor ac Decanus ecclie cathis Sci Patricij Dublyn, dns Cancellarius regni Hibernie, Qui assidebat a dextris dicti dni deputati.

Item, Thomas Butler alias Beckett [*sic*] Comes Ormond et Ossorye, vicecomes Thurles, magnus Thesaurarius Hibernie, Qui assidebat in sinistris dicti dni deputati.

Md that these two lords sat severally above by themselves, one either side of the said Lord Deputy, having their seats enrailed about, and hanged or covered with green, and the said Lord Deputy had steps or greeses made and covered for the seat of estate, being richly hanged.

Archiepiscopi et Episcopi

Archiepiscopus Armachaneñ Metropolitanus et tocius Regni Hibernie Primas

[1] The document is contained in a manuscript volume entitled *The Book of Heraldrye and other things, together with the Order of Coronacions.*—Egerton MS. (British Museum), 2642, No. 29 (fo. 282).

Dn̄s Archiepiscopus Dublyn
Dn̄s Archiepiscopus Casshallencis
Dn̄s Archiepiscopus Tuameñ Tomoneñ
Episcopus Midencis et Li
Episcopus Waterfordeñ et Limoreñ
Epũs Corkageñ et Cloneñ
Epũs Ossoriensis et Kilkenencis
Epũs Killdareñ
Epũs Elphinencis
Epũs Duanencis
Eꝑus Rosseñ
Eꝑus Clonforteñ
Eꝑus Ferneñ
Eꝑus Leiglinencis
Eꝑus Aladeneñ
Eꝑus Duneñ et Conneren aɫs Conn̄eñ
Eꝑus Arfertensis
Eꝑus Limerecencis
Eꝑus Ardachadeñ
Eꝑus Dromoreñ
Eꝑus Rapoteñ
Eꝑus Cloghrensis
Eꝑus Cluaneñ

} Archiēpi et Eꝑi xxiiij

DOMINI TEMPORALES

Comes Kildarie Admirallus Hibernie
Comes Ormonde Thesaurarius Hibernie
Comes Desmonde
Comes Tyron
Comes Clanricard
Comes Tomond
Comes Clincarre
Vicecomes Barrye
Vicecomes Roche
Vicecomes Gormanston
Vicecomes Baltinglas
Vicecomes Mountgarret
Vicecomes Deyesses

} Comites et Vicecomites xiij

Barones

Dominus de Kyrrey
Dominus Brymecham de Athrye
Dñs de Athynrii als Athanrye
Dñs Coursey dñs de Kynsale
Dñs Newgent Baron de Delven
Dñs Flemyng Baro de Slane
Dñs Plonckett Baro de Killyne
Dñs de St. Lawrencio Baro de Hothe
Dñs Barnewell Baro de Trymellston
Dñs Plonckett Baro de Donsannye
Dñs de Dongañon
Dñs de Donboyne
Dñs Plonckett Baro de Lowthe
Dñs de Kelleene
Dñs Michellpatricke als Barnaby Fitzpatricke Baro de Upper Osserey
Dñs Curraghmore
Dñs Powre als Powar
Dñs de Cahyre
Dñs obreyne Baro de Ibrecane
Dñs Garrott Baro de Offalley
Dñs Butler
Dñs de Fermoye

Summa Baronum xxij°[1]

Md that the Chief Justices of the one Bench, and the other, the Chief Baron, the Master of the Rolls, and the Queen's Majesty's Attorney General and her Highness' Solicitor, did sit altogether at a table in the myddes of the parliament house.

[1] Writing under date December 19, 1905, Mr. G. D. Burtchaell, Athlone Pursuivant, says: 'It seems to me that Commaundre endeavoured to reproduce from memory the official list which was, no doubt, as on previous and subsequent occasions, prepared by Ulster King of Arms. The Earls and Viscounts are right enough, but Viscount "Deyesses'" Patent was not passed till 31st January, a fortnight after Parliament met. This is, however, not of much importance, as the Queen's letter was dated several months previously, and his name may therefore have been entered as a Viscount on the Official Roll. But the list of Barons is certainly not in accordance with any possible Official Roll. There is no precedent for placing "Dominus de Kyrrey" first. The next two on the list, "Dominus Brymecham de Athrye" and "Dñs de Athynrii als Athanrye," refer to one and the same person. "Dñs de Dongañon" is

M^r that Mr. Stanhurst, Recorder of the city of Dublin, was Speaker of the lower house, and did wear for his upper garment, when the Lord Deputy sat in the higher house under the cloth of estate, a scarlet gown; and this Mr. Stanhurst was a very wise man, and a good member of the Commonwealth of Ireland.

Hugh O'Neill, whose right to the Earldom of Tyrone had not at this date been decided, so "Comes Tyron" among the Earls was an empty title with no person representing it in this Parliament. "Dn̄s de Kelleene" must be the same as "Dn̄s Plonckett Baro de Killyne" who appears higher up. "Dn̄s Curraghmore" and "Dn̄s Powre aℓs Powar" are one and the same person. The last four names on this list are peculiar: "Dn̄s obreyne Baro de Ibrecane" was the eldest son of the Earl of Thomond, and was not a peer. Possibly he might have been summoned to Parliament in his father's Barony, but in the absence of any evidence on this point, I do not think it likely. The next name, however, there can be no doubt about. "Dn̄s Garrott Baro de Offalley," the eldest son of the Earl of Kildare, was then only nine years of age, so he cannot have been summoned as a Baron. It was usual, however, for the train of the Chief Governor on proceeding to Parliament (on subsequent occasions) to be borne by the sons of Peers. I am therefore of opinion that Lord Ibricken and Lord Offaly were present, or were summoned, to act in that capacity. The last two names also probably refer to sons of Peers. The Lord Butler, probably the eldest son of Viscount Mountgarret, and "Dn̄s de Fermoye," eldest son of Viscount Roche. Of course Viscounts' sons were not known as "Lords," but Commaundre may be excused for not knowing this. I may also observe in addition to the Earldom of Tyrone being vacant, the Earl of Desmond was at this time in durance in the Tower of London, but that of course would not prevent his name appearing on the Roll. The list of Bishops is peculiar inasmuch as Elphin and Clonfert were at this date held by Roland de Burgo, who on the Roll of the previous Parliament is rightly described as "Clonferteñ et Elphineñ." "Duanencis" I take it is for "Duacensis" (Kilmacduagh), but that See was then held in commendam by the Archbishop of Tuam.'

APPENDIX C

John Hooker's Diary, or Journal, January 17 to February 23, 1568–69[1]

Md that one mone[day, the 17th of January, 1568–9] 17
the parlament beganne [in
Robert weston [
court adiorned vntyll the thurs[day following]
wch thursday beinge the xxth of Januarie [20
was assembled and there accordinge to the [
dyd chose theire speker namely Mr James [Stanihurst] Recorder of Dublin who forthwth was presented to the L. depute & made his oration before him, wch L: deputie awnswered verie eloquentlye.

On friday greate contention did growe yn the lower house, by 21
Sr chrestopher barnewell[2] & others of meth who thought not that assembly to be lauffull for sundry causses, fyrst because that some burgesses were returned for suche townes as were no corporations, then that some beinge shiriffes of countyes & some maiors of townes had named & apoynted them selffes, but specially because there were a number of englysshe m[embers] returned for burgesses whom the saide Irish m[embers] wolde not admytt because they were resyaunt [without] the townes for wch they were chosen. These [matters] were had yn greate questyon & miche stomake [dyd] growe thereof & dyd contynew from the [same] fryday vntyll the Twesday 25
folowenge the 29[th of] Januarie: at wch day the matter being before [referred] to the L. depute & Judges of the realme, the speker being sent to the saide L. depute for resolucion brought awnswere that it was concluded by the L. depute, that all suche shiriffes or maiors as had returned them selffes, and also all such burgesses as were for no corporatt townes sholde be dysmyssed out of the house /

[1] MS. Mm. 1, 32, Cambridge University Library.

[2] Sir Christopher Barnewall of Turvey, who was probably M.P. for Co. Dublin. See an interesting account of him in Lodge's *Peerage*, edited by Archdall, under Viscount Kingsland.

but as for the resydew w^{ch} [were not resident] notwthstanding they beinge returned [by the maiors and shiriffs] might sytt there lawfully so [ ] if any wolde fre them, upon the [ ] answere they wolde not credytt [ ] Luke Dyllon[1] the Quenes atturney was sent from the L. depute wth the lyke advertysement, who lykewise coulde not be credytted oneles the iudges wolde come them selffes / wherevpon a byll being redd they wolde not abyde the hiringe of it. On wednesday Sr John plunckett[2] Sr Robert Dillon[3] beinge the cheffe Justyces, M^{r} fynlas,[4] the Quenes sergent / Mr Luke Dillon the quenes atturney / M^{r} nugent[5] the Quenes sollycitor / came to the house and there affirmed theire resolucions wch they before had bothe saide & written / This same day at after none the lord depute willed the house to be before him at the castle savinge suche as were the dysturbers / neverthelesse some of them appered there wth the resydewe / where my L. havinge all before him blamed miche such vaunt parlers as beinge selff willed wolde not yelde to that that was reason / and notw^{t}standinge M^{r} barnewell[6] & others wolde scorne to humble them selffes / yet my L. gave this commandment that the house sholde assemble them selffs the day folowinge & to proceade to theire matters, willinge that such as wolde not be resolved to take choyse what they wolde do / And chardgd also the speker to have regarde bothe to the chardge comitted vnto him as also to see punyshment to be donne vpon such as dyd dysorder them selffes yn
27 the house /// The thursday the house assembled agayne / where one buttler demaundinge my L. resolucion was advertysed thereof / who saide he wolde yelde vnto it, but nevertheles his conscience dyd know the lawe to be to the contrarie / wch barnewell affirmed to be trew ; also the cavenaghts the same day had the overthrow / and the same daye there passed a byll for lymy[ting] places by the L.
28 depute & counsayle for tannyng of lether /// on ffrydaye there was adoo about the byll for the repeale of the L. poynynges act, but at lengthe dyverse were resolved //// about the byll ; on

[1] Sir Luke Dillon, Attorney-General, 1566–70 ; Chief Baron, 1570–93.

[2] Sir John Plunkett, Chief Justice of the King's Bench, 1559–83.

[3] Sir Robert Dillon, Chief Justice of the Common Pleas, 1559–93, and again 1594–97.

[4] Richard Finglas, Queen's Serjeant-at-law, 1554–74. He had previously held his office of Principal Solicitor.

[5] Nicholas Nugent, Solicitor-General, 1565–70 ; a Baron of the Exchequer, 1570–78.

[6] Probably Richard Barnewall of Crickstown, who was M.P. for Co. Meath in the next Parliament, erroneously styled 'Sir' in Lodge's *Peerage*.

thursday befor said the house was devyded by polls / and of thone
parte were xl^{te} for the negatyve & of thother L. englyshe affirmatyve 29
/ on saterday the saydė byll of poynynges being redd the third
tyme was miche debated & dyscorsed but at lengthe overthrowen /
for the polls of thenglysche were 44 / & of the irishe 48. /

one moneday a byll made that no capteyne nor lordes sholde vse
any lyberties oneles he were therevnto admytted by lettres patentes
was redd threes & passed / and then sent to the lordes.

on tueseday a byll passed that the L: depute sholde for x yeres februarij 1
promote & give all the dignyties in the churches of Monster &
Connagh / on saterday a byll passed that the L: depute may chose 6
skottes to serve wth in the realme notwthstandinge former actes to
the contrarie.

Item an acte passed one wenesday agaynst gray merchantes / 9
Item an acte that none shall foster children to irishe lordes / M^{d} this
day I spake yn the byll of impost & made an oration yn the des-
cribyng the offyce & authoritie of a prynce / the dewte of a Judge
&c. / wch was well lyked but by some myslyked / on frydaye then 11
folowenge buter[1] & bathe[2] laweirs & Sr Christopher b[arnewell]
claymed the lybertie to inveighe agaynst me chardgyng that I had
naughtyly compared phillip & the quene vnto pharao & that I sholde
name them to be kernes and that the Quene dyd tak bysid the lawe /
but they were willed to put yn wrytinge agaynst monday next / at
the same tyme also butler, being yn a coller, seyde if these wordes
had benne spoken yn any other place then yn this house there be a
great many here that they wolde rather have dyed then to have
suffred it / on saterday the byll passed for a subsyde of xiij^{s} iiij^{d} 12
vpon everie ploughe land &c. / On weneseday the 16. of februarye
the statute past for thattendure of Thomas eustac / on thuresday the 17
parlament was proroged tyll moneday foloweing / In this cessyons
ther passed these statutes folowing.

Item on moneday the 21 of february the parlament assembled and 21
that day the act for the repeale of poynynges act was passed & then
the parlament proroged tyll the wenesday.

On wenesday the 23 day the cessyons beganne & then iij bylls 23
were redd / & passed namely that the L. depute shall geve all the

[1] Evidently Edmund Butler of Callan, who was Attorney for the Liberties of Tipperary about that time, and who eventually became Attorney-General and Second Justice of the Queen's Bench.

[2] John Bathe of Drumcondra, afterwards Solicitor and Attorney-General and Chancellor of the Exchequer.

dignyties yn mounster excepte waterford corke lymerick & cassyle / also that none shall water any hempe or flax yn any rinnynge stream or ryver / And also that the landes of Thomas fytzgareld knyght of the valley beinge atteynted shalbe to the quene & hir heires.

Item the xjth of marche being fryday the parlament was proroged vntyll the xijth of october foloweng / and on saterday foloweng the xijth of marche S^{r} peter[1] was sworne one of the privie counsell / / /

[1] Sir Peter Carew, in connexion with whose claims to certain estates in Munster Hooker had come to Ireland.

INDEX

(The letter '*n*' after figures signifies note; Abp. = Archbishop.)

THE END